A DANGEROUS LOVE

A DANGEROUS LOVE

A DANGEROUS LOVE

A memoir by
Stephen Nicholson

Edited with notes on the unwritten chapters by
his friend
EDMUND MARLOWE

ARCADIAN DREAMS
London

First published by Arcadian Dreams 2023

ISBN 979-8-224495-34-4

Contents

Publisher's Note

The publisher is not endorsing the behaviour described in this memoir. It is being published in the belief that the frank description of such behaviour placed in the full context of an individual's life is so unusual as to make it a rare and extremely valuable contribution to human knowledge and understanding.

Editor's Note

At school, friendship is a passion ... All loves of after-life can never bring its rapture, or its wretchedness; no bliss so absorbing, no pangs of jealousy ... so keen! What bitter estrangements and what melting reconciliations; what scenes of wild recrimination, agitating explanations, passionate correspondence ... what earthquakes of the heart ... are confirmed in that simple phrase, a schoolboy's friendship!
BENJAMIN DISRAELI, *Coningsby*

One sleepless night when I was in my forties, I lay awake remembering my days as a schoolboy at Eton, some happy memories and some terrible regrets, all of them involving powerful emotions that had shaped my life in the special way that perhaps only adolescent experience can. I thought of all that had happened and all that might have happened, and suddenly I realised, "I can write a book about this!" Like millions of others, I had always thought of that as a fine thing to do without believing I could. Now, however, I *knew* I could. By dawn, the title, *Alexander's Choice*, and the outline of the plot had all come to me, and, bursting with enthusiasm to get on with it, I ran downstairs to begin.

What I wrote, and finally published in 2012, was the love story, ending in tragedy, of a boy of thirteen to fourteen and a young English master at Eton. I poured my soul into it, sometimes weeping as I recalled the memories that lay behind what I was writing. Evidently, with at least some very interesting people, it struck a deep chord, as it led to a multitude of correspondences, some of which have continued to this day.

These correspondents were of various types and the reasons my novel resonated with them varied accordingly. There was, for example, a particularly sympathetic and likeable woman my age who had been the daughter of a housemaster at a boys' boarding school and wrote a fine memoir she sadly never published, recounting how her own love affair with a boy at the school had ended with him being expelled for it. But most of my new correspondents were boy-lovers, who all believed their feelings were badly misunderstood by society, which, grossly unfair and often cruel, shied away from trying seriously to learn the truth. They felt I had spoken up for that truth in *Alexander's Choice*, and I, proud of this, struck up some serious friendships with a few whom I found particularly interesting and agreeable. The result was that I soon knew far more about boy-love than I had when I wrote my novel.

The most outstanding of these new friends was a retired music teacher called Stephen Nicholson, who began writing to me in February 2016, saying, "I have been haunted all my life by my memories of public school … and your often agonising descriptions struck a deep chord inside me. I have rarely read a book which felt so real, capturing the extremes of adolescent emotions." Somehow, Stephen, with his evident kindness, honesty and gentle wisdom struck a deep chord in me too, so that I was terribly saddened when, a year later, he wrote to say that he had been diagnosed as terminally ill with prostate cancer.

I finally met him during a brief trip to London in June 2017. Our three hours together flashed by, I went back to tell my wife about him and promptly afterwards wrote to invite him to stay in our home in France. He came two months later. He became close to my family at once. We confided in each other as old friends, which was unusual for us both, and soon both expressed our surprise at having struck up a close friendship at such a late stage of our lives. Thereafter, he came to stay several times a year and he came on holiday with my family regularly until his death in October 2020.

One of the things that most quickly became apparent about Stephen was that he was a brilliant raconteur. Every evening, over several bottles of wine, he would tell me about his adventures around the world. Besides opening up a new world for me, his stories were riveting, often very funny (part of his honesty was that he had no hesitation in poking fun at himself, as well as others). He was also a brilliant mimic, able to stage a richer array of accents than anyone I have known.

Though he was extraordinarily brave about his looming death and never grumbled about it, its shadow inevitably hung over us. I could not help thinking and putting to him that it, together with his unusual adventures, his gift for recounting them well and his having no close family left to be embarrassed, made him exceptionally well-placed to record for the near future, honestly and frankly, the life of an active boy-lover in the increasingly grim and repressive closing decades of the twentieth century.

He, partly I think out of his habitual kindness, succumbed to my persuasion and began writing *A Dangerous Love* in April 2018. By this stage, his life was being seriously disrupted by medical treatment and by the time the physical pain from his cancer and the effect of the drugs he was given made it impossible for him to continue, he had unfortunately only reached the 25th of March 1994. This, however, was a watershed date in his life, the climax of the crisis which led him to abandon England, so that his story as recounted here does come to a conclusion. (It was also incidentally the day I too abandoned England for a very different reason, to bring up my young children in the French countryside – one of a number of extraordinary coincidences in our lives that made our close friendship feel fated, despite the very different ways we had led them.)

The reader who is only interested in a coherent story should not read beyond Chapter X, the last he wrote. However, because in his penultimate email to me (by when he could no longer speak), Stephen wrote, "My biggest regret is not being able to complete the memoirs," I have done my best to make up for the loss, albeit with no more than morsels of what would have been the last four chapters. Thus I have collected together a bit of the last one that he wrote before anything else, along with some reminiscences from our correspondence and two documents that I know he had intended to include in the memoirs.

I have been given generous help by various people, of whom I must give special thanks to two. Stephen's Turkish friend, Isa Can, the boy with whom he forged the strongest bonds in his life, has helped me with the chapter about Stephen's years in Turkey. Perran Hereward proofread the whole manuscript with extraordinary thoroughness and made countless invaluable suggestions.

For the sake of historical accuracy, I should point out one change I think Stephen would have made to his first chapter had he written it a year later, when he suddenly, for the first time in his life, met the two half-siblings his step-mother bore his father. What he was then told inclined him to take a much gentler view of her and to place the blame for his father's treachery and neglect even more squarely on just the man himself.

There is no doubt the single most unusual and therefore interesting feature of Stephen's life was that he was an active lover of boys in an era which has singled out this form of love for the most severe opprobrium ever imposed on a sexuality in recorded history.

To understand why Stephen acted as he did, it is critically important to consider the appalling circumstances in which boy-loving men of his generation found themselves living. Just as he finished his education, his native land began to be gripped by a moral panic about children and sex which made loving boys infinitely more dangerous than it had been before. Many at the time believed that reason would soon prevail. When Stephen realised this was not to be and that he must travel abroad if he was to hope for a fulfilled existence, it was still possible in many countries for men and boys safely to have love affairs, in South East Asia quite openly. However, no sooner had he begun to explore these lands and to consider moving to one of them, longing for a love life such as people with different sexual longings could take for granted, than the writing appeared on the wall: the English-speaking countries were not satisfied with Gestapo-like repression of boy-love in their own countries, but were set on using threats and financial inducements to cajole every other country into succumbing to their new sexual order.

Stephen often said he wished he had been born half a century or more earlier. If he had been, with his affectionate and fun-loving disposition, I believe he would have been like the great writer Norman Douglas, who had a series of love affairs with boys lasting up to several years, the maximum span for this kind of love, and then evolving into lifelong friendships strongly felt on both sides. The enduring strong affection, gratitude and reverence these boys retained are touchingly recounted in a book, *Dear Doug! Letters of Norman Douglas*, and are echoed in this memoir by the words of Isa Can.

For the most part, however, the severely repressive times meant that Stephen and other lovers of boys were limited to sporadic and relatively fleeting tastes of what could have been in a freer age. It is this that explains their relieving starvation of the soul through resort to unsatisfactory substitutes like voyeurism and pornography, of which there is no mention in Holloway's frank and exhaustive biography of Douglas. One of the saddest ironies of the repression is that it is the noblest and most beneficial manifestations of boy-love that are most effectively banned, leaving only the most dodgy and useless to be carried on in secret.

By the time I met Stephen, he had stopped being a sexually active lover of boys for eight years and had come to terms with never being active again, for reasons to be explained in due course. But there is much more to eros than sex and he still loved boys. I shall therefore conclude with a few observations of the very little I witnessed of him in this capacity.

Our being sexual animals deeply affects our behaviour towards one another without forcing us to sexual acts. The faintest whiff of the possibility of a sexual outcome adds warmth and spice to our interactions with anybody vaguely the type of being we are attracted to, usually unconsciously. However, even when the attraction is conscious and mutually acknowledged, it can be accompanied by a determination not to act on it because it is felt not right or possible to do so under the circumstances concerned. Consider the chivalrous knights' chaste love of beautiful married ladies or the Sufi poets' chaste love of boys, both considered admirable in their time.

Therefore, by observing Stephen whenever he chanced to interact with a boy, I could still learn the broader meaning of loving boys.

I remember particularly a train ride Stephen and my family went on in Sicily. Standing together in the crowded corridor, I noticed sitting beside us (and noticed Stephen inevitably noticing) three attractive boys of about twelve with a woman who was the mother of one of them. Two were looking bored, while the third was positively soporific. I asked Stephen whisperingly, "Doesn't the boy sitting by the window remind you a little of Tintin?" (though he was really younger and incomparably better-looking). He took this as a trigger to introduce himself to the group with what I thought extraordinary daring, beginning by asking them if they were Tintin readers and then repeating my observation. As it happened, they were Russian and knew nothing of Tintin but, within a few minutes, Stephen had them so enraptured with his charm and lively conversation that they squeezed up to make room for him to sit down with them and the chat got more and more animated until we reached our destination. The mother appeared deeply moved by the effect Stephen had on the boys and became obviously warm towards him too.

To me it was an eye-opening demonstration that, in giving Stephen the romantic and sexual impulses it had, nature had designed him for the benefit of boys. It may be worth thinking about while you read his story.

Introduction

Down to Gehenna or up to the Throne,
He travels the fastest who travels alone.
  RUDYARD KIPLING

For someone who has always valued his privacy above anything, the act of writing a candid autobiography seems not only an unlikely enterprise, but unwise in the extreme. Any sort of self-promotion is abhorrent to him: you will not find him on Facebook or Twitter, nearly all his email addresses use pseudonyms, and he has always rejoiced in being unnoticed, invisible, not merely part of the crowd but well hidden within it. He's not "proud" in the way that a conventional (and probably married) gay man claims to be – the idea of gay pride marches seems particularly absurd, making a nonsense of the notion of equality; there are no straight pride events.

Forced by the need for secrecy into the shadows, his existence has been mostly a rather fraught and chaotic affair, which until very recently he has always considered of little significance or worth: at worst furtively egocentric, at best hedonistically indulgent. For the sake of mere survival, it has been a life clouded by necessary obfuscation, social reserve and incomplete "normal" friendships requiring a regrettable degree of deception whilst avoiding direct lies. As a journey of self-discovery, it has been travelled mostly alone, though, after finally fathoming and coming to terms with his essential Nature, it has been considerably enriched by like-minded soul mates met along the way.

Even amongst these, however, only a few select kindred spirits have been permitted unrestricted access into his private world. When he saw the BBC's extraordinarily gripping series *I Claudius* on TV in 1976, Herod's words to the title character resonated very strongly within him:

Herod: Listen Claudius, let me give you a piece of advice.
Claudius: Oh, I thought you'd finished giving advice.
Herod: Well, just one more piece, then I'm done. Trust no one, my friend, no one. Not your most grateful freedman. Not your

most intimate friend. Not your dearest child. Not the wife of your bosom. Trust no one.

This advice has mostly served him well, and some of his worst experiences have arisen from opening up to the wrong people, usually women. Of late there have been very few new friends permitted to see the whole shambolic mess which is him; one of the most recent committed suicide in 2014, thanks to unbearable persecution from our fine boys in blue. Financially independent at last, prepared and, he thought, content to live out the remainder of his otiose days in glorious inactive obscurity, drinking too much, overindulging in all the wrong sorts of food, reading trashy books and watching mindless TV shows and movies, something utterly unexpected, unlooked for and completely wonderful happened to him: a new friend walked into his life complete with his remarkable family. For the sake of protecting his identity, I shall simply call him Edmund, and you will hear more about him and the circumstances of our unlikely meeting in the relevant chronological section of this narrative.

It is in fact on account of Edmund's gentle but persistent persuasion that the writer is now laying bare every tawdry detail of an existence which is still mostly incomprehensible to Stephen the protagonist. There you are, he's already let slip a fact about his identity – his real Christian name, though mercifully there are many Stephens in the world.

Although he still feels that it is a supreme arrogance to imagine anyone would be remotely interested in following his idle ramblings, Edmund, remarkably, feels otherwise, and, as he is a well-appreciated author, his judgement deserves respect. The narrative will at times make for uncomfortable and maybe shocking reading. It is the account of a struggle to make sense of an identity instinctively understood and realised in one boarding school (1968) and then unhealthily suppressed by a second (1970). The narrator hesitates at this stage to give this identity a label or any sort of name, as any contemporary nomenclature will evoke false ideas of criminality and disgust in the sad deluded times we live in today.

What Stephen regards as a rather ignominious struggle to survive, Edmund sees as "a fascinating and unusual life". Whilst

Stephen wants to go to his grave an unremarkable nobody, Edmund talks of Stephen's "ticket to immortality". What Stephen sees as an act of hubristic folly, Edmund regards as an important record of times which have now all but vanished. Were he not now in his seventh decade, past the age of caring about his own safety or reputation, condemned to an early death by incurable illness, and, through a recent bereavement, without relatives to embarrass, Stephen would still resist the gentle pressure from his dear new friend to make his private life public in this way.

Now it's no good pretending you're someone else, Stephen, even if you can make that mental leap to imagine what it's like to be someone else and put yourself in their shoes, which, despite your habitual self-criticism, feel no more comfortable than your own. So, fess up and get this narrative into the first person, you can't hide behind a persona – you are about to emerge from the crowd, naked and unashamed.

OK, gulp, anything you say Mr Superego. Help! You've no idea how hard it is for someone who's always denied their ego, and been rather ashamed of their id to do this, but what the hell, what have **I** got to lose (there – done it!). *I I*, Eye Eye, Aye Aye. Ayes to the right, Nose to the left. Get used to it Stephen ...

So, were I unfortunate enough to be the same young man of twenty today as I was in 1977, with everything to lose, I would probably not even admit to myself the sort of feelings which have dominated and steered an important aspect of my life, let alone write about them. I would not be able to handle the social ostracism, persecution by moral crusaders, analysis and treatment (brainwashing) by "experts" who would seek to "cure" me by ridding me of one of the most important ingredients which makes me me. In 1977 I might have been thought rather sad, a sorry joke, even a raving pervert, but hardly a "danger to society". Little me, a danger to society – now that *is* a joke.

Almost a lifetime's involvement has finally convinced me that far from weird or strange, the challenging gift bestowed upon me has been a force for good. It is wholesome, natural and utterly compelling; it colours every aspect of one's relations with the world, demanding continuous recognition and action and, as an urge to cherish and protect our young, is latent within every human being. It is only the denial of this bountiful impulse that can lead to mischief, irrational rage, hatred, self-loathing and fractured relationships.

But I'm getting ahead of myself. Oh God, have you already guessed it? He's, sorry – *I'm*, one of *those*? Eek!

I'd love it if I could categorise myself so neatly. I've still not managed to do that after sixty-two years, but perhaps, as an intelligent observer, when you've finished reading about my experiences, reflected on my character and ambitions, have loved, despaired, grown, felt with me, actually *been* me, for the fruitful period you choose to spend with these memoirs, maybe, just maybe, you won't be so quick to find an easy, nasty word to dismiss me with.

Although every individual life is different, everyone is born alone and dies alone, we all have our unique destiny to fulfil and we can only do that according to our own special potpourri of innate characteristics. No one can live your life for you, no, despite what Auguste Villiers de l'Isle-Adam asserts in *Axël,* not even your servants.

I. Some Early Recollections

When I was a child, I spake as a child, I understood as a child, I thought as a child: and when I became a man, I *didn't* put away childish things.
    Adapted from *I Corinthians* 13:11

My entry into the world was not easy: I clearly felt that the warmth and comfort of my mother's womb was preferable to all the cacophonous hurly-burly which awaited me when I was finally forced to leave it. And, by all accounts, I was extremely reluctant to so much as poke my head out into this mess of a world: already significantly late, I was eventually prised out with forceps, kicking and screaming into the harsh lights of the hospital ward, no doubt to the immense relief of both maternity staff and pregnant mother.

My conception had taken a long time too. My parents had been screwing in vain for a good five years before their marriage was finally blessed with issue.

Please permit a little background here. My mother had two older brothers whom my grandmother was very happy to see married off, but, her husband having died soon after my mother was born, Granny most definitely did not want to lose the child who was going to tend her in her old age. Being a battle-axe of the fiercest sort, she succeeded in frightening off all of her only daughter's potential suitors until, reserved and rather insular (so I've been told, for I never met him), a man twenty years my mother's senior married her in 1951. Their wedding photograph is the only picture I have ever seen of him.

How ironic that having stood up to my grandmother's ferocity, this man should have been so easily ensnared by a predatory female who saved her most aggressive advances until my sweet faithful mother was well and truly pregnant; it was a subject which I could never get her to discuss.

1

Stephen in the arms of his mother, Diana, 1957

The ensuing divorce was clearly one of the single most traumatic and devastating events of her life, and even when I was trying to discover details of my father's occupation for an official document when my mother was ninety-one, the distress of talking about him, even sixty years later, proved overwhelming for her.

So I was born into an atmosphere of sorrow and tension, and vividly remember the naked horror of the shattering nightmares which troubled my sleep in those early years. The terror was as much auditory as visual, with grotesque noises seeming to come from the Devil Himself, and though no one had yet told me of the existence of pure Evil, an infant's supernatural awareness instinctively understands such things.

Despite her grief, my mother, ever capable and practical, soon found employment in the home of the large Catholic Cookson family, whom tragedy had recently struck. Mrs. Cookson had died whilst giving birth to her fifth child and only daughter, Mary, leaving a distressed and rather elderly colonel in pressing need of help to raise his daughter and her four brothers, and so my mother was employed as both housekeeper and nanny. My earliest memories are of growing up in this boisterous household and being part of a family. There was some concern that I did not speak for nearly four years, but, so the joke goes, once I started I never stopped.

Even today, though I have inherited something of my father's aloof reserve and stand-offishness, I do have a tendency to become garrulous when in the rare company of those I love and trust.

Early photographs indicate a happy young boy, playing naked on the local beach (I absolutely refused to keep on those oh so silly trunks, I've been told) and in the garden of the large house where I spent my first few years. The adopted family have remained firm friends and showed up in significant numbers at my mother's recent funeral.

Unlike her lackadaisical son, mother was always busy at some activity or other, be it golf, bridge, theatre-going, sailing or organising dinner parties (she loved cooking and was wonderful at it) and attracted a large amount of friends who tended to stick by her. Perhaps unfortunately, it was mostly women who fussed over me, so that I never really experienced the sort of healthy male bonding that "normal" boys do with their fathers or with adult males, even though I suspect I would have been hopeless at such hearty activities as camping out and kicking/catching balls, and been dismissed as a pansy.

When I was seven, mother was finally obliged to move into my grandmother's house, just round the corner as it happened, and look after her. I missed living with the family I had grown up with, but my grandmother had her wish and was cared for by her dutiful daughter for the next twenty years. These were difficult times for her as the old lady was difficult, opinionated, severely critical of others, always "right" and endlessly demanding. My abiding picture of her is of the cigarette always dangling from her lips (Embassy No. 1 for the coupons – "Stevie" was frequently dispatched to buy them) and the glass of neat whisky by the window seat where she spent much of her day playing patience and watching TV at full volume, as she became increasingly deaf. She related many stories to me about such (these days) non-politically-correct characters as Little Black Sambo, who was swallowed by a snake. Her favourite TV show was the now ignominious *Black and White Minstrels*.

The only ill effects she seemed to suffer from smoking was narrowly to escape burning the house down on two occasions when my mother was out working. Of the many anecdotes about my grandmother one of the most oft-told was when, after the second arson attempt, a fireman observed: "If we'd been 'ere ten minutes later, darlin', you'd 've been up with the angels." She replied: "Oh no, young man, the angels won't have me!" She died aged ninety-five in a nursing home where she was still allowed to indulge her lifelong habits of chain-smoking cigarettes and drinking whisky.

My early schooling was excellent and enjoyable. I was thoroughly grounded in the three Rs at a local PNEU school until aged seven by two stern and wonderfully humane spinsters: Miss Firth (pronounced Miss Firf by me) and Miss Jenkins. It was around this time that I was profoundly transfixed by melody, harmony and rhythm – Christmas songs such as "The Rocking Carol", "Away in a Manger" and "Once in Royal David's City" seemed like gifts from another world. Miss Firf apparently remarked on my musicality and sense of rhythm, but nothing was done about this until several years later. Music lessons at six might have resulted in a very different career, but not necessarily a better life.

As mother had to work, she was not always able to take me to school on her bicycle (where I sat perched in a little seat attached to the back) and various of her friends were enlisted to ferry me to and from Miss Firf's each day. I used to stay near the school in the house of one such friend, Betty Copland, who had, wonder of wonders, a piano. I'd spend hours making interesting noises on this and be told that I'd played an elephant, a butterfly, a thunderstorm or whatever. I'd memorise the noises I'd made with my hands and try to repeat them so that Betty always knew when the elephant, tiger or butterfly was being represented. Another regular feature of my life at this time was afternoon walks with "Auntie", a rather prudish spinster who lived in the next road to us. After our walk we would go back to her small house and she would provide afternoon tea while I watched her television.

I was transfixed, aged six, by the first episode of *Doctor Who*, and still remember the girl getting mocked at school for not knowing how many pennies there were in a pound. Later I was enthralled by the Daleks (and later the Cybermen) and wrote to the BBC asking for a Dalek suit, the ones being offered in Gamleys toyshop being far too babyish. I received a kind reply, but no suit, alas. At the PNEU school all the boys used to frighten the girls, as well as each other, by yelling "exterminate" in that characteristic electronic voice, with right arm extended fully and left forearm pointing from the elbow, upper arm firmly next to the body. I used to make my own teams of rival Daleks by sticking pins into sherry corks (there was always a plentiful supply of both), and then have fierce imaginary battles which felt real enough to me.

There was also *Crossroads*, a brand-new soap which was supposed to be for the adults, but I became hooked on it and fell in love with Sandy, Mrs Richardson's nephew, for his lovely gravelly voice and rugged good looks. Other TV programmes which thrilled me at this time involved space adventures and heroes. I was enthralled by *Space Patrol*, *Thunderbirds*, *Fireball XL5* and then later *Lost in Space*, featuring the Robinson family and their cute young son Will (played by Billy Mumy), along with a wonderful robot who answered questions with "affirmative" and "negative" and the evil Mr. Smith. I was a great fan of Batman and Robin and once insisted, the spoilt little brat that I was, that my mother buy me an expensive LP, which she could ill afford, featuring the pair along with characters such as the Riddler and Mr. Penguin – I played it endlessly and could even now recite passages from it.

I thoroughly enjoyed all the current cartoons such as *Bugs Bunny*, *Top Cat*, *The Flintstones* and *Yogi Bear* and once saw a feature film of the latter in the cinema: the small-screen black-and-white TV Yogi Bear looked so disappointing afterwards. I watched all the James Bond movies in the cinema as they appeared, and my model Aston Martin, complete with the guns at the front and ejector seat was the envy of my school friends. I used to feel so empowered when seeing such action films and was exhilarated by the great high dive at the end of *Our Man Flint*. I walked home alone completely energised pretending to take on, and pulverise, hordes of imaginary enemies attacking me on the pavement. Later at the Heene Road Baths where I learned to swim I wanted to dive off the top board like my hero James Coburn, and was very disappointed to be refused permission.

It was at about this time that weekend newspapers started producing colour supplements, and in that less inhibited era these often included a number of rather explicit naked photos which included children along with primitive tribesmen holding spears: shapely black bums, obscenely long cocks dangling (how thrilling; thus began a lifelong fascination). The dear spinster was offended by such pictures and I pretended to agree with her: "Ooh yes, dithgusting, auntie!", but secretly I was excited by them and I cannot remember a time when I haven't been entranced and fascinated by nudity – both in myself and in others.

Stephen aged six, 1963

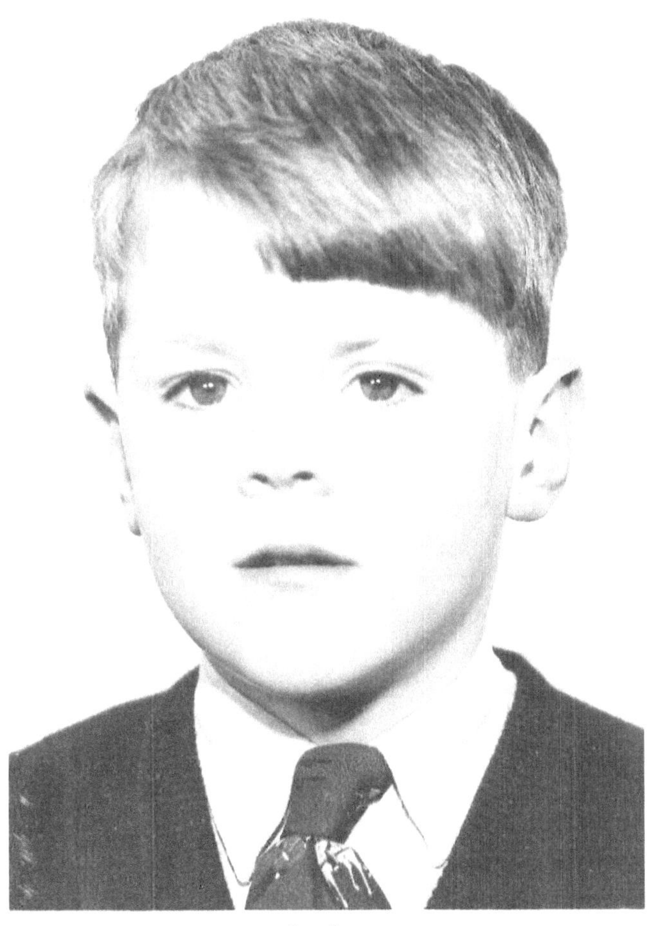

Stephen

I was given a cowboy suit when I was about seven and used to act in front of a long mirror changing into it from my usual clothes, lingering over my own naked body before transforming myself into Buffalo Bill, nifty with his trusty six shooter, "Pow wow you're dayad pardner, this two-horse town ain't big enough for the both of us" and such like. When I'd tired of playing cowboys, I would often remove all my clothes and rejoice in the freedom I felt, posing in all sorts of positions and admiring myself as unashamedly as any budding Narcissus, sometimes breaking out into a furious dance and proudly watching my fairly respectable willie jiggling about. Sadly this was well before the days of video, as I would have surely filmed myself and risked being the earliest ever victim to be listed in England's Gestapo-style sex offender register.

I often chose my friends for their looks too, and would try and engineer situations where we could be naked together. An early companion from these times was James Dickins (yes, with an "i"), who told me his family swam naked in their garden pool in the country. I found the outline of his bottom underneath his shorts interesting and longed to see it uncovered – oh, why couldn't his family take me swimming with them. Eventually I offered to let him try on my cowboy suit, and was rewarded with some marvellous sights.

Although I didn't know how to play any instrument properly at this time, I loved listening to records and spent much of my pocket money and tips from mother's friends building up an impressive collection of silly songs (such as "The Big Rock Candy Mountain") and stories, all of which I could reel off from memory. I then graduated to the latest pop singles by the Beatles, the Rolling Stones, Freddie and the Dreamers ("who wears short shorts – we wear short shorts") and many others. The singles cost six shillings and eight pence each, a vast sum in those days. There was a large collection of musical LPs already in the house, including various Gilbert and Sullivan operettas and *My Fair Lady*, which I adored: I was taken to see the stage show of this in London and was apparently enraptured. Later my mother took me to see *Mary Poppins* and *The Sound of Music* in the cinema, and after being given the LPs of the songs for Christmas I couldn't stop singing them. Much later still, aged twelve, I saw *Carry on Again Doctor* and *The Battle of Britain* in the cinema and still recall the frisson of excitement of the sight of Barbara Windsor's plump bum in the former and a brief nude scene in the latter – but I'm getting ahead of myself.

It will be apparent that, of necessity, much of my time during my first few years was spent alone. This never bothered me and still doesn't. I don't regard myself an antisocial loner or "git", as I was once called for refusing an invitation to a Christmas party where some young women were clearly planning mischief. Those self-sufficient days were a good preparation for the solitary life that all boy-lovers must expect in these censorious times. So, between the ages of five and eleven, before my first boarding school I was perfectly content to play by myself, listening to the radio, playing records or cooking little snacks: I made excellent chips and followed other recipes seen on TV, which I ate reading books by such writers as Jules Verne or Enid Blyton as well as comics. I loved *The Beano*, *The Beezer* and *The Dandy*: Christmas mornings when I was given the annuals to read were heaven itself.

I could also become absorbed by my Meccano and Lego sets and would make all sorts of useless contraptions, take them apart and turn them into other Heath Robinson-type functioning machines. I played endlessly with my Scalextric cars, creating long tricky Grand Prix tracks and having races with myself, but my real pride and joy were my two train sets. The first comprised the chunky Hornby clockwork models which were superseded, to my delight one Christmas, by a basic handsome electric set, which I gradually built up adding more and more track, stations, carriages pulled by different types of train. I adored all the fine engines of both sets and as with everything I loved I took great care of them, always putting the special ones (such as the expensive Winston Churchill model) back in their boxes afterwards. All these toys were eventually consigned to the attic, "to be given to my grandchildren", my mother always used to say: how it pains me that I was never able to provide her with that joy. The train sets alone would be worth a fortune today had I not, much later, entrusted them to a recommended collector/dealer for valuation. He absconded with them and I never saw him again.

We lived very near the beach in Littlehampton, just opposite a huge complex of amusements arcades owned by Billy Butlin and filled with penny slot machines, one-armed bandits and various rides such as a ghost train, dodgem cars and a particularly lethal looking roller coaster. From a very early age I was often given a handful of pennies and sent out of the house to spend hours there, sometimes by myself and sometimes befriending very dubious local boys. I once invited one of these, Hopkins, an older, bigger and rougher specimen than me, back to our flat and he stole all the carefully saved "lucky" threepenny bits from Doodi's Dimple bottle which would have amounted to a tidy sum of money. Doodi, pronounced Doo-Dye, was how I affectionately called my mother. She and I went immediately to the arcade, where we found Hopkins jangling lots of pennies and enjoying himself playing on the machines, but we could not prove these coins had been changed from the stolen threepenny bits, as nobody would grass on him. It was quite common then for local boys to offer sexual favours to men in return for some sort of protection, as well as monetary reward, and as Hopkins was such a compliant lad, no one wanted him to get into any sort of trouble. It was me who paid the price later with a thorough beating up from him for being a dirty sneak, not fair really as it had been mother who had seen him, not liked him at all and found the money missing.

I expect the reader is wondering if I was ever sexually propositioned by the men at the arcades. If I was I have no recollection of it, and was probably regarded as not streetwise enough and thus "unsafe". I did befriend many of the local adults in an ordinary way though. A delightful couple who ran a small arcade right on the beach had a young son I would play with, and they would let me have pennies to spend in the machines. I was fascinated by how the various types of slot machine worked, and would watch carefully when the attendants opened them up to repair some mechanical fault. As a result I became rather adept at removing money from certain models. There was one which involved flicking a ball using a certain technique and hoping it landed in a winning hole. If you had a win you would be able to twist the handle on the left once and be rewarded with tuppence. The mechanism also allowed the knob to turn twice or even three times if you managed to land in the middle 6d winning slot, which was almost impossible. I, however, soon learned how to "doubledetwist" and empty out all the pennies: the technique involved not allowing the knob to come right back and then suddenly twisting it clockwise again at just the right moment, with the indescribable satisfaction of finding umpteen jangling tuppences tumbling into the winning tray. This was by no means easy and required fine judgement and timing: something adults could never manage. I often hung around when a man was playing and when he won would offer to increase his winnings and earn a small reward myself: needless to say I was often evicted by the attendants when caught doing this and my pile of pennies confiscated. Protestations to mother that the nasty flunky had robbed me and then thrown me out were always in vain.

A good friend of mine, fifteen years older, tells me all sorts of stories of the fun he had with boys in Littlehampton during the sixties, mostly in the shelters on the beach near the end of the day before they went home. He also befriended some of the boys' families and would take their sons away for weekends. Being from a slightly better class of home, I was probably considered too dangerous to pick up, but to this day I've wondered what I missed out on. As recently as the late seventies and early eighties, when I used to return to Butlin's for nostalgic reasons, boys would latch onto me to partner them in Space Invaders or pinball machines, and allow me to buy them hot dogs and coke chatting away in a friendly easy manner. Slow on the uptake as I was in my early twenties to recognise a boy's availability, I hate to think of how many sexual opportunities I missed. Even as late as 1992, a boy befriended me in Butlin's and I said to him, partly in jest, "Haven't you been warned about talking to strange men?"

"Geez, it's so boring at home I wish some man would kidnap me."

His exact words.

By then I did recognise his clear invitation, and was sorely tempted. He was a good-looking twelve-year-old with a pleasant and relaxed demeanour, and he even admired and smoked my posh Danish cigarettes. But the danger of such friendships had by then increased exponentially in sad little England, and I was already experienced enough when it came to sex with boys not to take unnecessary risks.

Although much of my free time in those days was spent alone at home, I did make quite a few friends at school and locally from "good" homes. There was mad Charlie whose father was a dentist. He loved doing crazy things such as taking old television sets apart and throwing large pieces of them out of high windows – I drew the line at a huge cathode ray tube which he wanted to see smashed into smithereens. Then there was Adam Halliwell, a great mate with whom I used to go fishing, though we only ever caught crabs. One day by the river, we got trapped in quicksand and sank fast into gooey smelly mud. After finally extricating ourselves, we arrived home in a sorry state, stinking and filthy. Of course Doodi immediately whisked our clothes off before throwing us both into the bath together. I can remember to this day the shape of his little winkle and my general fascination with his naked body.

My first "girl" friend was Jackie Dickson, the daughter of the woman who took over as housekeeper for the Cooksons round the corner after mother had left to look after Granny. Mrs Dickson was a strict and unpopular woman and did not last long. She was not liked by any of the Cookson family and the youngest, Mary, whom I still regard as a sort of sister, particularly hated her, often coming round in tears to be comforted by Doodi after some great argument with Mrs Dickson. Jackie, very forward for her age, would also come round to see *me*, often early in the morning when I was still in pyjamas which excited her tremendously. She was the randiest little slut of a girl I've ever known and initiated various sex games with which I reluctantly and shamefully cooperated. It wasn't that she was ugly, but I would have much preferred to be doing these things with another boy, as is still very much the case. Unlike the Reverend Dodgson, I've never particularly liked little girls.

I should perhaps mention here Uncle Martin's (Colonel Cookson's) "companion" called Edgar, a bachelor whom he met at a boarding house where he worked as a cook: after a second visit to this boarding house Martin invited Edgar to stay in the big Littlehampton house after Miss Dickson and her daughter had been given their marching orders. Everyone disapproved of him because he encouraged Martin to drink too much, and was considered a dodgy character generally; the one exception to this general disapprobation was little me who found him great fun. In retrospect, I feel Edgar must have been a boy-lover, for he always made a huge fuss of me, lifting me up, carrying me about, playing physical games which often involved tickling (oh, how I giggled and then tried so hard to make him giggle): I was excited and flattered by his attentions.

Following Miss Firf's I was sent to an all-boys day preparatory school in Worthing where I was deliriously happy, mainly on account of the casual discipline, lax academic demands and fun to be had both in and out of the classroom, especially in those lessons "taught" by masters whose ability to control boys left much to be desired. I remember very little about old Mr. George other than the sight of him spending ages toying at his food with a fork at lunchtimes, mashing everything on his plate together into an unsightly pulp before he was able to eat it. A completely insane boy called Reynolds, who was fascinated with electronics, managed to wire up a compass, place it pointy end upwards on Mr. George's chair and plug it into the electric socket before the start of his lesson. Fortunately the ancient fossil was warned in time not to sit down by a boy with some sense of responsibility, who unplugged and removed the compass. Mr. George, however, hardly seemed to react at all, and there were no questions asked or repercussions for Reynolds. As ever, he barely seemed to notice what was going on, and commenced his tedious incomprehensible droning whilst we occupied ourselves in various nefarious ways.

Punishments were rare at this school, and Halliwell and I were unlucky and astonished to receive three whacks with a gym shoe on our backsides by Mr. Sams, the headmaster. It was the summer term and we'd been preparing for a game of rounders on the lawn; as the teacher was late, we suddenly had the urge to have a quick swordfight with the sticks before they were stuck into the ground, at which point the teacher arrived and reported us for causing malicious damage to school property. What a bastard! Nothing was damaged. When I told my mother that evening that I'd been beaten on my bottom, her only question was: "Trousers up or down?" *O tempora o mores* ...

Although I was always curious about nakedness in all its manifestations, it was at the age of eight or so that I first became really aware of the pleasurable potential of penises and bottoms – my own as well as my friends'. At school, there was a fair amount of mild sex play, though I don't recall that s-e-x was a word ever used to describe the fun to be had. Cocks would be displayed under the desks, squeezed into all sorts of shapes along with the scrotum and sometimes, to the delight of the owners, they would stick up proudly and demand admiration – all while some ineffectual teacher was vainly trying to decline French verbs on the board with his back turned. The instruction to be found below our desks was far more informative and interesting than anything the teacher had to offer.

There were several *National Geographic* magazines in my classroom which often contained nude pictures. One which I remember vividly, but have never been able to locate again, we're talking circa 1967, depicted the rear view of two naked blond boys in a field of corn. The boys' corn-coloured hair and amber bodies with their splendid bottoms made a very striking photo and caused great amusement to the class. How affronted I was when Harris thought it would be amusing to ink in the middle of boys' backsides with what looked like lumps of shit – to me this not only ruined the stunning effect of the whole picture but degraded the beautiful bodies of these two lads.

Stephen

Outdoor games, usually football, were played on a field requiring transport in the school minibus. Mooning was a very popular activity both in the bus and on the football pitch, and I became quite a connoisseur of the delightful variety of boys' posteriors, to this day retaining a mental picture of the very respectable rear ends of both Master Young and Master Blick as their shorts slid delightfully down. Unfortunately the school did not have a shower room, so it was not until I was sent away to board aged eleven that I was able to absorb the full glory of naked boys en masse.

One day the rather high-spirited Master Blick brought a small magazine into school called *Health and Efficiency*, which was nothing to do with diet or exercise as far as one could gather. It did, however, contain page after page of naked people of all ages playing outdoors in the sunshine. This caused great interest amongst the boys and during each break period that day we hurried to the changing rooms to pore over Blick's shoulder as he flicked through the pages to reveal big-breasted fat women with enormous thighs almost hiding their naughty bits and slim young girls with smooth slits, men with hairy bodies, especially round their groins, with large cocks and hanging testicles (the first time I'd witnessed this phenomenon, though I'd heard about them thanks to a mischievous and precocious friend called Andrew Bristowe) and hairless young boys who even then seemed to me the nicest-looking of all.

So Andrew Bristowe it was who first told me, aged seven, about the facts of life. Extremely eloquent on the size and hairiness of his father's cock and balls which he described in some detail to his fascinated friend, who wanted to see it for himself, he then told me in graphic detail about how a cock, when it got stiff, could be pushed between a woman's legs into her clit, and then some sort of liquid, but not piss, would be pumped out of the cock into the woman's tummy. After this extraordinary revelation, I rushed straight home to find out if there was any truth at all in what I had been told, and on finding my mother busy in the kitchen, asked her outright how babies were made. It was clearly the wrong moment and the wrong subject: there were some vague incomprehensible mumblings about passing on seed before the topic was hurriedly changed to something more wholesome. I was to find it always very difficult and awkward to discuss sexual matters with Doodi, though much later, in my twenties, it became necessary to have some heavy and frankly devastating conversations on account of my troublesome sexuality.

But back to cheerful wicked little Andrew. I suppose in Doodi's eyes he would have been considered a most unsuitable companion for her young son, and definitely not wholesome, though to me his company and lubricious imagination were a source of endless fun and discovery. Many games were devised which always ended up with us being naked together and indulging in all manner of experimentation. Just a couple of examples will suffice here to illustrate how these amusements would be initiated. I had a roulette wheel and for each number we landed on there was a task already thought up and written down by both of us varying in rudeness from merely displaying one's cock, balls or bottom, usually bending down to show off the hole, to more daring antics involving manipulation of oneself or each other. There was also a bagatelle board with similar actions required, depending on where the marbles landed. We soon became frustrated with the limitations imposed by the little pieces of paper we had prepared and they became a mere prelude to more earnest and committed sexual exploration. He once suggested that we should walk round the local park with our cocks dangling out of our shorts but I drew the line at that. When, however, I stayed with him and (what joy!) we were given a double bed to share, it was me who assumed control and stripped off completely as soon as the door was closed, prancing around the room, Andrew looking on with considerable interest. It didn't take long for him to follow suit and, pyjamas abandoned, we enjoyed ourselves, and each other, immensely.

Perhaps it was fortunate that we were never caught with our pants down, or we might have learned what spoilsports adults can be in believing that sexual pleasure is only to be enjoyed above a certain age (what age? why? who can decide this? does this mean that sex is bad when it felt so good?), and even then, for the strictest, only when you are married. To paraphrase

William Blake, I was born to sweet delight and made for joy, not woe. Although I did think, speak and play as a child I also took huge pleasure in my little body and believed the fun and joy to be had from it would never end.

Everything was to change, however, when I failed the entrance exam for the junior department of the special public school for which I had been entered, an institution which offered generous bursaries to "deprived" children, which adjective included those boys who, for whatever reason, had lost a parent. No more idling: I'd have to be sorted out in a boarding school paid for, I was to learn later, by my rich uncle.

To this day I don't know whether I should have been grateful for this chance, but my days of true innocence ended the very day I, aged eleven, bade my mother a stoic farewell (that moment of abandonment will never leave me, what did she think she was *doing*? – but cry I wouldn't) at the front door of Beatemup Manor Prep School for Boys near Horsham, and entered a jungle of wild savages overseen by an unbalanced screwy headmaster assisted by his team of kinky matrons and eccentric bachelor masters.

II. First Boarding School

Shades of the prison-house begin to close
Upon the growing Boy
  WILLIAM WORDSWORTH, *Intimations of Immortality*

My first few daunting hours in that school will stay with me forever. It was the Summer Term of 1968, I thought I was the only new bug in the place and, for the first time ever, felt utterly lost and lonely, despite being surrounded by so many (too many) other people, all of whom seemed to know each other. Dumped like an old sack of garbage in an alien environment with no one to stand up for me, I understood intuitively that in order to survive I'd have to pretend to be hard and unfriendly, to show no weakness. It being the final term of the academic year, there was no warm welcome to parents and new boys from the head-master, and no guidance at all other than being shown where one's dormitory was: just twenty metal beds close together separated by lockers. We were introduced to Matron, whom I disliked on sight. So Mr. Tough Guy strutted around aimlessly, trying to display the self-assurance he certainly didn't feel inside, and at one point a rather gawky older boy, all freckles and large glasses dared to approach and ask:

"So what's your name, then?"

I didn't recall him telling me *his* name. "M-Y-O-B," I boldly retorted, pausing dramatically between each letter. What a brave Devil I was.

"Oh come on. I'm going to find out sooner or later, aren't I!"

MYOB strode off wondering if he'd perhaps been a bit abrupt; after all, the boy seemed decent enough. By seeing enemies everywhere, would I soon be making them?

The next encounter was far more positive. A thin bony twinkly rag doll of a boy with jet-black hair and an amused expression clearly observed my misery as I was sorting out the padlock on my tuck box.

"You new too?"

"Yeah." Hooray – I wasn't the only one. I might have even managed a smile.

"Not much fun so far, is it?"

"No," I agreed. "It isn't."

"Well, we've gotta make the best of it. I'm Tyrrell."

"I'm Nicholson."

"Oh good, I've made a friend now."

We solemnly shook hands, and friends we remained right through our time there.

The third unforgettable encounter of that day occurred in the dormitory. One soon learned the evening ritual which involved stripping to one's underpants and going to the bathroom to wash and clean one's teeth under the watchful eye of Miss Roe, the aforementioned witch of a Matron, who also busybodied herself in as many dormitories as she could before lights out. Once she was satisfied that you were clean, you were permitted to get into pyjamas and bed to read, chat or whatever (there wasn't much else on offer) until the duty master turned the lights out. It was still too early for the dormitory prefect to be in bed, and there was virtually no supervision once the lights had been put off.

Boarders at Beatemup were made to retire ridiculously early, and the late April sun had not yet set. If I'd still been at home it would have been another two hours at least before I would have had to go to bed – two hours which would have been spent profitably, enjoyably, cosily, comfortably. What *was* I doing in this squeaky metal bed with its thin lumpy uncomfortable mattress? I wasn't at all sleepy, but pretended to close my eyes and ignored the excited chatter which arose around me as soon as the rule breakers deemed it safe to do so. I was to learn that almost anything was safe after lights out. The closest one came to being supervised was when certain duty masters, usually the decent ones, prowled around hoping to get a glimpse of something going on, but never troubling to put a stop to it.

If one of *those* masters had chosen to spy on my dormitory that night, he might have been gratified to observe something which initially shocked and surprised (not so) little Nicholson, but was probably a fairly everynight sight to *him*.

A boy called Glover suddenly announced that he was feeling sexy, removed his pyjamas and climbed into my bed.

"You know what people do in bed together, don't you?"

"Erm … Well, sort of."

"Do I have to explain, or shall I just show you?"

"Erm … Well … Erm."

"They do this, and while they're doing it, they make lots of groaning noises, like this."

"Oh, right …"

I'll leave Glover's dramatic groans to the reader's imagination – he won't need much.

I couldn't say I found the experience unpleasant, though in retrospect it was clear Glover, as a mere eleven-year-old, was no student of the Kama Sutra: his sexual skills and repertoire left much to be desired. However, he did lie on top of me and bounce up and down enthusiastically, thrusting his pelvis forward and backwards in a playful, and really rather agreeable manner, emitting those strange guttural noises with gusto, and pretending some sort of build up of excitement. Where *had* he learned even this, I now wonder: from a wicked uncle? At the time I wasn't particularly curious or bothered.

Neither were the other boys in the dormitory. It was more a case of "Oh, there's Glover up to his funny tricks again." After he'd left me and gone back to his own bed, I lay awake for some time, in an altogether better frame of mind. I hadn't been at all sexually aroused by Glover's antics, which were no more than just a piece of puerile playacting, but I'd enjoyed them: enjoyed the physical contact, the sheer animal exuberance of it.

So this was what boarding school was about, was it? Perhaps I could possibly get to enjoy it after all.

As I sit here in the comfort of my warm bungalow with an early summer's sun streaming through the open window, Haydn playing on Radio 3, my body free of all clothing and my head free of all the petty everyday distractions which prevent adults from enjoying the quality of each passing moment, my difficulty is not so much in recalling those crucial days of late boyhood, but in controlling and ordering the torrent of memories and associated sensations. As these pages unfold and the author's nescience becomes increasingly tarnished by worldly knowledge and experience, so will he impose the necessary structure on his storytelling, as he had to do in his life. For now it is simply a matter of getting down these elusive recollections of that summer term as quickly as possible, reliving them now with the same clear-eyed innocence regained through nearly a lifetime's struggle.

Following this account will be some more sober reflections on staff, friends and my own emotional and intellectual development.

The subsequent days and weeks didn't really live up to the rather dramatic start described above, and as I zoom back the telephoto lens to consider those seven terms as a whole, there was no single day which is so seared or engraved on my mind as that first one. I recall incidents, impressions, friendships, conflicts, bizarre adults and, overall, the extraordinary license, even freedom, which was granted to us within the confines of the prison in which we were necessarily held. Half way through my stretch there I started keeping a diary, and became meticulous about recording the events of every single day, much to the disparaging amusement of Chalkie White, the lunatic headmaster. Rereading this so many years later is both revealing and disappointing: much of what I wrote in those emotionally stable days is simply a factual account of what happened in lessons, what the meals were, things we did and so on. I couldn't then step outside myself to observe the significance of particular feelings, though even in those tender preteen years I grasped that certain matters should definitely *not* be written down for anyone to discover, or if they were it should be in some sort of oblique way or even in code. Perhaps I already had an inkling that what Life held in store for me was not something too many others would approve of, and that if one wasn't going to conform, it was better to keep one's apostasy secret. This was in effect the tentative start of a double life which I sensed would be necessary for survival in an uncomprehending and often hostile world.

Despite my later inevitable questioning of religious indoctrination, a naïve belief in a benevolent all-seeing Deity did sustain me through those first difficult weeks. For example, I had been something of a bedwetter in my infant years, and this was still occasionally a problem at home. Oh, how I prayed to my God each night not to let me wet the bed here (*"Please!"*) and, Deo gratias, I never did. Poor little Amery in the bed opposite mine, used to suffer all sorts of ridicule from his contemporaries on account of his bedwetting, and so I nightly gave thanks to the Almighty for sparing me that humiliation. There was enough to cope with as it was.

As two new bugs arriving near the end of the academic year, both Tyrrell and I came in for a fair amount of casual, though not entirely malicious, bullying. Any little idiosyncrasy that could be discovered in one's mannerisms would be seized upon and exaggerated mercilessly by gangs of taunting boys. Apparently I would scratch the back of my neck, quite unconsciously, and so when we played on the lawn I had to endure gauntlets of goading neck-scratchers chanting "Nich-ol-son" in rhythmic chorus during free time, of which there was plenty. This seemed horrible enough, but I was constantly warned that there was to be worse to come, that everyone was in fact being easy on me because I was new, but *"Just you wait* until next term, your second term – the *bashing-up* term". I was to hear so much about this ritual bashing-up that seemed to be being reserved especially for me, that I could not but believe it. Needless to say, when that dreaded term arrived, everyone had quite forgotten their threats, as they were having far too much fun trying to get a rise out of the fresh intake of new bugs: myself, I regret to say, included, and shamefully perhaps all the more so for the way I had been made to suffer.

There was so much to assimilate, so much that seemed uncomfortable and strange which however soon became an accepted part of the routine. One thing I'd taken for granted at home, for example, was being able to wash myself in private – I certainly no longer needed my mother's help for this. The notion of communal bathing was completely alien to me, but at least I was introduced to it gradually, and not thrown in at the deep end. That first term there were only baths, and a rota for mornings and evenings was pinned up in the small washroom, which comprised a row of basins and three rather ancient tubs, accommodating two boys each. In the evenings, these were supervised by Matron, the headmaster and anyone else who cared to stroll in to watch us at our ablutions, but, early in the morning, one was, amazingly, trusted to get on with it by oneself. So that is how I remember my first shared bath with Horton, a tall, tanned handsome lad, casually pleasant of manner and most easy on the eye. I was shy at first, and after running the hot water so that it reached a decent level and testing it with my hand, I rather awkwardly took my pyjamas off hurriedly, bottoms first, thrust them onto the floor and quickly hopped in first.

From this position of relative safety I was able to observe smoothie suave Horton as he, in contrast, nonchalantly removed his own top and bottom, turned and placed them carefully on the nearby chair before finally deciding to join me. Facing me, he first lifted one stunning leg over the side followed leisurely by the other, affording me a full and prolonged vision of all that lay in between. He then stood for a few moments, perhaps deciding if the temperature was OK before finally lowering himself slowly into the water. I couldn't then have explained why, but the sight of this miraculous glowing naked body gradually accompanying me into the bath was pure heaven, and every inch of its magnificence is indelibly etched upon my inner eye.

Everything was of course all very proper; after all, this wasn't Glover. Somehow it was all the more thrilling for that: the initial "accidental" touching with one's toes ("Ooh sorry") and then being touched back ("That's OK, don't apologise"), and later hands unavoidably brushing against feet, legs, thighs ("Oh golly, that seems to be *your* leg") and then – yes, you're there before me. Do I really have to spell it out? OK then, if you insist, we did coyly feel each other *there*, under the soapy water so that should someone come in suddenly our explorations wouldn't be too obvious. When we reached this point all conversation ceased: it somehow seemed too serious for words.

Bath time in the evenings was far less fun.

But people also spoke of the *showers* – everyone naked in the same room together, all clothes to be left in the dormitory. What? No! Unbelievable. But surely they were never used, were they? A relic of a bygone age before real baths could be afforded … For indeed I'd *seen* them in the downstairs washroom. I can see them now, six little sprinkle heads which wouldn't now reach my shoulders, sadly drooping through neglect. In the summer term boys swam and played cricket and had normal baths – no need for these showers. Ah, just you wait until the winter term, Nicholson, after games. You'll see.

So this was something else new to be anxiously awaited in that dreaded second term, though perhaps with less foreboding than the legendary bashing-up.

Although slightly apprehensive when returning for my first autumn term, I had more or less become used to the way things worked and waving my mother goodbye was not nearly as traumatic as before. Physically, I was growing fast and felt I could handle a fight or two, should anyone care to try and administer the bashing-up which was apparently due to me. But boys' memories are short: not only was there no mention to me of the second-term tradition, but there was to none of any of the new arrivals either. I made two close friends during that 1968/69 academic year: the first because his good nature refused to rise to the mild ragging I was trying to inflict on him, the second just sort of happened naturally – we simply clicked.

I encountered Williamson, usually simply Willy, whilst playing outside one break time: a rather slow, deliberate individual with a ponderous gait and very round face. I immediately nick-named him Pieface, hoping thus to incite his wrath and give me an excuse for a fight. He merely laughed, however, and pointed out that his eyes could be cherries and his nose the funnel in the middle supporting the pastry; it was all rather disarming. He somehow became devoted to me and I must confess I did tend to dominate him, especially when he came to stay in the holidays and we engaged in various sex games … but I'm getting ahead of myself. Tyrrell also remained a firm friend, and he too was to play an important part in my sexual awakenings.

My closest buddy throughout my time at Beatemup was a boy who lived on a farm not far away. He had ruddy features, a cheerful disposition and one of those first names that could also have been a girl's, Lindsay. In those days, luckily for him, first names were never used so he was always referred to by his surname, Eccles. Even back then, aged eleven, I was starting to make the distinction between boys whom I liked as people and those to whom I was drawn for their looks. I would be curious about the latter and relish seeing them naked, mildly titillated by the strange tingly stirrings the sight aroused in me. I can still see gorgeous Muller arriving in the dormitory dressed only in a towel which another boy suddenly grabbed and tried to remove. Muller's reflexes were quick enough to snatch the end of the towel and he was left struggling in a frantic tug of war, cock rapidly bouncing up and down, as he bravely, but vainly, tried to repossess his property. With Lindsay however, there was no such curiosity – he was a mate, not particularly good-looking and, so I thought, rather ignorant or prudish about sex. Not that I was that advanced: amazingly, given my explorations with Andrew Bristowe, I wasn't even aware yet of the pleasure to be gained from self-stimulation.

My judgment of Eccles' innocence was entirely misplaced, as I discovered to my surprise one holiday when he was staying with me.

Before continuing with my relations with other boys in the school, this seems a good place to consider some of the teachers.

Apart from Chalkie, there are four members of staff whose names immediately spring to mind when I think of Beatemup Manor. I will list them in order of the lasting mental impression each made upon me and the influence they had: A V Plommer, David Sillince, Finlay Cornish, and P O Newman. The latter, known as Pongo, was hopeless at keeping order, but still much loved by the boys. Of lesser significance were Mr. Brown, who, besides a dormitory prowler, was a chain-smoker who normally got through at least four fags per lesson; Brian Barst, who was always late for class bearing a freshly made steaming cup of coffee; pathetic Mr. Paine, whose ability to maintain any sort of classroom discipline was notable by its absence (Pongo was a martinet by comparison); "Pervy" Purvis, who replaced Sillince as French teacher in my last year (arriving with a boy called Noble from a prep school which had closed down and where the boys swam naked – I still retain a vision of Noble nonchalantly stripping off in the dorm whilst engaged in idle chat with me) and finally young Mr. Fletcher, also only there for my last year, teaching English to the scholarship class. He enlightened us as to the public schools at which anal intercourse on the young boys by the bigger were most commonly practised: top of the list was Hurstpierpoint, where "you go if you want to get really well and truly buggered."

With the possible exception of Fletcher, all these men in retrospect were clearly devoted to us in various ways. As bachelors and boy-lovers, none of them would be likely to qualify for a teaching post in today's dreary, sanitised, conformist world, and yet through their very eccentricity they probably had far more to offer to the quirky puerile mind than the boring average *Mr. Look-at me-aren't-I-ever-so-decent-and-conventional* square of today.

To my knowledge no boys were ever "had" by any of these teachers, and I suspect this had more to do with the geography of the school than the morals of either adult or child – there was simply nowhere private enough to go. The Masters all lived in, their rooms either dotted around the school in very public places or located in the staff bungalow. There is a strong memory however of when the school doctor conducted a full medical of the whole school. What a job; someone had to do it I suppose. We queued in underpants and were felt all over by this man under the watchful eye of Matron, who didn't demur when he held our cocks and testicles in his hand and asked us to cough. I found this rather pleasant, but I do remember one boy objecting violently to it though there was no way he could complain officially. That was the way things were done, end of story.

Mr. Purvis resided in the "bungalow" and I frequently visited him to see and experiment upon his organ, a wonderful old harmonium. I always had to pass through a gauntlet of often disapproving-looking staff to get there.

Pervy used to spend nearly every evening in the local pub and, much to my mother's misgivings, told me that the place had an old harmonium which they were chucking out and which I would be welcome to have. It was, in the event, a much smaller organ than his and fitted easily into the car. I played endlessly on it, and still have it though it is being looked after in a friend's house in Belgium. But in my second term, I still knew nothing about music; I have Mr. Plommer ("Plom") to thank for opening a door into a whole new wonderful world of sound and creativity, a discovery which was eventually to become my career.

Plom was a true original with a brusque manner and a heart of gold, loved and feared by all. He played several instruments, including the 'cello, clarinet, piano and organ with foot pedals. In the summer term he would frequently sit outside playing the clarinet; this was how I first came to hear Mozart's wonderful K 622 concerto. His room was next to Chalkie's study and when the senior boys gathered there in their dressing gowns, as they did every evening after their baths, his pleasant light baritone voice could often be heard floating through the closed door, joyfully executing some well-known Italian operatic aria. He was an effective games master and charismatic mathematics teacher, though often he would be lured into red herrings and tell one of his many fascinating stories which held all of us mesmerised, hanging on every word. He drove a classic Austin 7 which he kept in spankingly clean condition, and would take parties of boys out in it for a spin: such a treat when I was eventually among the honoured chosen ones.

My serious involvement in music started one day when Plom came up to me and fixed me with his terrifying stare, moustache twitching, barking interrogatively as he did to so many: "So Nicholson, are you a passenger?"

"Sorry, Sir?"

Much louder and impatiently: "Are you a passenger, boy?"

"I don't know, Sir."

"Well what do you do?"

"Do, Sir?"

"Do you play for a school team?"

"No, Sir!"

"Do you sing in the choir?"

"No, Sir!"

"Do you play an instrument?"

"No, Sir."

"Then you are just a passenger. Do you *like* being a passenger?"

Almost tearful by now: "N-n-no, Sir."

"So what are you going to do about it?"

"Erm, I'll play an instrument, Sir."

And so I did, finally earning Plom's respect and approval, and more importantly deriving huge personal satisfaction and confidence from discovering I could do something really well. I taught myself the recorder first, speeding through the books finding out simultaneously how to read the notes and play them, followed by the clarinet where progress was equally rapid. Plom's praise for my abilities, never lightly bestowed, fell like balm on my soul: the more he said things like "You're getting really good, Nicko," the more I wanted to improve and the better I got. After two terms he entered me for grade 3, which I passed with distinction and, after that, grade 5 (likewise). I inspired Willy and Eccles into taking up the clarinet as well, and together we formed rather a competent trio, even providing background music for the school play; a great honour. Plom never allowed complacency to set in though, and was often harshly critical of my public performances, upbraiding me on aspects such as rhythm or intonation. It is from Plom that I learned never to be satisfied with any personal achievement, as there is always the possibility of doing better.

Although the behaviour of many masters, beginning at the top, was odd, it never seemed so to us. This was school, not home: another universe. Different things happened here which didn't occur in the real world, but we never thought them that weird or strange. It was just the way things were.

So when Chalkie White madly rampaged round the school rubbing his hands together, mouth opening and closing rapidly, spittle dribbling down his chin and his whole body quivering with rage, one just knew to stay out of his way until the episode had passed; usually his fits lasted about two hours. It was rumoured he'd been blown up in the war and had a plastic chest, so it seemed to us quite reasonable that he should explode himself, which he did about once a week. He had an old Italian car which would take over half an hour to get going whilst he sat throttle pushed to the floor, engine screaming at maximum revs with the vehicle completely immobile. Because of this I will never forget the Latin word for "immediately", *statim*. Finlay Cornish, our classics master, wryly observed that "Mr. White's car always starts *statim*."

I heard of Mr. Cornish years later in the early 1990s when working in rather a good prep school myself. He'd successfully applied for a teaching post there and his name was announced in a staff meeting – he'd be joining us the following term. When I piped up that this was my old Latin teacher, the head and second master had an immediate private conference and checked dates with me afterwards. In the event, his appointment was cancelled and I never did discover why, though it wasn't because of (and I felt very bold asking the question) "little boys".

Mr. Cornish's influence was twofold. He was another chain-smoker and the fingers of his right hand were badly stained yellow. Because of this I made sure, when I later took up the delightful habit, that I held my cigarettes so that the smoke would not pass over my hand, with the result that after forty years of daily smoking my hands are still unsullied.

More significantly, his calligraphy was wonderful: a beautiful left-leaning Italic script that I just had to emulate. My handwriting became almost a replica of his, and earned me for a while his favouritism. There was much experimentation with different thick nibs, and my diary shows a swing between the new style and the traditional joined-up writing I had learned at Miss Firf's of the PNEU school, with sometimes a blotchy mess in between. My public-school housemaster later forced me to change this into a more "legible" style. The compromise between the script I had to adopt and the urge to go back to the former style resulted in the illegible scrawl my handwriting became when I was an adult. I wonder in this computer-controlled age whether children ever pay as much attention to their handwriting and pens as I did aged twelve.

"What's going on?" I can hear the reader who's managed to stay with me so far ask. "There's been at least three pages and the dirty-minded bugger hasn't mentioned sex at all!" We'll get there, just be patient, there's yet another unique teacher who needs to be mentioned in some detail first.

I remember David Sillince (DS) as the most exciting and inspirational of the masters during this year. Naturally charismatic, he attracted boys the way bitches on heat attract dogs, and was always surrounded by a crowd of the more dominant ones – weaker boys somehow never got a look in. Apart from his enjoyable way of teaching, in which he once made me take over the class whilst he sat in my place, I remember his French lessons for two specific reasons. When he set work to be done in class, he would often produce a sheet of manuscript paper and spontaneously compose music using a fountain pen. Not yet able to read music fluently I was struck by the beautiful shapes of the notes as they appeared on the five lines, along with all those other funny squiggly symbols, stylishly written by DS and clearly heard in his head. How I longed to be able to understand what was being written and to do it myself.

The other memorable action was his tendency to stamp on any hint of bad behaviour by ordering the culprit out in front of the class. DS would then remove one of his large leather brown shoes and beat the offender hard on the backside with it, after ordering the unfortunate lad to lower his shorts (the whole school wore shorts) and bend over the master's chair. In the mornings modesty was preserved as underpants were worn, but in the afternoons boys were often in games kit and the strict rule was "no pants underneath". There was a breathless shocked hush in the class when this happened for the first time and a rather naughty (and nice-looking) boy called Lochhead, crimson with embarrassment, had to bare all to be whopped. We were all very careful not to cross DS during afternoon lessons, but there was sometimes the occasional victim, much to the schadenfreudish delight of the spectators.

To help me refresh my memory I was able to access some comments from old boys on the now defunct website Friends

Reunited. Lochhead recalls how cruel the system was, so maybe he is still smarting with embarrassment from the humiliation of those bare-bottomed public whackings from DS.

I was fast becoming quite a connoisseur of the endlessly fascinating variety of boys' intimate parts, for those much anticipated and simultaneously dreaded showers were now regularly happening after games exactly as foretold. We changed into sports gear in the dormitory, immediately after lunch, and football or rugby would happen after the first two sessions of afternoon school. After the game, all the dirty muddy little creatures (I somehow managed to avoid getting muddy even on the wettest days) were expected to remove everything, walk to the washroom and queue for shower. It was normal protocol simply to hold one's towel rather than wear it during this entire operation. Any attempt to cover up would have attracted derision and merciless taunting.

What an eye-opener it was! Previously I had only been aware of long and short cocks, and the phenomenon known as Roundheads and Cavaliers. I'd never even seen descended testicles. As for the shape of bottoms, I had by then only distinguished between plump ones with dimples at the top and flat, less interesting ones, but now I was dazzled by the infinite variety of nudity, and nobody seemed to mind anyone having a good look. It was even discussed how much the master taking showers was enjoying himself, and whom he was enjoying, by where his eyes roamed: a teacher who used to pretend not to be looking was soon rumbled as he used to focus his gaze on the large adjacent mirror.

My initial reluctance to be seen naked myself was soon overcome by the sheer joy of being amongst such a large number of infinitely enthralling young bodies. I saw pubic hair for the first time, huge cocks on rather small boys, smaller ones disappearing into large hanging ball-sacks which swayed as their owner moved around washing himself. I saw high-placed cock-and-ball arrangements which seemed to form a single unit and permit a view between the legs of that heavenly join between the front and back. With some boys you could see their equipment from behind as it hung down low with a sufficient gap between the lower part of the bottom and the meeting of the thighs. Occasionally a boy would bend over to pick up the soap … Heaven! I could meander on, but you probably get the idea.

The ecstasy induced by this early experience of drinking in the infinitely variegated delights of naked boys has remained intense throughout my life, and the determined pursuit of these visions has been the source of both unbelievably intense excitement and utter catastrophe: the sheer exhilaration of the moment takes complete hold of you, and all sense of caution and danger is thrown to the winds. Before I discovered that real sex between boys and men was not only possible, but often welcomed by the former as pleasurable and uncomplicated fun, I was resigned to the fact that scopophilic activities would be my sole sexual outlet. They would be less likely to lead to trouble and could cause no harm to pretty boys, innocent and unaware of the lustful turmoil aroused by sexy little bodies.

During barren boyless times I have often had to resort to the rather recondite and tricky sport of observing without being observed observing, and even this really rather harmless pleasure became increasingly fraught with difficulties as opportunities for it gradually dwindled. This theme has played a significant role in my life: the challenging awareness that the ineluctable love of boys will always form an essential part of one's nature, knowing that it is a dangerous love because of the incomprehensible irrational hostility of society and yet, paradoxically, realising it as a mutually beneficial one. At eleven, I had no idea of the storms ahead; the shades of the prison house were then simply a limitation on my immediate freedom to set foot outside the school. Progressing through adolescence I came more and more to realise that I inhabited a foul world in which I had to hide my feelings in order to survive. By sixteen, I was fully aware that these incarcerating shades were not only choking self-expression and causing untold mischief by the necessity for sexual repression, but astonishingly could result in my being sent to a real prison if I acted as my urgent emotions told me was natural. With no one to turn to that I could trust, I knew the path ahead would be lonely and full of pitfalls.

But that was all in the future. At Beatemup sex was, as it should always be, pure innocent fun. To conclude this chapter I will describe how I first heard about masturbation officially, and my own early attempts at it as both a solo and shared activity.

It was a boy called Adorian, who subsequently went to Eton and was extremely unhappy there, who first described wanking in detail while we were in a classroom awaiting yet another late master. Young master Adorian was clearly an adept himself, for his account of rubbing his willy to make it stiff (even I knew about *that* aged twelve) but then continuing, and continuing, until "this most amazing feeling goes right through your whole body" was something I'd not yet come across. I can see the look on Adorian's face and hear his awed tones to this day, and had the sense I must have been missing out on something truly epic. I resolved to experiment with this at the first opportunity, and dashed to the toilets during the next break period to test out the truth of Adorian's account.

For once I'd been given entirely accurate information and the overwhelming shattering sensation of the climax, far from disappointing, exceeded all expectations and was richly different from anything I'd hitherto experienced. I wonder how many readers can remember the defining moment of their first orgasm, whether self-induced or, and how I wish mine had been, brought about by an obliging companion, and the sheer bliss of the then-still-dry explosion which one longed to prolong forever. If there was a disappointing aspect to it, it was that the feelings went away far too soon and, even though I optimistically continued rubbing away enthusiastically, the organ which seconds before had produced such exquisite pleasure merely shrivelled up and frustratingly refused to respond. I soon learned that, for some reason, my pecker needed some time to recover before performing this magnificent service again. With practice I found ways of shortening these recuperative periods, and learned how to stimulate my precious boycock as much through erotic imaginings as by purely manual stimulation.

As with any new piece of knowledge or skill one acquires, I couldn't now imagine ever *not* having known about it and became suddenly aware that wankers were everywhere, especially in Beatemup Manor. A fact of life which, in my innocence, I had simply not noticed soon became abundantly obvious. I was of course familiar with every inch of every boy's body in the school and knew not only which ones had huge cocks proportionate to the size of their bodies, but also which of these impressive weapons had a little moustache or sprinkling of hair just above them. What I hadn't realised was that it was these magnificent specimens which were capable of producing that mysterious white fluid which my mother had been so reluctant to tell me about all those years ago, and that this marvellous liquid spurted out of the cock at the exact same moment as the blissful feelings surged through one's entire being.

More things began to make sense. There was an extremely well-endowed handsome boy called Addison who, I now realised, was prepared to give exhibitions to members of his select circle; sadly I was not one of these. Previously I had been puzzled that a gang of curious boys should huddle in awe round Addison near the end of the large playing field, making sure that he was hidden from sight, far enough away to warn him of approaching masters. I soon learned that he had been producing spunk for a good few months and was not only extremely proud of the fact that he could ejaculate when his friends couldn't, but was delighted to demonstrate his skill to them.

To begin with, masturbation was for me a purely solitary activity and I developed my own special technique, whereby I would pull the foreskin over the top of the glans and tug away wildly on it. This always produced the desired result, but was not, I was to learn later, the most effective method of creating and prolonging the pleasure. This was still my penultimate year at this odd little school and most of the boys in my dormitory were still relatively naïve. Such sex play as went on, as with Glover on my first night, was fairly inconsequential. It was during my final year that veritable orgies would spontaneously take place well after lights out, with much imaginative use being made of torches. With my tendency to shyness, I always pretended to be asleep when these public performances were going on. Anyone awake was expected to participate, and your forfeit was worse if you were caught shamming slumber. I kept my eyes firmly shut when the torch was shone in my face: "Feeling sexy Nicholson?" I made sure however that I didn't miss a single piece of the action and can still see these naked antics in my mind's eye. It is absurd to reflect that had anyone managed to capture these naturally exuberant group manifestations of boyish sexual experimentation on camera, the images would be rated as grade 1 child pornography today, and earn their possessor a lengthy term in jail. How puritanically evil the world has become.

But back to Stephen's life-changing discovery and how it progressed through that year of growth and increasing self-knowledge. I was now becoming far more sexually curious about my contemporaries, and began mentally to categorise them more according to a composite of their physical attributes and personalities: not just sizes of cock-and-balls and shapes of bums but also the level of sexiness in their behaviour. Some boys seemed to be utter weeds with no sex appeal whatsoever. Perhaps as a mere observer I was then one of them, who knows. Others exuded a magnetic playful energy which I started to find enchanting and irresistibly attractive, and have continued to do so since. I admire this quality in a boy even when no sex play has taken place nor is likely to. It is infectious and life-enhancing and the world seems a far better place when you are in the company of such an individual. Any boy-lover reading this will know exactly what I mean, for this impish trait remains a part of their own emotional make-up, latent until triggered by that increasingly rare specimen in these ugly times: a real boy.

Many examples of such a boy at Beatemup at this period flood my memories. There was Keene, for instance, who often played with himself after lunch when we were supposed to be reading improving literature silently on our beds for thirty minutes. A senior boy would come round with a tin of sweets – three each, though brave souls who knew where this container was kept would often risk disgrace by raiding it. One day a virtuous booky lad mentioned that he was reading an excellent novel called *Moby Dick* and Keene stood up on his bed, proudly pulled his shorts down and displayed his rock-hard erection with the words: "This is *my* Moby Dick!"

There was always a fair amount of casual nudity at the end of this rest period, as the less inhibited boys would strip off completely prior to donning games clothes. Spoilsport Nicholson was always careful to do top half first and then bottom half – what a whopping wetty he was, clearly not a real boy at all. I always preferred the Cavaliers, but one particularly striking Roundhead called de Courcy-Hughes was a notable exception. He once removed everything and was just about to put on his jockstrap when he remarked casually that he wanted to be an actor when he left school. Someone immediately replied that he would have to do a lot of work in the nude, whereupon he threw his jockstrap to one side and sensuously adopted various provocative poses to show his wonderful physique off to its full advantage. Another boy asked him, "How does that feel?" to which the immediate reply was a languid "Just great, man."

There was little Brownlow, a well-proportioned but diminutive boy in all respects bar one. He was on a special medicine which was supposed to stimulate growth but, everyone was convinced, only seemed effective on one part of his body – the size of which exceeded anything I have witnessed since on man or boy, and I've seen some whoppers in my time. He was extremely proud of his enormous truncheon and was happy to give demonstrations by arrangement of what it could do, whilst incredulous onlookers gaped and marvelled.

One of the strangest exhibitions I witnessed was when I woke up in the middle of the night and wondered if I were still dreaming. A rather tall, posh and stuck-up boy called Swinyard, not particularly attractive, was walking up and down the length of the dormitory. He seemed untroubled by the fact that he was completely naked and that his respectably-sized member was sticking up rigid, and bobbing from side to side under a beam of light from the dormitory captain's torch carefully focused on it as he made his steady way up and down the catwalk. As usual I pretended to be asleep whilst this was going on and wondered if it were a nightly occurrence; also whether Lochhead senior, the somewhat sadistic dorm captain in question, was forcing Swinyard to do this as a form of forfeit. If so, the latter was complying magnificently and with admirably cool insouciance.

But back to Stephen's tremendous new revelation: masturbation soon became part of my daily routine, normally at least once during the day and always in bed after lights out. I thought I was being terribly discreet here by raising my knees so that the rapid up-and-down movement shouldn't be too much of a giveaway. How easy it is to deceive oneself. I soon discovered that my nightly exertions had earned me the reputation of a dedicated Olympian wanker, though this didn't involve any disapproval – quite the reverse. One night when I was hard at it, dear Tyrrell suddenly appeared on the floor by my side, having silently crawled the length of the dorm under all the other beds. He told me matter-of-factly that he knew what I was doing and would I please do it to him.

Well, ever happy to oblige, I wanked my first boy to orgasm, while he sat and purred happily, thumb in mouth. It was the first time I'd experienced another person's pleasure as my own and was something I was determined to repeat. Tyrrell declared my technique unusual, though he seemed quite happy with the outcome and scuttled back to bed contented.

So, I wondered, who next? Tyrrell had really behaved rather boldly, and I sensed that however vigorous and noisy I made my nightly ritual it was unlikely to attract others to my bedside curious for a hand job. So what should I do? Ask every attractive boy in the school if they fancied a free wank, deftly administered by Yours Truly? I was far too timid for that. In retrospect I could probably have had lots of fun, but even in those free and easy times gaining a reputation as a nifty manual manipulator might just have led to trouble from spoilsport adults. But ah yes, of course, there was young Williamson, two years younger than me and always eager to please.

I worry today if my behaviour was exploitative and whether I was using Willy purely for my own pleasure, though he never complained or needed much inducement. It was usually easy to find places where we could play together unobserved, often in the music room or the dormitories. Here we were once caught with our pants down by pathetic Mr. Paine, who had clearly noticed us creeping off at an unusual time of day and guessed our intentions. I hope he has pleasant memories of what he witnessed before we both scarpered, hurriedly pulling up our shorts as we went. I suspect he saw such opportunities as perks of the job; he certainly never attempted to pursue the matter or punish us.

If I were writing one of those pederastic fantasy books rather than recalling events as accurately as possible, I would have had Mr. Paine gleefully rubbing his hands and declaring something like "Gotcha!"

"Oh golly Sir, where did you come from? Don't tell anyone about us, pleeeeeeeeeeeease!"

"Well that depends. You're both behaving in a disgusting, beastly way and deserve to be punished – severely. I shall report you to the headmaster. Both of you pull your trousers up and come with me."

"Oh, please don't report us, Sir. We'll do anything for you if you keep this to yourself, Sir. Anything!"

"*Any*thing, you say? Mmm, perhaps we could come to some arrangement."

I don't think I need continue except to observe that Paine (Keene called him that mockingly to his face) was far too much of a wimpy weed to take that sort of advantage of the situation. I might have respected him more if he had.

So, fun though furtive gropes with Willy were, it was during the holidays when our serious sex play would take place as he came to visit frequently. My mother often left us alone together because of her work or visits to her own friends in the evenings. The sex consisted in me being the mostly active partner: I'd have all Willy's clothes off as soon as I could and explore his body thoroughly with my hands. I'd like to think I used my tongue too, but my memory of this "sex" is of him standing or lying placidly whilst Stephen gazed and felt in all those naughty places. As ever, it was that luscious area between the scrotum and backside that received my full attention.

Rather selfishly, I didn't really want him doing stuff to me, which being of a gentle disposition he was mostly fine with. But I do, to my shame, recall him using his sexiest voice almost pleadingly: "C'mon – 'smy turn now." What a nasty, selfish brute I was to refuse him, and without wishing to analyse my twelve-year-old self too deeply, perhaps this had as much to do with the wish to dominate someone as with sex itself. There was a more unlikely encounter with my other close Beatemup friend later on, which took me completely by surprise and was to be a much more equal, spontaneous and joyous romp in my bedroom.

Along with sexual awareness, my general emotional make-up was also rapidly maturing during this crucial period between the pinnacle of boyhood and that turbulent period of hormonal pandemonium when one's comfortable world of certainties is cruelly and incomprehensibly overturned, necessitating a recon-struction of one's individual set of values and beliefs. Sadly, one of the commonest occurrences in this process is a rejection of one's parental conditioning as one begins to apprehend that most of one's opinions are second-hand and require thorough review and verification before one can adopt them as one's own. This is inevitably distressing both for parents and teenagers, but real growth is seldom achieved without pain.

The first evidence of this new maturity was a broadening of my musical tastes. Until the age of twelve and before Plom's goading of me into taking up an instrument, I used to listen to all manner of popular music and never missed the round up of the top thirty on Radio 2 every Sunday afternoon. Hits such as the Hollies' "Jennifer Eccles" (wolf whistle), the Scaffold's "Lily the Pink" and the Beatles' "Ob-La-Di, Ob-La-Da" take me straight back to those long evenings of my first summer term at Beatemup when I would listen to my little transistor radio out on the lawn, content and at peace with myself. When working through the two *Tune a Day* clarinet books, however, I discov-ered all sorts of extracts from composers I hadn't heard of before, with funny names like Brahms, Schubert or Dvořák and soon discovered a whole exciting new world of sound which had to be explored.

Henceforth all my pocket money was spent on building an impressive collection of classical records, which at that time cost in between 19/11 and £2 8/6. That's 99p. and £2.42 in decimal currency, a huge sum then. It became a joy when, the following

Christmas, I was given a stereo record player by my wealthy uncle so that I could listen to these in solemn silence at home and be transported to a new magic and exotic world. Such was the pure delight of this that I felt if life offered me nothing more than the ability to sit and listen to great music in solitude mine would be a happy existence indeed.

As well as music, my other solitary joy was reading. Before being sent away to school, I would have already devoured all manner of literary styles, including Jules Verne, Robert Louis Stevenson and Aesop's *Fables*, in addition to the comics already mentioned. The forbidding prospect of boarding school had led me to such stories as Antony Buckeridge's *Jennings and Darbishire* and the many public-school yarns penned by the highly prolific Frank Richards, including Tom Merry's adventures and the *Billy Bunter* stories, which I collected avidly.

Once on my bed during a rest period after lunch I was completely absorbed in a *Tom Merry* book, only to have it suddenly snatched away by a bullying prefect, the elder Lochhead who "persuaded" Swinyard to do his nude catwalk. On pain of some dire punishment, the prefect demanded to know what page I was on. Of course I was not able to tell him, but ever since that incident my delight in reading has been slightly clouded by the illogical compulsion to check page numbers regularly, just in case this information were to be urgently required.

My reading was thus still relatively superficial, but my emotional life was becoming increasingly enriched and prematurely deepened through the experience of romantic composers such as Chopin and Tchaikovsky. Along with attempting to play the Mozart clarinet concerto, I was having a go at the works of Weber, which were enormous fun with their virtuosic pyrotechnics and operatic slow movements. I'm sure my playing of them was dire, but listening to recordings of such diverse performers as Jack Brymer, Gervase de Peyer and Benny Goodman was a huge inspiration.

My academic work was also improving and I was, amazingly, considered capable of trying for a scholarship for the special public school, whose entrance paper I had failed just over four terms previously. This meant that in my last year I was in the elite top class with boys much brighter than myself, trying for scholarships to the most distinguished public schools. It was not an altogether happy experience as I, and a few others, were not able to quite hold our own in the competitive mental gymnastics and were frequently subjected to humiliation. Six years later, at a social function in the school where my mother worked, I happened to meet again a particularly obnoxious boy called Onslow, who apologised for his nastiness back then. But I had completely forgotten about it, and only had eyes for his younger brother who had blossomed into a stunningly attractive blond fourteen-year-old.

In the hothouse of after-lights-out dormitory sex displays, the intimate friendship with Willie and Eccles, masturbatory fumblings with the former and daily private wanking, my first wet orgasm in June 1969 came with a confusing mixture of achievement and misgiving.

This insipid spurt of colourless liquid, collected in my foreskin because my technique had not yet moved on, was not at all what I'd been expecting. Wasn't spunk supposed to be white? Why wasn't there more of it? For the first time too, I began to experience a strange sense of anxiety about it as the lows following the still shattering climaxes, which I wished would go on longer, became tinged with notions of shame and guilt. I still retained this simple belief in an all-seeing God, the one that had helped me and answered my prayers. What did *He* think of this? Was I offending Him?

This simple shame generally lasted only as long as the short downer following the increasingly productive and messy orgasms, and despite silly promises to the Almighty that I would try to abstain and be a good boy, I never could. The sexual feelings were still experienced purely for themselves too. Despite my increasing awareness of the attractiveness of boys' bodies, I was not yet linking my enjoyment of sexual pleasure to specific objects of desire. Although I could now add lust to my list of new and exciting emotional experiences, I did not yet lust *after* anything or have a masturbatory focus. I just enjoyed the wonderful sensation of it all.

It would have been the summer holiday following this that I had my totally unexpected, fully nude frolic with the person I had, up until then, not had any sexual curiosity about. Eccles was staying over, which was always great fun, and one evening we found ourselves alone in the flat, as my mother had, as usual, gone out. We had all manner of ways to entertain ourselves: cards, board games, records, TV, model trains sets and the like, and I was wondering what Eccles would like to do when he simply suggested mischievously: "Why don't we do sex?"

My surprise at the time is difficult to convey. There had hitherto been very little dirty talk between us and he'd struck me as someone utterly uninterested in erotic play; he was not particularly good-looking, though not ugly either, and I'd never even been curious about his little cock, though I suppose I must have seen it before. It was this sudden enthusiasm on his part which so completely threw me, but I was certainly not about to let the opportunity slip away.

"Yeah, OK."

All clothes were eagerly abandoned in seconds, and Eccles' rather small member was already rigid and ready for action. Oh, the fun we had on my bed that evening, romping away doing whatever came naturally: vigorously bouncing about on top of each other, rubbing cocks against cocks, cocks over and between buttock cheeks and generally delighting in the feel of our nakedness as we explored each other's bodies. I can hear Eccles' whoops of delight as I tap now. This would have been the first time I experienced serious sex with another person on an equal basis.

I can't even remember if either of us reached orgasm, but that wasn't really the main point. One's whole being was tingling with erotic emotion anyway, as we both discovered just how good shared sex could feel. At the time I did not appreciate just how remarkable this experience was. I would have been dismayed to have been told that as my need for sex would become more urgent, so my environment would strive to repress me and my contemporaries from experiencing it. The misguided, and very British, view was that sex would corrupt and pollute the mind of a developing teenager, whereas precisely the opposite is the case. The emphasis on ghastly compulsory games to burn up energies and purify thoughts which would otherwise be directed towards "dirty" behaviour could not be more erroneous. I'm certain that when Juvenal declared *orandum est ut sit mens sana in corpore sano*, he had no idea of the degree to which these words would be quoted out of context and misapplied over the centuries.

I will close this chapter with a few random important memories of events which occurred before I was sent off to Reed's, the public school for which Beatemup had done such a lamentable job of *prep*aring me. I'm sure one of the reasons that I was so dismally unhappy during my first three years at this brutal and forbidding institution was not just the primitive philistinism I encountered, but my own sensitive nature. My character was at the time utterly unsuited to such an environment. Adorian instinctively realised this with astonishing prescience when one day, a propos of nothing in particular, he told me seriously and earnestly that Reed's was not the right place for someone like me and that I wouldn't fit in there. There were quite a few rumours of torment and bullying of new boys at this school which mostly proved to be unfounded, but Adorian's wise words seemed to be based on some sudden insight he'd received about the sort of person I was in relation to the rough reputation which Reed's had managed to earn.

I visited Reed's at the end of the summer term before I was due to go there and had a fearful premonition of how ghastly it was going to be. The atmosphere felt cold, even hostile. During a swimming match, I saw a great lout push a smaller, fully-dressed boy into the water seemingly without any repercussions, though I like to think he was severely reprimanded later. I was also measured up for games clothes, which I so didn't want, by a sexually frustrated spinster from the school shop. She informed me that the fashion was to have games shorts "as short as possible", and I was given a ludicrous garment with virtually no crotch at all. Given that one was still not allowed to wear anything underneath, this caused a fair amount of embarrassment during PE periods and exacerbated my loathing of compulsory sport.

I was later kitted out at Gieves & Hawkes in London with an extremely expensive school uniform which I was pleased to have. The oleaginous shop assistant was very attentive, almost trembling as he unctuously took his measurements, quivering hands lingering unnecessarily on thigh and waist: "Quite the young man, aren't we, Sir." I was still naive enough not to twig the possible reason for his odd behaviour.

When I was twelve, my mother nearly died.

In the summer holiday of 1969, following Eccles' memorable visit, we were due to go on holiday to Devon. I anticipated this with huge excitement, as it was virtually another planet for little me who'd hardly travelled anywhere. Doodi had been complaining of extreme fatigue and her hopeless doctor, whom she never went to see unless really ill (he was ironically named Dr. Best), had pooh-poohed her complaints, declaring that she simply needed to get out and play more golf. When the symptoms became intolerable, she again went to consult Dr. Best only to find that he was away. She was seen by a locum, Dr. Haywood, who took the symptoms more seriously, performed various tests and took a blood sample, effectively saving her life.

He called round the same afternoon, as the immediate analysis had revealed a critically dangerous blood count with such a low level of haemoglobin that death from anaemia could not be far off. She was immediately admitted to hospital, where she spent the remainder of that holiday whilst I was farmed off to the houses of various friends, Eccles' included. That visit ended unhappily as his older brother took a huge dislike to me and resented the fact that I was staying in their house, eating their food and so on. It was the first time I'd encountered such irrational rejection, and it helped to prepare me for the inevitable disappointments which so often accompany human relations when people have different understandings and conflicting expectations of each other.

Much of that summer holiday was spent visiting Doodi in hospital; my home still contains some of the many ornamental gifts that I bought her when her life hung in the balance. I would cycle many miles each day along busy main roads, including dual carriageways. I'm sure it would be unthinkable today for a child to be allowed to cover such distances alone on a bicycle, but it seemed normal then and I never had an accident. For a thrill I would sometimes ride a friend's sports bike, complete with speedometer, as fast as I could down steep hills, always trying to reach a faster speed. I certainly hit 40 mph on one occasion – it was lucky the brakes didn't fail!

One house I stayed in was that of Doodi's friend, Mrs Hill, whose two sons were at Beatemup. This was truly grand, almost a mansion after our small flat, with luxurious bedrooms, a big kitchen where we took our wonderful meals and a huge garden where I played with her boys. These outdoor games included, to my shame, shooting birds with a 2.2 air rifle. One was supposed to aim for sparrows and starlings, as they were considered a nuisance, and when I once accidentally shot a chaffinch and saw the disapproval this aroused, I vowed never to hurt a living creature again.

Nothing sexual happened between me and the Hill brothers, but once, when I had the chance to explore the house alone, I unearthed a pile of girlie magazines in their father's study with titles like *Penthouse* and *Mayfair*. I was delighted to discover that they contained naked pictures of young ladies and devoured them greedily. I had seen nothing like this since Blick had shown everyone his *Health and Efficiency*. I don't, however, recall using them as wanking fodder, despite the fact that I was by then indulging regularly in that delightful activity. My sex play was still unrelated to any sort of sexual fantasy, but, as long as I can remember, I have always been fascinated by nudity, enjoyed the sight of people with their clothes off, whatever their age or gender, and felt liberated when I was in a situation where I could remove my own.

I had no formal sex education, apart from what Andrew Bristowe had told me all those years ago, and my dear mother was still too hopelessly out of touch with the nature of male sexuality to advise me properly.

I once discovered some white sausage-shaped objects seemingly made of stiff cotton wool in Doodi's bag. I asked her what they were and why she had them. She was far too embarrassed to tell me direct that they were called tampons and were needed when she had what was known as monthly periods. Instead, she talked vaguely about blood and making babies and our small dog Gigi, which left me more confused than ever. I later managed to acquire a "complete manual of sex instruction" when looking round local bookshops, and felt very bold buying it. I still have this, a collection of cards with graphic no-nonsense explanations, though with much left out. I showed it to my mother, who remarked: "I can give you all the sex instruction you need," but when I questioned her about words used such as orgasm, she was again very evasive.

The final excruciating time the subject of sex was raised at this stage of my life was by my mother herself – a conversation she'd clearly been dreading, but felt it was her duty to have with me. It was the traditional warning about boarding schools and some of the things that went on in them, but again it was tantalisingly inadequate, and I soon put her out of her discomfort by assuring her I already knew all about this stuff. I didn't of course, but I understood the mechanics of buggery and so assumed she was telling me to be careful about getting fucked by nasty big boys. There was no practical advice as what to do should I be forced to submit to an older boy's amorous advances – what position I should adopt and so on. Jesting aside, she was clearly horrified by the thought of me getting buggered, so I simply told her I wouldn't be, not to worry, end of story. This turned out to be the case at Reed's, not because I was a strong person capable of looking after myself, but because the atmosphere there was so anti-homosexual. Boys were terrified of being thought "gay", which was equated with inadequacy and sheer perversion. On reflection, the legalisation of homosexuality three years earlier might paradoxically have contributed to this: same-sex acts were no longer a bit of illicit fun to be enjoyed on the side, but a serious lifestyle choice defining the sort of person you were. No one wanted to be thought of as a fairy.

As my clarinet playing was improving, I attended a small music summer school shortly before going up to Reed's and was entranced by the playing of Colin Lawson, related to a friend of my mother. He performed the Mozart clarinet quintet on the final evening, a piece I then knew virtually by heart and still do. I was utterly absorbed in the performance, but was distracted every now and then by the intense looks of a man who also appeared absorbed, but seemingly in me rather than the players. His ogling eyes were fixed upon me, but I was still too immature to read their lustful message.

At one level I did understand, however, that his way of staring at me had somehow been sexual. It was the first occasion on which I was aware of being given what I later discovered was called the glad eye, sustained for more or less the entire four movements of the Mozart piece. Who knows what might have happened had that man visited me in my room later that evening? He would certainly have been pleased with what he saw as, excited by the attention, the first thing I did was to strip naked and arouse myself into a state of sexual excitement which I was able to prolong for much longer than usual. I'm certain that I didn't even bother to close the curtains of windows through which anyone in the school yard outside would have had a fine view of my masturbatory antics, and I like to think that I at least gave that man a visual treat that evening, as boys have so often unknowingly done for me.

Had he dared to knock on my door and ask to join me, when I was clearly in such a frenzied state, I still wonder what I'd have done. Perhaps I'd have been scared, lost all desire, screamed for help and slammed the door in his face; or maybe, just maybe, if he had been brave, gentle, cajoling, experienced and skilful, who knows how my life might have been transformed. I hope he would have remembered to close the curtains first.

After several blood transfusions and a hysterectomy my mother had mercifully survived, and we did make it to Devon the following year, 1970, about a month before the incident at the concert happened. We stayed with my big-hearted godmother, Barbara Williams, in her charming cottage in Ivybridge and made delightful outings, including many to various seaside places, in Doodi's new red Mini Minor, a present from a rich appreciative friend. Unfortunately, Barbara, jolly, fun-loving woman that she was and always so generous to me, strongly disapproved of homosexuals and in particular men who fancied boys. This later prevented me from being as close to her as I would have liked, and is a sad example of how people's prejudices can blind them to what is good and real in others.

It was during one of those trips to the beach with Doodi and Barbara that I had two further important insights about how my life was probably going to unfold. I felt apprehension about how I would cope as an adult, so much wanting to remain a boy forever. In the words of W. H. Hudson, "If the question had been put to me then, and if I had been capable of expressing what was in me, I should have replied: *I want only to keep what I have*". Michael Tippett's musical outburst at the beginning of *Boyhood's End* captures this hopeless longing so wonderfully.

The first incident was trivial enough. Two boys were playing on the sand in life jackets and a couple of men sitting in front of us were watching them; one was overheard remarking to the other: "I don't know why their parents need to dress 'em up like that for; mollycoddling I call it." Barbara became incensed by these comments and remarked to my mother that life jackets were very sensible by the sea, and that these were clearly a couple of "queers" who liked looking at young boys in as little clothing as possible. When I asked what queers were and why they would want to do this, both my mother and Barbara became strangely silent, but their disapproval was obvious and I became rather uneasy and thoughtful.

The second incident confirmed my fears that I might be growing up into one of these queers myself, and would thus be disapproved of by two women whom I loved more than anyone in the world. It was not a comfortable premonition, but one which reinforced the need for secrecy when it came to intimate matters, and the importance of hiding my feelings, even from those who were closest to me. Again the event was trivial enough in itself, but it was a defining one for a thirteen-year-old sensitive emotional male on the verge of puberty.

A beautiful blond suntanned boy of about twelve had been playing on the beach and it was time for him and his mother to go home. I had been already eyeing him up in an idle fashion, aware of his attractiveness and wondering if he was English.

There was an exoticness about his features which could well have been Nordic or Eastern European, but the pair were not close enough for me to catch any snippets of conversation between them.

While I was still gazing at him, admiring his perfect skin and body shape, he suddenly tugged down his brief swimming trunks prior to getting changed and the effect upon me was immediate, electric, shattering. Maybe it was the unexpectedness of this brazen behaviour in a public place, or perhaps it had something to do with the particular quality of this boy's outstanding glowing beauty, but my spontaneous reaction to his total nudity was dissimilar in nature and intensity to any feeling previously aroused in me by the sight of a naked boy, and I'd already seen many in my short life.

The sight of the perfect whiteness of his "private" area, contrasted with the brownness of the rest of him, made his handsome peachy bottom and respectable penis and balls seem somehow forbidden and hence intensely desirable. I experienced a huge, hitherto unknown and hence bewildering surge of sexual attraction and desire. Had he had an overall tan acquired from a naturist holiday in, say, France, I doubt I'd have reacted as powerfully as I did, but the vision of the most essential components of his boyhood in their virginal white glory came as something of a revelation and provoked an aching erection which I had difficulty concealing. The boy was in no hurry to dress and I was permitted an extended gaze at this rare and exquisite, yet troubling vision. Why on earth did I feel like this? What did it mean?

That was the first time I really *grasped*, not only that I fancied boys, but all that might be implied by this knowledge. It was the first time I can remember deliberately retaining a mental image of another human being who excited me sexually and, inevitably, it was the first time, later in the privacy of my bedroom, that I consciously masturbated myself to orgasm, releasing as best I could the sexual tension which the vision of this naked godlike wonder had stirred within me. I relived that glorious sight in my feverish brain as the unavoidable climax shook my helpless body: it was a personal revelation of the powerful, ineluctable fascination which the sight of naked boys in all their dazzling variety would henceforth exercise over me.

I was saddened and appalled, confused and empowered, ecstatic and frightened about becoming a man.

It was the true end of innocence.

III. Second Boarding School

ora puer prima signans intonsa iuuenta.
his amor unus erat pariterque in bella ruebant
    VIRGIL, *Aeneid*, Book IX

Just as my first day at Beatemup is indelibly engraved on my brain, so the misery and feeling of abandonment when deposited at Reed's on that first day has never really left me. There I was in my smart new uniform, emotionally impressionable and sexually precocious yet sensitive and malleable, wishing I could be anywhere but in this new prison.

Everything was Spartan, ugly and cheerless; how on earth was I going to live in such a godforsaken place? My boarding house was coincidentally named Bristowe, though there would be none of the fun offered by that cocky individual. It had three upstairs dormitories containing about thirty beds separated by small lockers. Large curtainless windows, through which anyone outside could view the whole dormitory, looked out onto the drive and main school building opposite. The communal washroom was at the end of a corridor with a small anteroom on the left just before, where Matron's workroom was located and where we hung our towels. Downstairs there were two large common rooms, the only place one was allowed to be in the house when not sleeping, changing for games or showering after them. Both rooms had a large wooden table spread around three of their sides and a huge window looking out onto the main building and drive. Above the table were rows of lockers, below were rows of plastic uncomfortable chairs and each boy was allocated his study area in alphabetical order. The other rooms downstairs were prefects' studies, and there was a small single room upstairs where the (always unmarried) assistant housemaster lived. The housemaster himself was expected to be married and occupied a bungalow attached to the building. One entered the house through a main central door and turned right. If one turned left one would be in an almost identical house, geographically-speaking, the mirror opposite of Bristowe. The two other boarding houses, contained within the main school building, were even rougher and run solely by bachelors.

The first words our housemaster uttered in his welcome address at the beginning of term were intended as a joke: "I won't pretend I'm any more pleased to see you than you are to see me." Was that possible? I wondered.

There were no instant friendships as there'd been at my last school. I loathed the place on sight and hated everything and everyone I saw, my only thought being how soon I could escape this grim den of primitive savagery. There was just one small kindly light amidst the encircling gloom as that dark day came to end, but oh such an important one. After my year had changed into their pyjamas, at the ridiculously early hour of nine, it was announced that all the new boys were to gather in the tiny room of the assistant housemaster, John Leach, who also happened to be the director of music. "Just say no to everything!" was the advice given to us by the old lags who'd come up from The Close, as the Junior School was known and into which I'd so spectacularly and mercifully failed to gain a place two years before.

As with everything else said to me that day, this sounded like sheer nonsense. Thanks to Plom, music was one thing I felt I could do well and I certainly wasn't about to make a secret of it.

I could devote a whole book to John Leach, with whom I am still in touch; he phones me regularly for updates on my medical news. (My condition is deteriorating, so there is a greater urgency to get these memoirs down whilst I still can, before that glorious oblivion.) JML, as I will now call him, was the embodiment of firm gentleness and compassionate wisdom. I loved him on sight. A small, wiry and apparently sexless man with a cultured, rather high-pitched voice, he was affectionately known as "Gosh Leach" (pronounced Gawsh) as he was supposedly always in state of surprise at the things boys said and did. As with many such nicknames, it was apt and amusing, but I really never remember JML uttering this word, just as the film critic Barry Norman never said "And why not?" despite all the impressionists of the day using the phrase liberally when mimicking him.

Music soon became far more than something I enjoyed doing. It was a refuge, an escape from the house to the five underused practice rooms (just *five rooms* for the whole school – I ask you!), a place where I could be alone, where I could be creative and meet some of the few friendly musicians from other houses. Under JML's gentle guidance, I started the piano that year, having my first lesson on my fourteenth birthday. I then started playing the violin, but avoided the choir for two main reasons. The first of these was that I didn't particularly enjoy singing, but the second had much more to do with my ever-shrinking self-confidence.

I was soon singled out as *different* from the rough-and-tumble of average, "normal" boys. I didn't join in the free-for-all ping-pong games in the junior common room, for example, when every boy would grab a textbook and walk round the table-tennis table attempting to return successfully a little white plastic ball over the net in turns (how pointless, I thought) until there were just two boys left. Nor at first did I attend the compulsory rugby sessions, which were *every* afternoon except Fridays and Sundays, for Christ's sake. I declared myself off games, and got away with this for two blissful weeks until my absence was noticed. I was then forced to change into those oh so hideous games clothes and show up for what was one of our glorious traditional public school's most otiose time-wasting rituals. I showed up on pain of being caned: one was forced to do everything under the threat of the *fucking* cane. I made every effort to avoid any contact with the ball or anyone else running with it; how much more sensible if I'd been allowed to take my exercise by going for a brisk walk and then using the rest of the time practising one of my instruments. How much better a performer I might have become, how much happier I would have been.

My differentness soon made me the target of bewilderingly malicious verbal bullying and unwanted attention. I wasn't hurting anyone else; why couldn't I just be left alone? My voice was still unbroken, along with those of quite a few others who escaped humiliation for it. In my case, however, it became an easy way to torment me: "Hello Nicholson," boys would squeak in a mockingly high-pitched falsetto, "how are we today?" I was also frequently asked, squeakily, "Are you a *eunuch*, then?" before I even knew what a *eunuch* was. Such baiting would happen incessantly, morning, day and night: in the breakfast queue, in the lunch queue, in the supper queue, moving between lessons, waiting for lessons, coming out of lessons passing some moron in the corridor, changing for games, changing after games, changing for bed, in the washrooms, in bed – everyfuck-ingwhere, all … the … *fucking* … time. It caught on amongst boys of other houses whose names I scarcely knew, and my house-master gradually became aware of the misery it was causing me.

"You must fight!" he urged in his sniffy tedious whiny voice. OK, I thought, I will then. I was quite large and well-built for my age and had some physical strength too, so I lashed out at the bullies. This only added to their amusement, though I did manage to inflict some satisfying damage on a few of them. Far from stopping the baiting, however, my reaction seemed to cause an increase in unwelcome attention (so much for *that* advice, you plonker of a housemaster). Boys became more daring and ready to defend themselves by attempting to duck and block my punches before hitting back, I got into quite a few unwanted scraps, and, most unfairly of all, was punished by the prefects for it – just *me*. I was the one punished, not the one who started it, usually with "whites": essays of a certain number of words to be written on foolscap paper provided by the prefect on a subject he chose. I can't recall the topics I was given. I'd like to think that some of these tyrannical sixth-form oafs might have chosen Gandhi's philosophy of non-aggression and passive resistance as something fitting the crime, but I suspect none of them would have had the imagination for that; it would have been something more prosaic such as "why I must not break school rules". There was a thick booklet of the latter hanging by a thick piece of string on the main notice board in the school and one was supposed to remember them all.

Fagging had been abolished some time before, and in its place was a rota of tedious jobs for the third-form boys to perform each day after breakfast: chores which would normally be done by paid domestic staff such as cleaning classrooms, and sweeping the ramp at the back of the house – always filthy with mud from the previous day's games. Although they could not officially force boys to do tasks for them, prefects would, in the name of punishment, perpetuate a type of slavery which came close to the old fagging system. During my first week, I was woken up by a prefect switching on the lights and hollering: "I can hear talking in here, everybody line up outside the dormitory." After being made to stand for nearly an hour we were told that everyone would be punished for making too much noise, as no one had owned up. I was given a messy study to clean out before making the prefects their coffee and toast and then cleaning their mugs and plates, every day for a week. This was on top of the "official" duties, which were also unpleasant. I don't remember ever being physically mistreated by these swaggering and frighteningly big Neanderthals, even though one was constantly shouted at.

Some of them used to give an early morning cold bath as a punishment. Before breakfast, the culprit, often a pretty one, would have to wake up the despot who had imposed the penance and together they would go to the bathroom. The bath would be filled with cold water and the boy had to strip, lower himself into it and stand up again. This process would be repeated several times under the ogling sadistic eye of the monitor. Perhaps I wasn't sufficiently attractive, or naughty, but this never happened to me so I can't say whether anything more interesting or indecorous occurred, though I suspect not.

Of course my work during that miserable first term suffered, and I always came very low in what was known as the three weekly orders, except in French. This was one of my favourite subjects, not just because of memories of Sillince (how I missed all those odd, friendly teachers), but because an uncle by marriage, Leslie Braedon, whose Yugoslavian wife was a very fine pianist, took the top stream in it, and I often saw them in the holidays. Leslie was urbane and amusing, an excellent teacher and disciplinarian who showed no special favouritism. He awarded me lines for being late to the very first lesson, but then "forgot" to chase them up; he'd known me as Stephen and sometimes became muddled, addressing me as Stephenson, which caused some amusement to the other boys. He lived in a pleasant staff house, well away from the main buildings, which was to become another important refuge on those

Sundays when I would be invited to tea. Auntie Vera's teas were superb; afterwards we played music together, me on clarinet while she accompanied me. I would also listen to her play Beethoven and Chopin, then watch some TV or play card games with her daughter Michelle who, at thirteen, was already extremely beautiful and much desired by many of the boys. This did in fact later add to my kudos as, when I'd eventually found my feet at the school, I was greatly envied my easy contact with her in a place where nearly all the females were ugly old termagants.

Two subjects I simply could not abide were geography and history, mostly on account of a loathing of the teacher in the first and the lazy method of teaching in the second. This consisted of wittering on and on about some battle or other while I gazed absent-mindedly out of the window thinking my own fine thoughts, the droning voice of the teacher, AW, floating over me. But then, horror of horrors, came the end of the lesson and the fatal words "Write it up for prep." Help! Write *what* up? I hadn't even the faintest notion of what he'd been blathering on about, which made writing it up an almost impossible task. He was one of those teachers whose tedious delivery, even when I tried to listen, invariably had a soporific effect.

As for geography, this was taken by an arrogant young master, GM, fresh from college and eager to establish himself as a disciplinarian. Young Stephen's behaviour never gave any of the masters an ounce of trouble in those early days, but that didn't prevent him from being an easy target of this particular teacher's heavy sarcasm. It was because of GM that I came as close as I ever would to being caned for bad work. I also had to put up with his verbal abuse on many occasions. One example will suffice: he asked me where the river Nile was.

"Africa," I replied nervously.

"Africa!!"

"Mmm," even more nervously.

"Nicholson, you are the *stupidest* person I've ever met."

Guffaws of laughter from the rest of the class. He never even bothered to correct my "mistake".

At my lowest point in that first term, I was called into the headmaster's study and lectured for thirty minutes about standing up for myself, joining in more, et cetera. All I can remember of this pi-jaw was a story he told of a boy who refused to use the swimming pool. That sounds a good idea, I thought, and, throughout my five-year stretch, followed this example as best I could. I did so even though I loved swimming for its own sake at this time – swimming because of the delightful near-naked young male creatures to be found in swimming pools was a later obsession. The odd words intoned by William Burroughs in his gravelly metallic voice as a tape loop throughout his short surreal movie *William Buys a Parrot* encapsulate the influence this strange monastic institution had upon an impressionable teen in his formative years: "Boys, school showers and swimming pools, full of them."

Yum yum.

It was entirely thanks to JML that I not only survived that first year, but managed to gain some grudging respect from my contemporaries. In the spring term I was chosen to play the junior solo in the house music competition. I came top in this category, my high mark just ensuring that Bristowe won the competition overall. This was something they hadn't done for some time but, on account of my determination, continued to do every year that I was there. The housemaster, BG, was delighted and all the important participants were invited to partake of fizzy wine afterwards. I don't think it can have been real champagne, but BG managed to break the top of the bottle whilst removing the cork, which didn't stop any of us drinking from the large silver victor's cup as it was passed round. "Mind the bits of glass," he said, "I think I got them all out, but I can't be sure." As BG was head of chemistry (very thorough, but oh *so* boring), one smart aleck in the sixth suggested he fetch some filter paper from the lab before pouring, a proposal which provoked much merriment but struck me as admirable.

The praise heaped on me by boys in the house was veritable balm of Gilead. "Well done, Nicholson," (no squeaky high voice – rapture!) "I wouldn't have had the guts to stand up in front of the school and play like that," and such-like.

At the end of the summer term I achieved the distinction of winning the then-coveted Copland prize, a cup awarded in a yearly competition to find the best instrumentalist in the school adjudicated by a visiting musician. The praise and genuine admiration I received for this were even greater, as I managed to beat some senior boys who were more advanced technically on their instruments. Who knows what other musical heights I might have scaled in the ensuing years had I not, one morning in the corridor, as I was emerging from the dining room after breakfast, received the worst possible news from JML.

"I just need to tell you something before it's formally announced. I am leaving Reed's at the end of this term!"

A surge of grief and sadness shot through me; it was all I could do not to burst into tears there and then. The happiest times of that year had been spent in his company: going to his room and listening to classical records (just the two of us, probably unthinkable now), studying for grade 5 theory so that I could take grade 6 on the clarinet at the end of that summer term, as well as concerts and shopping trips to London by train, listening to his gently humorous stories. Once when he, a very small boy, was on the escalator in the London underground carrying an enormous tuba to a musical repair shop, someone shouted to him: "Give us a tune, mate."

He took boys to many local concerts too, even if only two or three were interested. Fourteen-year-old Nigel Kennedy, such a pretty boy at the time, played Bruch's first concerto with the Surrey Philharmonic. It was in this concert that I heard Shostakovich's extraordinary fifth symphony for the first time, in the company of a blond boy a year above me called Mark Eynon. To my ears, Mark was a phenomenal pianist and I'm still not sure why he didn't win the coveted Copland Cup for his rendition of the Chopin A major polonaise. He also had a much-better-looking, sandy-haired brother, Jeremy, who joined the school when I was in the sixth form. Jeremy was a pianist too, though of much lower calibre and it transpired later that his tartish interests were more geared towards seducing French masters: he was uniquely responsible for the abrupt dismissal of two of these in successive terms.

Under JML, musical life in the school had been vibrant, an amazing achievement considering the lack of both facilities and talented pupils. He exacted a high standard from the orchestra and there was a flourishing music society, with regular chamber music concerts given throughout the school year. Sometimes these featured children from the Yehudi Menuhin School which was just down the road. One event included a divine performance of Brahms' string sextet in B♭ major in which the first cellist, a startlingly attractive boy of thirteen, looked and played like an angel. When I asked JML about this forty years later he could recall both the concert and the name of this cellist, Felix Schmidt, who now teaches at the Royal Academy of Music in London. He was the youngest protégé of the late Maurice Gendron, an excellent mentor who apparently took a benign pederastic as well as musical interest in his young male pupils.

Here is a sketch of Schmidt at about the age he would have been then:

JML went on to teach at the now celebrated specialist music academy in Manchester, Chetham's, although when he first joined the staff it had only just become a school for promising musicians and was apparently experiencing many teething troubles. The standard of music in Reed's suddenly dropped dramatically with the promotion of the very immature and narrowly talented assistant director to the top job. He only understood choirs and readily admitted to me he was not suitable for it. The idea that I might follow JML to Chetham's was seriously entertained.

In the next autumn term, during the long half term break, I took the train north to visit him there, staying in a hotel in Manchester, as the school would not provide accommodation, and completely fell in love with the place. There was plenty of top-class playing with marvellous pianists, who took the Brahms opus 120 E♭ sonata in their stride. I met many of the sophisticated and civilised students there when, for example, JML went round to supervise and help during their practice periods. There were no compulsory games, there were cosy little bedrooms with two or three people sharing, and both staff and pupils treated each other with mutual respect – what heaven! I was auditioned by their woodwind specialist and offered a place, which for some reason I was never able to take up. JML made much of the teething problems, which seemed to impinge far more on the staff than the pupils, to sweeten the bitter pill of disappointment, but I suspect the main stumbling block to my attending Chetham's was financial. There would have been no way my mother could have afforded the fees, and asking my rich uncle for further help would have been too much.

How different my life would have been had I left the nightmare of Reed's after two years. How, in a gentler, more humane environment, might I have avoided all the subsequent emotional turmoil, the hopeless confusing passions exacerbated by the monastic single-sex lifestyle as I lusted after certain boys I believed to be unavailable. How on earth I kept a lid on this explosive simmering volcanic whirlpool of conflicting feelings, cultivated by what Royston Lambert called, in his study of the effects of boarding school, *The Hothouse Society*, is beyond imaginings. I gradually reinvented myself and adopted a persona by which I might survive, becoming thoroughly unpleasant, arrogant, cynical and disrespectful of authority in the process. As I became more anarchistic, I also became more popular and came to believe that this mask was my true self, thus acquiring a rather dubious circle of friends.

Because sex was unavailable, it began to preoccupy me to an even greater extent than it would the average teenage boy whose body is awash with hormones. Certain pieces of music could still overwhelm me with pure emotion, but music began to take second place to finding ways of achieving sexual gratification without letting on to anyone that beneath my false cheerful hard veneer I was a filthy disgusting pervert, an oddity who would have sold his tainted soul to Beelzebub for a good session of raw sex with GS, DS, IR, NB, MS … The list was so long!

Boys perceived as "fairies" in this school were given an extremely hard time, but I, in my adolescent turmoil, couldn't honestly identify myself as gay anyway. I certainly didn't find men's bodies in any way attractive, and was also dying to fuck a presentable female just to see what it was like. The readily available girlie porn mags made for reasonably satisfactory wanking fodder, but when alone one day with a boy called Ridsdale who was immersed in a much-thumbed copy of *Health and Efficiency*, the magazine with which Blick had amused everyone five years previously and which still contained naked boy photos, I knew what my preference was. Ridsdale was quite unfazed about the young nude boys and even, in a rather dispassionate way, made factual observations about the various shapes and sizes of boys' penises: "Look at that one, it's just about to go erect."

During the Easter holiday in this second year I went by train to London and met up with one of my dubious friends. I can only recall his surname, Mathelone. He was an ugly brute of a boy in a different house from me – I certainly didn't want sex with *him*. The previous term he'd become anxious to improve his piano-playing and was inspired by my attempts to plough through Beethoven's *Waldstein* sonata. Beethoven, or any sort of culture, was the last thing on his mind that day however, as he was already familiar with the decadent seedy cinemas around Leicester Square (sadly long gone) which screened non-stop X-rated movies. How a couple of callow fifteen-year-olds gained admission to one of these places I have no idea, but the films we saw were an eye-opener in every respect. I think they were German or Scandinavian and dubbed very poorly into English with minimum plot and maximum depictions of all manner of sex acts with all manner and ages of people. The first film opened, for example, with a group of teenage boys coming into the changing room after swimming and removing their trunks prior to showering, and then getting up to all sorts of mischief with each other. Two of these became especially intimate and were the stars of that particular show, as we followed their antics with teachers, each other's parents, sisters, brothers – you name it.

I ended up staying at Mathelone's house that evening and had to phone home to report that I would not be back that evening, which was no problem. As money was running low we hitched a lift from Surbiton station to his house, something else I'd never done before, nor since.

There was much private discussion between us about the content of these hard-core porn movies, and Mathelone urbanely remarked that there was "something for everybody", whatever you happened to be into: women, girls, men or boys. Without letting on about my own preferences, I certainly couldn't argue with that. Replaying some of those unusual scenes in my mind provided many a pleasurable wank over the following week or so back at home and later on at school.

But at fifteen I was desperate for real sex. I devised many techniques for prolonging the feeling and delaying the orgasm, experimenting with various grips, my first method having long been superseded. I found visual stimulus in the form of pictures in ordinary publications of boys in sports gear and swimming trunks. I never felt bold enough then to seek out copies of *Heath and Efficiency* or any other magazines which might have naked boy pictures in them. They were fairly specialised and required ordering anyway. By the time I did try to buy such material, it was well-nigh impossible to find, even in an infamous "gay" men's shop in Cecil Court. When at home I would improvise various fucking apparatuses by arranging pillows and cushions on the floor, along with a tall plastic picnic mug which I would line with spongy material and Kleenexes. When everything was prepared, I would remove all my clothes, carefully place my rigid member inside the mug and hump away with my eyes closed, imagining I was screwing all the boys I most fancied at school, especially those whom I had seen naked.

It was an exquisite thrill when you first got a revealing eyeful of someone you particularly fancied, and I began to list the names of those I had already viewed and those I so longed to – mostly from other houses, those unobtainable Adonises that I would have killed to spend a night with. One useful stimulus was house photos or those of various sports teams, which I would scan with an almost X-ray vision, focusing so hard on certain individuals whose entire bodies I had witnessed that arousal came about without any manual help whatsoever. This could be prolonged in my mind into a whole sequence of sexual events which inevitably ended in a huge ejaculatory climax.

At the time I knew no different, no one had told me that boys reach a sexual peak at fourteen. Seen from the perspective of so many years it now seems a colossal waste of what was a tremendous sexual appetite to be forced to play these furtive solitary games about which I often felt so shameful. Where was Eccles now? Where Williamson? Tyrrel? Andrew Bristowe?

It was apparent when I returned to school for the summer term of 1972 that Mathelone must have told others about our cinematic adventure, and word rapidly spread about *those* films we had seen together. Bizarrely, I once again gained a new respect from this as various boys pumped me for details of the content of the movies, their titles, the name of the cinema and so on. It was known which boys had supposedly already experienced sexual intercourse at fifteen, and they were revered as real bloods, whether or not their claims were true. Watching hard-core porn in a public cinema came a pretty close second to having done it for real, and had the advantage of being verifiable. I kept very quiet about the parts which had really turned me on: my double life was beginning in earnest, and I was becoming more and more aware that one's private sexual feelings could be the cause of much misunderstanding, misery, persecution and even actual danger in this mess that adults, especially English ones, were making of the world.

I was slowly beginning to sense that the institutional environment in which I had to spend most of my time was choking my individuality, but helpless to know what to do about it. Most painful of all at this time was a sense of growing alienation between myself and my mother: she was the one who had sent me to this awful place and would not allow me to leave. Her argument that the period of five years represented such a small portion of my life even then seemed spurious, though I was not aware then of the term "formative years" and that the experiences one has during this crucial time are never forgotten, felt as they are so intensely. One event from this time which brought us together in a common grief was the death of her dear little griffon dog Gigi. Rescued by her from ill treatment, Gigi was devoted to my mother, and my mother alone, and spent all the time she was out of the house hiding under a large cabinet and whining – the time mother spent in hospital was particularly difficult. In the telepathic way that certain animals have, Gigi knew when she was on her way home and would be at the window in joyful tail-wagging anticipation a full ten minutes before the familiar sound of the Messerschmitt bubble car, and later on Mini Minor, arrived outside the house.

What a marvellous car that Messerschmitt was. My mother sold it in 1969 for £80, and working models now sell for tens of thousands of pounds.

Gigi was run over by a car in 1971, and the motorist was decent enough to bring the body to the house explaining that she had simply run straight out into the road and there was nothing he could have done. Though one doesn't like to apportion blame, it was in fact Gran who let her out. When I arrived home for the next exeat, we hugged each other and wept, and that is the last time I can recall being emotionally close to Doodi for a long while. I was still very aware of her wonderful qualities, but her very goodness was what made it so increasingly difficult to be close to her. She had, for example, an irrational hatred of the word "sod" and when I once described Gran as a "sod" mother flew into a rage and asked me if I knew the meaning of the word.

"No."

"It's short for sodomite."

"Oh."

"Yes," – meaningful nod – "so don't use it!"

Such were the gaps in my sexual education that whilst I knew perfectly well what buggery was, and was curious to try it, I had not come across the word sodomy for the same activity. Anyway I had meant the word as a vague term of abuse, and afterwards, when I consulted the dictionary and found that a sod was also a piece of earth with grass on it, felt that I had very unjustly been the object of my mother's wrath. I had been similarly chastised, many many years previously, the first time I had used the word "fuck" in front of her, also in the context of my grandmother ("fucking Granny"). I didn't stop using the word; after all, everyone else did, but simply made sure it wasn't within her hearing.

By the time I reached the fifth form, my third year at the school, I had acquired a new self-assurance founded on acting out the sort of person who seemed to get on alright at this school – not a very likeable person, somewhat arrogant and abrasive with a sharp tongue and a ready cynical wit. My true self remained buried underneath this façade, but would not allow itself to be forgotten.

I began to develop serious crushes on certain boys, mostly in the year younger than me, and the feelings they aroused were so intense that I would physically tremble when in their presence. Finding very little in contemporary culture to endorse these powerful emotions, I discovered that ancient civilisations had not only recognised such attraction, but applauded the resultant friendships as something enriching and special.

I regretted not having studied ancient Greek to any sort of standard, but came to enjoy Latin more and more. We were studying, amongst other texts, book nine of Virgil's *Aeneid*. The words which introduce this chapter made a huge impression on me as I could identify with Nisus, and longed to have a slightly younger Euryalus as a friend and lover. By sixteen I already had to shave frequently, something I hated doing, and was becoming fairly hairy compared to others in my year group: perhaps my desire to remain just on the verge of manhood attracted me to the qualities of those boys who were. Furthermore, although he was married, the Latin teacher, Mr. Savage, had a certain reputation for liking boys; for instance he also took my year for PE and made sure that all the fifteen- and sixteen-year-olds showered under his supervision afterwards. This was a delight for me, as I unexpectedly got to view naked many boys whom I fancied in other houses.

Savage treated the pederastic theme in Virgil in a purely matter-of-fact way, and ensured there were no silly titters from our rather small group. We all understood, even if no boy was brave enough to articulate it, what this form of love was about and respected the teacher for talking so directly about it.

It was around this time that I discovered Oscar Wilde; the first complete work of his I read was *The Picture of Dorian Gray*. Ideas such as this resonated with my own ideas of youth and beauty:

But beauty, real beauty, ends where an intellectual expression begins. Intellect is in itself a mode of exaggeration, and destroys the harmony of any face. The moment one sits down to think, one becomes all nose, or all forehead, or something horrid. Look at the successful men in any of the learned professions. How perfectly hideous they are! Except, of course, in the Church. But then in the Church they don't think.

The critic is he who can translate into another manner or a new material his impression of beautiful things.

The highest as the lowest form of criticism is a mode of autobiography.

Those who find ugly meanings in beautiful things are corrupt without being charming. This is a fault. Those who find beautiful meanings in beautiful things are the cultivated. For these there is hope. They are the elect to whom beautiful things mean only beauty.

The idea that a picture could grow old and bear all the outward signs of gradual corruption and decay while its subject retained all the freshness and spontaneity of youth struck me as a brilliant one. I was also becoming increasingly aware that my own sexuality was not proceeding the way others expected it to, and felt I had little control over this. My masturbation fantasies tended to be imaginative recollections of boys I had recently seen naked, or pictures of semi-clad or naked lads which were still to be found in the mid-seventies. The Green Shield stamp catalogue, for example, featured two snaps of a charming nude blond boy in its bathroom section, and years later I was able to find a digital photo of this from someone who'd been a lifelong collector of such material. During the Christmas break of 1973, I saw the adaptation of M. R. James's *Lost Hearts* with the adorable Simon Gipps-Kent and was haunted as much by his beauty as by the spookiness of the tale. I am still an avid collector of any film or TV show in which he featured during his absurdly short life.

I longed even more for the real thing however, and now grasped that although I was still curious to try sexual intercourse with a girl, this would be very much second-best to what I really craved. Given the atmosphere in the school, I despaired that I would ever achieve my dream of sex with a teenage boy and consequently tried to repress the desire as being something troublesome and dangerous.

I started reading books on psychology and discovered the theories of Sigmund Freud concerning the different levels of consciousness, and how the divided mind chooses what it will allow into everyday consciousness and buries the pain resulting from any trauma experienced in one's life. However, these unwanted feelings do not remain quietly suppressed, but lurk unrecognised in the subconscious mind, constantly influencing our behaviour in all sorts of unconscious ways. I learned to my alarm that, if not given natural expression, powerful sexual urges would be released in other ways – through violence or nervous disorders such as tics, and that, in extreme cases, this could lead to serious mental and even physical illness. I read R. D. Laing's *The Divided Self* around this time too and was deeply disturbed by it. When I later saw Laing on a TV programme, drunk and mostly incoherent, it occurred to me that he was probably madder than most of his patients, but at sixteen I had a great fear of insanity and wondered if my deviant feelings were a prelude to complete mental breakdown.

It was at this time that I began to develop very serious acne, not only on my face but in various places on my body, especially my back. In consequence I became more and more worried about taking my clothes off in front of others and began to experience serious embarrassment whenever I had to do so. I attributed the acne spots and my hypersensitive state to sexual frustration, and cursed the world I lived in for forcing me to live a lie by hiding the most important part of my Nature.

And of course I couldn't fully hide it anyway. One cannot conceal the look in one's eyes when one beholds beauty which prompts lust, and the changing room, with its baths and showers, drew me like a powerful magnet so that I devised all means of lingering there as long as possible. It suddenly became very important to clean one's teeth thoroughly and the dreaded shaving became a pleasurable duty, something requiring time and attention, especially at peak times, when the room was crowded. I would pretend to be studying my face and apply the razor with enormous care whilst I was really drinking in all the wonderful nudity reflected in the mirror.

Then there were the crushes, boys whose physical beauty utterly overwhelmed me and in whose presence I literally trembled with lust and desire. One of these by the name of Geoffrey Starr haunted all my waking moments, a vision, an Apollo, a star in every sense – the sight of him in games clothes reduced me to a quivering jelly. But, curse it, he belonged to another house. Oh, those lucky boys in Capel who got to see him naked every day in the showers: one heavenly glimpse and I could have died a happy soul. I contrived all sorts of ways of being in his company, including taking up bridge and joining the school club. I was determined to be as fine a player as possible, so that on those joyous occasions when we shared a table I could demonstrate a skill and competence which he would appreciate. Sometimes I "accidentally" let my leg brush against his under the table.

How much healthier would it have been if we could have simply gone to a room together and had a steamy session of raunchy love-making, culminating in me fucking him in every position possible? This is intended as a serious question, but of course Geoffrey probably had his own unfulfilled desires; such is the tedious way human beings are made. It would have been nice to have been given the chance to try it out though: I don't know if he ever realised the strength of my adolescent feelings for him.

Somehow, despite my emotional turmoil, I managed to achieve a batch of nine fairly decent O levels and went up to the sixth form to specialise in three of my favourite subjects, English, French and Music. School life suddenly got a whole lot better.

During the preceding summer holiday I had discovered the liberating effects of alcohol and, in order to minimise the still horrible wrench of leaving my comfortable home for the Spartan surroundings of school, I consumed four cans of strong lager on the way back at the beginning of the 1974 academic year. Without realising that the smell would be on my breath, I addressed my housemaster in an overfamiliar and jocular way. Fortunately he took this in good part, probably relieved that I wasn't the miserable creature I usually appeared to be on arriving back in Belsen.

This uncharacteristic boisterousness also communicated itself to my coevals on that very first night, and it was apparent to all that a very different Nicholson was starting the final two years of his school career. From being a timid, rather withdrawn person I suddenly adopted a devil-may-care, almost reckless attitude, little troubling about what other people might think of me, shouting out in class, starting playful cushion fights in the study I shared with three others and generally treating life as the enormous joke I still now believe it to be.

"What's the point of living if we're simply going to die?" was the familiar question posed by one of my contemporaries. Someone else countered with: "What's the point of dying if we're going to carry on living as Christianity claims?" I simply shortened this to: "What's the fucking point of anything?" and, at this stage of my adolescence, regarded human beings as glorified machines which eventually stopped working. I began to read the work of atheists such as Nietzsche and Bertrand Russell, and found inspiration in the negative existentialism of French thinkers such as Camus and Sartre, the notion of the absurd and the futility of all endeavour. Despite the intensity of my passionate spiritual nature, all religious faith now struck me as nonsense. I once deliberately shocked my closest friend at that time by coming out with all the worse blasphemies I could think of in the school chapel, cursing Jesus and daring God to do His worst to me – I felt He'd already done so by lumbering me with a criminal sexuality and thus perpetual ostracism. This boy, a fellow musician, is still a very good friend even though I wasn't able, then or since, to discuss my sex life with him. That was Stephen's deep dark secret which he thought he'd never be able to share with another soul and survive the humiliation.

My clarinet-playing suffered tremendously at this time. This was partly on account of my emotional turmoil, as successful wood-wind-playing requires a calm mind, but also because a friend of my mother, an author of books on basic piano technique and a professor at the Royal Academy of Music, thought I should study with her colleague John Davies. He was initially happy to receive me as a pupil – at a huge cost per lesson. In the event, he turned out to be the worst teacher I could have had at this time, criticising all the bad habits which lingered from when I'd more or less taught myself at prep school and dogmatically forcing me to change my embouchure into something which felt entirely unnatural. I persisted in doing it his way, believing that my hard work and practice would eventually produce the sort of tone quality I wanted, and used to have before. Instead of this, I struggled to play at all, producing a harsh sound and many ugly squeaks.

This frustration, on top of the denial of my sexual instincts, also caused me huge anxiety.

My new what-the-hell approach to life probably helped me here. I could still practise the piano with enjoyment and, having given up the violin after grade 5, switched to the viola. I adored this instrument for its rich mellow sound and its forgiveness of less than precise intonation. I discovered that this was Mozart's favourite instrument, and whilst I could never compare myself to that God of music, I could certainly understand his preference and the feeling of being inside the music when playing in an orchestra.

Some time previously I had been refused a highly competitive place as clarinettist in the West Sussex County Youth Orchestra. I re-auditioned on the viola and was accepted, enjoying many residential holiday courses in which I hankered after the pretty young boys. I was never bold enough to proposition any of them, even though a handsome young bassoonist had a certain reputation. Some of the older teenage girls, some of them definitely slags, chased after me – what a situation! There was a sweet blonde viola player who did attract me, however, and I later wrote her a love letter. She did not reply.

During the summer holiday before my final term at Reed's I went to stay with a French family south of Bordeaux. They lived in a remote house in the middle of the countryside and took in schoolchildren from all over Europe who were studying French to a high level and wished to improve their skills. The father was a violinist who spent much of the day practising when not tutoring his young guests. He would fly into violent rages when anyone used their native language rather than French and had high "moral" standards deploring, as *père de famille*, films such as *La vie sexuelle* then showing at the local cinema, and the increasing amount of youthful nudity to be seen on beaches.

His two sons, by contrast, were far more liberated. The elder boy, sixteen-year-old Didier, was always talking about sex, displaying himself – "Tu aimes mon cul, Stephen?" (Yes, I do as a matter of fact, I thought) – and sharing his porn mags, one of which particularly delighted him as it featured the head of the Queen of England photoshopped onto the body of a stunningly pretty nude model. "Regarde, Stephen, la reine d'Angleterre – ha ha ha!" Didier was a fine oboe player and inspired me musically too. The younger son, twelve-year-old Laurent, was a good violinist, though he was always arguing with his father when it came to making him practise. He was an exuberant character and quite unfazed by nudity, as I discovered when I shared a room with him for the first couple of nights. He slept naked, and paraded around the bedroom *au naturel*, once getting out of bed to close the shutters when there was a storm brewing and never bothering to cover himself.

I did in fact believe that I might finally score with a boy here for the first time since leaving prep school, and kept him amused with all manner of jokes and naughty stories after we had gone to bed. Sadly, this only resulted in my being moved to a room of my own, not because his parents were worried about my corrupting influence, but because they had simply decided that I clearly needed less sleep than Laurent, and was keeping him awake with my talk.

In between O and A levels, one was able to take AO levels and perhaps it was my top grade in French Literature which first decided my teachers that I might be a realistic candidate for Oxbridge. In my heart, I knew that my musical abilities were not up to this, though things might have been different had I studied with John Leach throughout the school, rather than with his chorally-obsessed replacement. I enjoyed the non-music part of the Cambridge entrance requirements far more than the drudgery of aural tests and strict harmony and counterpoint one was supposed to study. It all seemed so detached from the reality of music itself, unlike the Use of English exam and original essays on quirky subjects such as "If it is hot weather, why should people not be allowed to be naked in any public place if they want?"

I relished spending an extra term in the sixth form with almost no classes, little responsibility and, as a school prefect, eating lunch with the masters and finally being treated as their equal. I was free to leave the school when I wished and used to go to New Malden to have extra harmony lessons with an organist from the Royal Academy, Michael Austen. He spiced up the lessons by talking at length about his sexual conquests and introducing me to the piano-playing of Alexis Weissenberg. Michael regarded an effective musical performance as akin to sexual congress, another novel concept for an impressionable eighteen-year-old, peppering his descriptions of Weissenberg's playing with terms such as "erotic phrasing" and "orgasmic climaxes". I once brought him a rare recording of Prokofiev's third concerto and he declared enthusiastically that the aggressive entry of the piano was "like being raped".

He put my sexual inexperience down to that fact that I was at a boys' boarding school with little chance to meet girls. I hadn't the courage to tell him about my attraction to boys, as he'd already made his views on effete "queers" very clear. Perhaps he'd have told me to go for it, who knows. I learned later that there'd been some sort of scandal when he was organist at Wimborne Minster, with the implication that boy choristers were involved, but this remains hearsay.

That final term at public school was passed in a dreamy haze of poignant nostalgia. I had finally made it. I was liked and respected and wore my mask of detached cynical indifference convincingly, whilst harbouring huge crushes on boys from all year groups. I devised ways of seeing them naked whenever I could, brazenly entering the washrooms when I knew they would be showering. I would pretend to pee, shave or impart some important message to one of them, then linger whilst engaging in idle conversation. I'm sure many twigged me, but there was little animosity; in fact, one or two boys I didn't particularly fancy used to hang around while I was having a bath, making their interest plain. Perhaps I should have been bolder, but such was the layout of the house that it would have been well-nigh impossible to find a private place to indulge in sex play.

Occasionally when I was practising the clarinet in the small music rooms, pretty younger boys in their sports kit would come in for a chat and pointedly stay longer than necessary. Perhaps timid Stephen might have managed a quick unsatisfactory grope inside their miniscule games shorts, but he was too "wet" to risk the shame if he'd misunderstood the boys' intentions. It would have been all round the school.

Although I made it through the first round of papers and attended Cambridge for the auditions, interviews and fiendishly difficult aural tests, my musical standard, as I knew, was not good enough. Disappointed as I was to fail, I don't think I would have flourished there, finding the atmosphere rarefied and the undergraduates who deliberately got me drunk the evening before all my interviews a tad pretentious and insular.

So whilst the Christmas of 1975 was not as merry as it might have been, the beginning of the new year was spent visiting many of the second-choice universities for Oxbridge rejects, such as Manchester, Durham and Bristol. I eventually settled for a place at the latter, which impressed me for its beautiful setting, friendly professors and quite exacting entry requirements, which a few more sessions with Michael Austen had prepared me well for.

Such was his charisma that before going up to Bristol, I continued visiting him each week in New Malden, and this was now about my development as a person as much as a musician. The gentle insistence that I should be fucking someone now I was nineteen, "for Christ's sake", and his promise that another student of his, Debbie, was also going to be at Bristol in October and would certainly be interested in having sex with me were effortlessly mingled with exercises in Fux counterpoint, Bach chorales and attempts to teach me to play the organ using the pedals, a skill I never mastered. I would accept glasses of wine to help the lesson along, but refused his cigarettes. It was three years later that a profound emotional crisis led me to embrace the comforting weed.

My personal confidence was at an all-time low, and I had developed terrible acne, especially on my back, which I attributed to sexual frustration. I was missing all the pretty boys from school and the easy opportunities for nudity, and knew that no female was going to do it for me as a boy could. No girl I passed in the street would cause that rush of desire that a boy would. The summer of 1976 was particularly hot; one frequently was allowed prolonged glimpses of nude boys changing on the beach, and occasionally whole families playing naked on the more secluded sandy beach on the other side of the river. It was from this time that I became resigned to the truth that voyeurism was going to be my lot. I enjoyed many a prolonged wank while recalling in the privacy of my bedroom the stunning beauty I had witnessed. I longed for magazines with boy pictures, probably available at this time, but not in my provincial seaside town. A defining TV moment was an episode of *The Glittering Prizes*, unthinkable now, which depicted naked boys misbehaving in the

showers after a football game. My orgasm was swift and powerful and I knew at that moment that boys must always feature in
my life.

However, before that I had to endure three boyless years as a
student, a role in which I never felt comfortable.

IV. University

But though I had found out about myself, no one else would ever find out as long as I lived. That stigma and keeping it a secret were the fundamental core of my mind, from which all other thoughts and actions flowed.
JOHN REID, *The Best Little Boy in the World*

I do not propose to dwell too much on my three years as an undergraduate. The fourth, spent working for a Postgraduate Certificate in Education, which included a whole term resident in a delightful Berkshire boys' boarding school, is of far greater significance in terms of how my life unfolded.

After a long drive to Bristol, I arrived at a student house in Cotham Lawn Road, where I was to spend the first year sharing with a slightly mad philosophy student called Patrick, another Oxbridge reject. This was a time of exceptional mental expansion, but also of torment, as the persona which had served me so well at school and which had taken five years to construct was of little practical survival value at all here. The tedious business of sorting out who I really was, and what I was doing on this planet would have to begin all over again.

Patrick and I created a surreal fantasy world in which all Oxbridge rejects rode on huge motorcycles with high handlebars to compensate for their personal inadequacy, and spoke in la di dah accents – the bigger the machines they rode, the more affected their voices. Instead of speaking as ourselves, we often conducted conversations based on the numerous characters in our imaginary world. There was the drab middle-aged couple, Ethel and Bert, whose opinions on everything were formed by reading *The Daily Mail*. There'd be a lot of shaking of heads, funny faces and voices with negative opinions always expressed as "Isn't it disgusting", "It shouldn't be allowed" and "Something should be done about it". Bert was oversexed, and impatient for it as soon as he came home from work, threatening to "do yer on the table" if Ethel didn't immediately shut up her talking, drop all she was doing and move straight to the bedroom. There was also the religious freak who, in his high-pitched American drawl, was always trying to convert you to some strange belief system, imploring you to bury your prejudices and embrace love in the form of Jesus, Vishnu or whatever: "Hey man, don't proscribe, open your heart to the reality …"

None of the other residents of the house escaped our parodies, and we made caricatures of them all, which probably didn't endear us to them. Mrs. H., the cleaner, came in for especial mockery with her broad Bristol accent and lascivious chat. If one was eating large sausages or small frankfurters for breakfast, she would talk about "big boys" or "little boys". Another favourite topic of hers was the number of students who killed themselves at exam time by jumping off Clifton Suspension Bridge: "Ooh arghh, there were another couple this mawnin'."

The arrogance I had learned to hide behind at boarding school manifested itself in a rather unpleasant opinionated critical attitude towards musical performances (based on what I had picked up from Michael Austen) and towards most of the lecturers. It was a small department, and I would frequently interrupt lectures demanding clarification of a point, or challenging what had been said. Surprisingly this was mostly met with good humour, and I earned something of a reputation for boldness as well as the admiration of the more callow students who were away from home for the first time in their lives.

But all the while I remained aloof, and felt obliged to rebuff all the various offers of friendship in case my mask be uncovered. Inevitably students soon began pairing off, many losing their virginities, whilst I remained alone with mine firmly intact, though my masturbatory fantasies became more intense than ever.

An early visit to the vast university library confirmed beyond doubt where my sexual preferences were now beginning to crystallise. A friend of mine has a hypothesis that wherever there is a large collection of books he will be able to find a picture of a naked boy within ten minutes, and until recently he has always been successful. Back in 1976, it didn't take me long to find several fine examples in various photographic albums, and I particularly remember a book devoted to the work of Frank Meadow Sutcliffe. The author describes how Sutcliffe paid the boys of Whitby a penny to pose naked, and added the amusing detail that with clothes discarded they had nowhere to put the coin. The erotic charge produced by these ancient nude photographs was really quite staggering.

Showing at the cinema around this time was Derek Jarman's *Sebastiane*, with a poster depicting two naked youths. I just didn't have the courage to go in and watch it: what if someone saw me there? My whole arrogant persona would be blown apart … In the event, I did see this film a few years later and realised that it held little interest for boy-lovers. In fact, my form of love just didn't seem to be acknowledged anywhere except to be mocked as a sickness.

And yet there were boys everywhere in the city. The local school did their running very near my student house, the boys dressed in tantalisingly short shorts. There was a children's hospital near the department building, and one caught glimpses of the patients through the large uncurtained windows. The student union building had a huge swimming pool, and one could often observe school lessons in progress. One got to know the times when the place would be full of boys of all ages in the skimpiest of swimming trunks, as was the fashion in those days. I would be drawn to the viewing area, book in one hand, drink in another, hoping that my interest was not too apparent. One began to feel like the archetypal dirty old man.

Through Patrick, my world view began to expand enormously. He would share much of his reading and interesting lectures with me and, silliness forgotten, there would be some quite deep discussions. Topics included Bertrand Russell and his pupil Wittgenstein, A. J. Ayer and logical positivism, religion, death, and different civilisations and their customs, including ancient Greece. Occasionally, our imaginary characters would intervene and offer opinions, and I remember that happening when Patrick told me about Greek pederasty, on which he was reluctant to comment. Ethel had plenty to say here however, condemning it to Bert as something which "shouldn't be allowed" (which it wasn't of course). I like to think that these alter egos provided an escape route for such uncomfortable topics as we felt were just too awkward and difficult to discuss as ourselves. We never confronted each other directly with questions relating to our own sexuality, but one of our characters would never be at a loss for words.

Throughout my time at Bristol I was beset with the question of what I was going to do with my life. I was fortunate in some ways in finding the best possible clarinet teacher to sort out the mess caused by John Davies and his dogmatic approach. Angela Malsbury was an up-and-coming young player, vivacious and beautiful, who managed to restore my dwindling confidence to the extent that I was able to perform Nielsen's notoriously difficult concerto with the university chamber orchestra in my second year and pass the external Associate of the Royal College of Music examination which I had narrowly failed the year before. I achieved a first in my third-year performance option, but knew that because of the lack of certain skills, such as flutter tonguing, I could never aspire to be a pro.

Besides, what chance did being a professional clarinettist give you to work with boys? During my wanderings around Bristol, I would frequently find myself outside Clifton College, yearning for the sort of environment in which I could spend as much time in the company of boys as possible. Despite my difficulties at Reed's, I was now missing it. I had left on something of a high note, despite the Oxbridge failure, producing the house play in my final term. The entire cast smoked real cigars in the opening scene, regardless of my housemaster's protests ("Is it *really* necessary Nicholson, sniff?" "Yes, it's in the stage directions."). I had been back a few times before coming up to Bristol and been greeted warmly by masters and boys alike. I now felt curious about what it would be like to be on the other side of the fence as an Assistant Director of Music, with not too much responsibility. One trait Stephen has always lacked is ambition, worldly success seeming a shallow and ephemeral goal.

But first of all I needed to establish who I was. I needed to find my own Truth, my own raison d'être based on my own discoveries. I was so conscious of my existence as second hand, many of my ideas, opinions and beliefs about the world being simply borrowed. Borrowed from my mother, from my teachers, from the books and authors I had been made to read. Many of these were fine; Camus' *L'étranger* made a huge impact on me when studying French literature, as did Sartre's *La nausée*, Gide's *La porte étroite*, Zola's *Germinal* and Alain-Fournier's *Le grand meaulnes*, to name but a few. I had also been enthralled by English writers such E. M. Forster, George Orwell and even Jane Austen, and, as was my way, made a point of reading everything they had ever written.

During my first year at Bristol I discovered allusions to boy-love in some of these prescribed writers which were, or at least seemed, positive. In Forster's *Maurice* one of the characters is bowled over by the sight of a naked boy asleep on his bed and, in his memoir *Si le grain ne meurt*, Gide described his excitement over a young lad procured for him by Oscar Wilde. Wow, I thought, Oscar Wilde was attracted to boys too. Perhaps I should feel exalted rather than ashamed to be in such company.

Gide's description of that encounter is also seared on my brain. My Penguin copy of *Si le grain ne meurt* had every page in which boy-love is mentioned indexed at the front of the book. A highly important friend I was to make in my third year, and to whom I confessed all, remarked that he was surprised the book didn't open itself on the page where this description occurs:

Long after Mohammed had left me I stayed there in a state of quivering jubilation, and although I had reached the summit of pleasure five times with him I revived my ecstasy many more times, and back in my hotel room I relived its echoes until morning …

How I longed for a little Mohammed, just to hug and cuddle if need be. There was clearly a message of vital importance in this yearning for boys, and it was something which was never going to leave me alone. I knew that, whatever the cost, I would have to explore it if I was to feel complete as a person. But I was still left with three major questions which troubled me.

1) How much truth is there in any religion, or had they all been forms of social control throughout the ages? I was also at the time much preoccupied with the famous quotation from Voltaire: "Si Dieu n'existait pas, il faudrait l'inventer."

2) If there was no God, did life still have meaning? Should we all not just kill ourselves and be done with it?

3) Were there other boy-lovers open enough about their sexual attraction to describe articulately all the sentiments and finer feelings which accompany the condition?

I refused to consider myself pathological, I knew my feelings were good. Over the course of time as an undergraduate, I was able to find answers to all these questions for myself, helped by three important writers and, most importantly, writers I discovered by myself. Through them came my first tentative step towards personal enlightenment and authentic existence. I had to be who I was whatever the cost, which would often prove considerable.

The first of these questions was answered for me when I discovered amongst my mother's books a slim volume of talks by someone I had never heard of, Jiddu Krishnamurti. His message seemed one of brilliant simplicity: Truth, Love, God or whatever you wanted to call it is a fundamental reality which we cease to perceive when the mind, full of chatter and abstract ideas, obscures our direct perception of "what is". He insists that no teacher (or "guru") can show you or lead you to this reality, which is not of thought. It is a matter of entering into a state of "choiceless awareness" and directly apprehending the beauty or otherness which is always out there. There is no system or method for doing this, and though religions often start off with some sort of marvellous insight, this becomes clouded by a shroud of dogma and meaningless ritual in which the symbol becomes more important than the truth it represents.

I was impressed that one of his books, *The First and Last Freedom*, had an introduction by none other than Aldous Huxley, another author I knew well. The quote from the *Observer* review on the pure white dust jacket, "for those who wish to listen, this book will have a value beyond words", intrigued me. I bought a new copy from George's Bookshop when I returned for my second year and, with a room to myself now, would read portions of it each night before going to sleep. The wisdom of those pages transformed and sharpened my perception of everything, and it became too precious to share with Patrick, who might make fun of it as, for example, another cult promulgated by our religious freak.

Much later, on reading a biography of Krishnamurti, I found out about the pederast Bishop Charles Leadbeater who discovered the thirteen-year-old Jiddu on a beach in Adyar, and was so impressed by his aura that he knew this boy would achieve great things. There is a famous scandal surrounding Jiddu and Leadbeater, who helped groom the boy as a World Teacher, a role Jiddu completely rejected on the day of his inauguration in a wonderful speech beginning "Truth is a Pathless Land".

Another book I stumbled upon was a second-hand paperback copy of Colin Wilson's *The Outsider*. I had heard of this author at school when a friend who was trying to convert me to Christianity lent me a popular Billy Graham-type book about being born again in Christ, a concept I've never understood. It contained a misattributed quote on the cover: "according to Colin Wilson 'man is useless passion, it is meaningless that we live and meaningless that we die' ...", something the book would set out to disprove. I now learned that this was in fact Wilson quoting Jean-Paul Sartre and that Wilson himself was also keen to disprove it.

Wilson's compelling writing did far more to ignite my interest in spiritual matters than any Christian book, and I'd read a fair few of those. His work was directly concerned with man's quest for meaning, and he had an amazing ability to absorb the world's most complex philosophical writings and reproduce the essence of them in everyday language. I also discovered his early autobiography, *Voyage to a Beginning*, which described his humble Leicester upbringing and gave me huge hope about my own ability to manage and cope, whatever circumstances I found myself in.

Regarding question 2, it was not so much a matter of whether there was or wasn't a God out there, but of reconnecting with the part of us all which we call God, Spirit or, in the words of Wilson's favourite author George Bernard Shaw, the Life Force.

Through Wilson, I grasped the fundamental absurdity of suicide, as well as the contemporary malaise of the small man feeling defeated by life, as portrayed in much of the work of Samuel Beckett. I read the entire *Outsider* cycle of six books covering religion, world literature, sex, the individual in society and philosophy. I was impressed by the logical way each book developed Wilson's central theme of personal freedom through phenomenology, the awakening of perception and what Edmund Husserl called Gestalt theory. *The Age of Defeat*, with its focus on Heidegger's concept of authentic versus inauthentic existence, made a particularly deep impression.

So whilst Krishnamurti demonstrated the danger of allowing aimless abstract chatter to obscure our sense of reality, I learned through Wilson how to use and exercise my mind, and then to rest it just as one rests any other part of the body. Ideas could be thrilling and illuminating, causing the brain to explode with excitement as the synapses connected, but it also became important to switch the brain off, or it would overheat like a computer when the fan has stopped working.

So, Stephen, you were making some progress here. You'd successfully addressed the many issues surrounding the Spirit and the Mind and learned to apprehend subtle new meanings in everything around you, including music, the experience of which could now be sometimes overwhelming. Like Blake, you were again able *to see a World in a Grain of Sand. And a Heaven in a Wild Flower. Hold Infinity in the palm of your hand. And Eternity in an hour …*

But what fucking use was any of that without a boy to love, or at least someone open-minded and sensible with whom you could talk about your feelings for boys, discuss that love which in the words of Oscar Wilde normally "dare not speak its name", though "it is beautiful, it is fine, it is the noblest form of affection." I was fully aware that "that it should be so the world does not understand. The world mocks at it and sometimes puts one in the pillory for it." However, it wasn't about to go away, was it, Stephen?

This fatal attraction I came to see as my hamartia, something which was preventing me from growing and evolving because of the impossibility of any personal fulfilment. This was sometimes the cause of profound misery, especially in the vacations where I had few companions and could no longer relate to my mother in the easy way I used to. I know this caused her distress. It was as if university had turned me into a different person, someone she failed to recognise, and I knew that she still saw me as her little boy – perhaps *the best little boy in the world* of the chapter title quote. How could I begin to explain all the conflicts going through me?

One evening she virtually forced me to make some sort of confession. "What on earth is wrong, darling? Please talk to me: even if I can't do anything, I can listen." Even then I couldn't reveal the full extent of what was troubling me, but I was able to blurt out something about being terribly worried I might be homosexual, which was at least partially true. I, probably most unfairly, prefaced this revelation with a lot of stuff about never having had a father, and going to a single-sex boarding school. Her first reaction was predictable. I was reading too many books, it was just a phase, I would meet the right girl and so on. She had made some efforts to set me up with girlfriends when I was in the sixth form, and none of them had gone anywhere, so she must have had an inkling.

But what really hurt me was when she said sadly, "So I've failed," with all its dreadful implication that there was something wrong with homosexuality. She also sorrowfully remarked, "But you'll be so *lonely*," an emotion almost unknown to me up until then, or since. I've always enjoyed my own company immensely, and hate being with people who bore me.

I'm not sure how much our little chat helped, but it did emphasise to me the hopelessness of my condition. If my own mother couldn't fully accept a *gay* son, what chance did I have as a *boy-lover* in the wide wicked world?

And then, one glorious summer's day again amongst my mother's books, I discovered Forrest Reid.

It started with a Radio 3 broadcast about E. M. Forster which I had been listening to the evening before, and Reid was mentioned as a friend and fellow writer. After so many years, I forget the exact words the broadcaster used. The essence was that Forster admired Reid's work but felt uncomfortable about the way he always wrote about boys and his sentimental attraction towards them.

I was delighted to find a copy of *Young Tom* on the book-shelves. I read it in one sitting, transported by the lyrical style of the writing and the way Reid brought the eponymous character to life. This became my third "special" writer, discovered by myself. By the following term at Bristol I had acquired *The Retreat* and *Denis Bracknel* as further bedtime reading.

Reid's books were notoriously difficult to find in these pre-internet days, and each new discovery made in a second-hand bookshop was a joy. At last I'd discovered a man who had had young boys as companions in a friendlier age, when such rela-tionships were still considered mutually beneficial. OK, he didn't touch any of them sexually, but the sort of friendships he achieved, as described in, for example, Russell Burlingham's biography, were unimaginable to me in those dark days of uncertainty. I would have loved to have such a friend.

My confusion over my sexuality or orientation, which I was given to believe was a distinct part of my identity which should by now be firmly formed, was exacerbated by the fact that I was emotionally drawn to a few girls. There wasn't the same intense passion which boys excited in me, but I would have been inter-ested in sexual experimentation with a certain type of young woman, as I wouldn't in any of the male undergraduates. How-ever, I was simply too awkward to approach any girl. Annoy-ingly, it was the ones I found repulsive who often tried to pick me up.

In my second year I did attend a few parties and got very drunk. I then felt emboldened enough to kiss the less unappeal-ing girls, who were also pretty sozzled, fairly comprehensively, but this never went any further.

One day I fell helplessly in love with a girl whom I shall sim-ply call Miriam. I had a sudden surge of emotion when I first saw her in the student's common room early in that second year.

If ever I was going to settle into a normal life, it would have been with her, but she resisted all my efforts at seduction even though she did eventually allow me to become her friend. It truly hurt me when she found herself a boyfriend whom I and many others considered one of the ugliest people in the department, both physically and character-wise.

So I had to settle for respectable friendship, and having been told that real friends share everything and have no secrets from each other, I told her about my feelings for boys. This was a big mistake, and one from which I didn't learn. She pretended to be fully understanding and assured me that it was "our secret", but it became plain towards the end of my second year that she had not held her tongue. From being a reasonably popular person, I became increasingly aware that I was being shunned, and of the reason why.

Why oh why, Stephen, could you not have realised then that this sexuality is something women can never understand, however much they may pretend to? Confiding in women has always been disastrous for me, and especially so when, in my thirties, I opened up to a lesbian who later on was the cause of a major downfall.

Towards the end of my second year, increasingly ostracised as I was and forced to rely on my own dwindling inner resources, my despair deepened. I wasn't going to jump off the suspension bridge and be one more amusing statistic for the sensation loving Mrs. H., but the alienation was becoming unbearable. The kindly professor who ran the music department befriended me and would often flatter me about my powers of intellect and perception. I became the person he selected to go with him to special evenings when distinguished speakers would visit the university, and this did something to restore my confidence.

I scraped a 2 ii in the end-of-year exams which were Part 1s of the final degree. Although I had expected to do much worse, I was becoming disillusioned with university, music and even life itself. I really did begin to feel everything was pointless; despite my exciting literary discoveries, there had to be something more.

During that summer break I attended a woodwind course in Canterbury at which all the luminaries of the day were present: Tony Pay, Thea King and Keith Puddy, for example. I remember the latter as a fat little man who spent a long time coaching a rather poor female clarinettist, which slightly bemused me until a few days later when she complained bitterly about the sexual advances he had made to her. Well, love, he sure wasn't attracted to your playing!

There were also a fair number of attractive adolescent boys on the course, and had I had more confidence in myself, I would have certainly attempted something with one or two of them. I was green with envy when, on a trip down to the beach, I saw a blond flute player I fancied horribly in the company of an old man who'd accompanied me on the piano in a Debussy piece only the day before. The man and boy, who was about fifteen, were clearly on intimate terms and became quite furtive when they realised I'd seen them, beating a hasty retreat into the crowds. What had I missed? Should I also attempt to pick up this boy, or was he now spoken for? If only I had someone more experienced to advise me.

It was near the beginning of my third year when a truly unique individual became part of my life and rescued me in every sense.

My first piece of luck in my final year was to become first clarinettist in the university symphony orchestra, as the person who would have continued in that role had broken his arm over the summer. The second piece of good fortune was to secure excellent accommodation on the top floor of a large house owned by an organist called Ivan Fowler. The rent was reasonable and, as it was a detached house, I could make as much noise as I wanted listening to music and practising. Ivan was out most of the day teaching anyway, but the place was big enough for me not to disturb anyone.

The previous summer vacation I had bought a small portable TV, which worked excellently at that high altitude. My taste for alcohol was growing, particularly for whisky which I would sacrilegiously mix with ginger ale. I also took up smoking at this time, largely under the influence of Miriam who told me she found it relaxing. I preferred cigars to cigarettes though, and probably made myself very unpopular with Ivan by stinking the place out. After finishing all my coursework for the day, I would often relax in front of my little TV, whisky in one hand, cigar in the other, and feel that life couldn't get much better, especially as I caught some remarkable films such as *Le souffle au cœur* with the gorgeously nude Benoît Ferreux. One saw a fair amount of boy nudity on TV in those enlightened days, and there is still one film with a particularly memorable shower scene which I have never manage to trace.

My evening whisky consumption was fairly copious and must have eaten up much of my student grant. However, even after a really heavy session, I would awake refreshed in the morning, and I have been lucky in that I have never suffered hangovers.

Ivan's mother came to stay quite early on. Good with little old ladies as I am, I managed unintentionally to charm her, being able to chat freely with her. It was something I was never able to do with her son, whom I found rather creepy and whose company I tended to avoid – another big mistake, as I was to learn later. He had wanted a music student staying in house for company, and, I later learned, possibly for something more. I was therefore something of a disappointment. I will come back to Ivan a little later and describe his character and looks in greater detail, as they are relevant to the extraordinary man I was soon to know very intimately indeed: my third and positively largest piece of luck.

It all started at a chamber music evening in the home of an eccentric old man with a passion for baroque music. He would invite groups of students to play through the string parts of Bach and Handel concerti, whilst he took the leading role on the harpsichord. I was playing the viola, an instrument I was never able to master. There were four others in the group, including a young blond man playing violin who made funny faces and outrageous comments throughout the evening, especially over the splendid supper which was provided in the interval, complete with bottles of fine Hock. I'm not sure how it came about but this man, called Gabriel Strider, ended up driving me home, as he knew where Ivan, of whom he had expressed a low opinion, lived.

The following day in the library, I met one of the girls in the group who had been completely bowled over by Gabriel's personality and looks, and went on at some length about them. That same day I bumped into Sue G.; I was always "bumping into" her, as she had a crush on me and would invite me to accompany her to dinner dates and the like. I only did this once, innocently oblivious of her designs upon me; she came into the category of repulsive for me and was, maddeningly, a close friend of Miriam. I happened to mention meeting Gabriel Strider to her, and she clearly knew him, going into a partial swoon and sighing, "Oh he's so dishy, what a pity he's gay."

I pondered this for a few days. Although I couldn't see the dishiness, I had been excited by his obvious charisma and sexual energy, which came off him as a sort of fragrance one could almost describe as bewitching. Perhaps it had something to do with pheromones …

Just a week later I was to hear his voice again in the large sitting room below my room, next to the kitchen used by everyone in the house. This sitting room contained a grand piano which I often played when Ivan was out, and Gabriel was, coincidentally and unusually, being entertained to supper and an evening of listening to music. We met on the landing and he managed to slip up to my room for a brief chat, after which he left me his phone number.

I dithered for a day or two before finally deciding I had nothing to lose, and rang him from a call box. We arranged to meet at the Catholic cathedral after evensong the following Sunday, and he suggested I bring my clarinet and some music for the benefit of any suspicious neighbours. I did not quite know what to make of this, but was happy to comply, little knowing that this would be an evening which would change my life.

I was very prompt and slightly uneasy about what I was letting myself in for. Gabriel was clearly a popular man, and I stood for some time enjoying the faint aroma of incense which hung in the air whilst he chatted with various people who had buttonholed him after the service. Eventually he simply nodded for me to follow him. I climbed into the passenger seat of a rather battered VW Beetle which he drove fast and erratically, frequently mounting the kerb when turning corners.

His basement flat turned out to be a magical place with an atmosphere of what I can only call sanctity about it. Apart from a fine upright piano in the bedroom, the other striking item of furniture there was a large water-bed, something I'd never encountered before. There was one other room, quite large with a kitchen alcove. The bathroom was a small room just off the bedroom. No amount of description could begin to portray what this small flat came to mean to me. It was a true haven, and soon a place where I could feel relaxed and entirely myself.

We duly played through a few of the clarinet sonatas I had brought with me. Gabriel proved an excellent accompanist which inspired me to play better than I usually did. He was full of genuine praise for my skill and equally scathing about my lack of ability on the viola. He made it plain that he hadn't invited me to his flat to play music, as the dear old man in whose house we'd first met had, so my musicianship on the clarinet was a pleasant surprise for him.

We then sat and chatted over coffee and snacks. I was feeling completely relaxed by this time: there was something hypnotic about Gabriel's soothing voice and gentle manner which inspired trust. We chatted idly about such topics as composers, the music department, the sort of books I'd been reading, and he berated me gently for keeping the conversation "safe". He subtly sought entrance into my carefully guarded private life by asking me about my friendships and affairs, telling me much about certain people in the music department about whom he seemed to know a great deal. He was genuinely witty and forthright about the people he found ugly or screwed up, usually those who had been to all-boys public schools. He also told me intimate stories about the professors, and young musicians in the orchestra, one of whom had been a male model at thirteen, posing in underpants for advertising purposes, and who at twenty-one was still obviously attractive – about the only male undergraduate I'd found remotely sexy. It was no surprise to learn that Gabriel had had plenty of sex not only with him, but with many other young men, both in the university and elsewhere. I also learned that he'd been married, which was a surprise.

At one point he asked me why I'd agreed to come to his flat, and I admitted to curiosity because of rumours I'd heard that he was gay, which seemed to amuse him. Whilst he gently probed into the nature of my own feelings and dreams, I found myself opening up fully to him in a way I'd never done before to anyone, not even Miriam. I didn't only tell him of my attraction to boys, but was very specific about my type and spoke of the crushes I'd had at school and much, much more. Part of the conversation went along these lines:

"So tell me, how it was, having sex with these boys?"

"Er, well, I never managed to do that with any of them."

"What! Never? Someone like you should be having plenty of sex, why on earth aren't you?"

"Er ..."

"And is it just boys? Don't you find anyone else attractive, have you never felt a young woman's tits in your hands and fondled them?"

"Er ..."

While this and similar things were being said, I barely noticed that his right hand was caressing my thighs and working its way closer and closer to my groin. To my surprise I had an erection which he gently fondled over my trousers. I'd never been seduced before and found the novel experience rather thrilling and indeed flattering, as I did not regard myself as that good-looking, especially as years of sexual frustration had resulted in acne over my back and partly on my face.

Of course, it wasn't too long before we were naked together on his wonderful water-bed and I experienced all sorts of delightful explorations, including my first real blow job. Although I remained stiff, something – perhaps years of lack of intimacy with others – held me back from orgasm. When I started doing the sort of things to him as he was to me, he warned me to go easy or he would come too soon, which was in fact what happened.

I felt entirely comfortable being naked with him and we remained that way playing more music, and then chatting easily. I ended up staying the night and sharing the huge luxurious bed. It was as if I'd known him for years.

This was the start of a friendship which lasted way beyond my time at Bristol. Although I knew he had many lovers, this didn't worry me at all. There was usually one or maybe two nights a week when I could spend the night with him. His phone would often ring, and when it wasn't switched to answer-phone he nearly always phoned the person back to save them money.

Gabriel was the first one to lecture me about the *dangers* of relationships with young boys, and how this was becoming more and more precarious in England. He told me of many others he knew who had come to grief, lost careers et cetera over their affairs with boys, including a celebrated local organist with whom I had been considering having lessons. Often when Gabriel would visit his house, the door would be answered by this man in his dressing gown, and there was clearly a young friend upstairs in the bedroom.

Gabriel also told me of his own encounters with boys, always at their instigation. He was genuinely not attracted to anyone under about seventeen, but would go with preteen boys as a favour to them: "The little pillocks would be in heaven, and it meant nothing at all to me."

"Pillock" was his favourite word for me too, which he said could be either an insult or a term of endearment, and I could take it as I pleased. He once revealed that his chief fantasy about me was that I was a young wood nymph he'd met in the forest. I had a lot of body hair which he adored, although I detested it, so all in all he did much to improve my self-image and sense of self-worth.

A few weeks later Ivan's mother died and he left me alone in the house for about two weeks whilst he was away sorting out all the necessary arrangements. It was then that Gabriel visited me. We played music together in Ivan's sitting room and I was able to show Gabriel all my books, including the Gide autobiographical volume mentioned earlier.

I learned that Ivan had intended to chuck me out because I wasn't friendly enough towards him, but that his mother had overruled this decision – how lucky that I worked my unintentional charm on her. I also learned much about Ivan's private life, including the fact that he used to go to public toilets for sex with men, something I found incomprehensible. We both agreed on his ugliness and Gabriel had me in stitches when I casually remarked that I could imagine Ivan with a nut and bolt through his neck, as in portrayals of Frankenstein's monster. Gabriel's swift, wicked response was: "That's all he'd need!"

Throughout the rest of that academic year I didn't attempt sex with anyone else, but did tell a few people about my affair with Gabriel, which again was probably a mistake. One of these was a young man in the year below me called Graham who wore a badge with I AM GAY emblazoned upon it. A sweet girl called Jo who used to visit me, with whom I became good friends and whom I entertained to dinner a few times, called him "Gay Gray". Jo never tried to probe my secrets, though she did make an offhand remark about the absence of a father often being a cause of homosexuality. I did not rise to this; besides, she was far more interested in telling me of the gradual progress towards first-time intercourse with her lover Paul.

One evening Gay Gray and myself were the last two drinking together after an orchestra rehearsal, and somehow I found myself going back to his flat with him. Bad move. It wasn't long before he'd taken off all his clothes for casual sex, and was expecting me to do the same, but I just didn't find him in the least sexy or attractive and had to apologise. I knew I would never manage an erection with him.

It wasn't quite a case of "hell hath no fury" but, unsurprisingly, he became distinctly cool to me after this and, along with Miriam, spread a fair amount of nasty gossip. By the end of my last year at Bristol, there were few people I could really regard as friends apart from a closet gay called Julian Grant, who also played viola in the local youth orchestra and was a serious composer. He can now be found online, living as an openly gay man and successful musician.

One other friend was a nervous chap, also called Paul, a fervent Christian and Michael Tippett fanatic. On one of our trips to the local second-hand record shop, he confessed to me that he was gay and directly challenged me as to my sexuality:

"Someone asked me if I was homosexual, and I said, 'Yes I am.' So Stephen, I'm putting the same question to you: are you or aren't you?"

I hummed and hawed and obfuscated by saying I wasn't yet sure, and I still didn't feel my sexuality had crystallised. It more or less had, but I did not feel I could trust him with the truth of my attraction to a certain age group. This was, anyway, something for which I didn't yet have a word, but *gay* just didn't feel right. Another reason to be careful with Paul was that he was clearly struggling with himself, and regarded his orientation as a sin. He prayed constantly that his gayness might be cured.

When I met him at a reunion the following year, he was distinctly hostile towards me. I gently asked him if his prayers had been answered and he retorted, "No, but at least I don't fancy young boys!" I was also to hear one or two other snide remarks from students when it was announced that I'd been offered a job in quite a prestigious boys' Catholic public school as Assistant Director of Music.

At the end of the final year my mediocre 2ii became a respectable 2i (only one person achieved a first), mainly thanks to a thesis I did on Penderecki and my performance recital on the clarinet in the final exam which earned me a high first.

Largely through Gabriel, my self-respect had been restored and I slept with him one last time on the night before my graduation, whilst my proud mother and her close friend Rachel stayed in a local hotel.

I had obtained a place at Reading University to do a postgraduate course in music teaching. I was very much in two minds about it, though I did know I wanted boys to feature in my life despite Gabriel's dire warnings about the way the world was changing. And this was 1979, for heaven's sake, when things were still comparatively civilised.

I hadn't succeeded in keeping "that stigma" from the title quotation completely secret, but at least I had a fair idea of the price there was to pay if the wrong people learned of it.

V. Teacher Training and First Job

I have to confess right away that I have never considered myself a natural teacher, though there have been some pleasing successes. Much of it seemed like drudgery, and had little to do with the musical skills I had striven so hard to acquire. One-to-one instrumental teaching was bearable and even enjoyable with talented pupils, but finding activities to interest and absorb a classroom of ordinary boys (and later girls too – shudder) was a continual challenge and stretched my imagination to its limits.

I was not a natural disciplinarian either, and probably would not have survived long in a typical British comprehensive. I was fortunate therefore in that I was sent to a pleasant local public school to do my term's teaching practice, or I would probably never have made it into the profession at all.

Reading was a pretty ghastly place after Bristol, but the Music Education department was well-organised and the year passed agreeably enough. I was in a large hall of residence along with quite a few other postgraduates doing the same course, including a few familiar faces from Bristol. I kept a detailed diary at this time and am surprised on rereading it to see how apparently interested I was in some of the girls, but, yet again, always the wrong ones: my feeble advances were always gently rebuffed as they had other boyfriends or girlfriends even. Perhaps I didn't really have my heart in it, and was in truth quite frightened of any sort of commitment. I also felt that those years of repression at boarding school, involving tremendous will-power to resist my natural urges, really had caused some sort of blockage where sexual expression was concerned. This had only been partially cleared by my relationship with Gabriel.

I knew I wanted to go back into boarding schools, not only to experience the life "from the other side" but because I now ironically felt an aching nostalgia for that sort of environment. In a sense I had become institutionalised, and craved a simple monastic existence protected from all the hassles of real life in an all-male environment. I did visit a monastery at this time on the

Isle of Wight, as one of the Cookson sons had become a monk; he is still there. I was quite bowled over by the apparent simplicity of the monks' existence, and moved in an almost mystical way by the sound of gentle plainchant.

I will not dwell too long on the details of the first term of the Postgraduate Certificate in Education course, which involved many of the then trendy new approaches to music education. Basically this meant encouraging students to make as much noise as possible and try to control it – some of the girls got rather upset when it came to bashing piano keyboards and fiddling around with the strings inside. There was also a fair amount of emphasis on pop music – this being a way of pandering to the tastes of "ordinary" children, which fortunately I had never been subjected to in classroom music. Traditional ways of educating young people such as "music appreciation" and learning to read music were much frowned upon.

The person running the course, Tony Kemp, was meticulous about choosing the right schools for each person to do their whole term's teaching practice, and whilst some more idealistic students were happy to go to local comprehensives, I was delighted to be sent to an all-boys' boarding school. Kemp's typically dry remark to me was "I think you'll enjoy Bearwood", and he was absolutely right. I was given a large room to myself where I installed my portable TV, which still worked despite being once dropped on the floor in the hall of residence. I acted as an assistant to the charismatic director of music, Malcolm Pierce, from whom I learned far more than I would at the university.

I kept in touch with Gabriel, who urged me to find "willing" boys in the school, of which he was certain there would be many, and "do things with my lips and tongue other than play the clarinet". This went somewhat against his previous comments about how dangerous sex with boys was becoming, but as the worst that might happen in those days was that a teacher would be "moved on" and plenty were getting away with it, the risk was far less than it would be today. I read Jonathan Gathorne-Hardy's *The Public School Phenomenon* at about this time, and was quite startled by some of its revelations.

However, just as something held me back from approaching girls, the same mechanism continued to operate with boys. I didn't feel it was wrong as such for a master to have a relationship with a pupil, but it was something I just didn't feel I could, or should, do. In retrospect, with so many historical cases now emerging from the woodwork, it was just as well I kept my hands to myself.

On looking back, there were opportunities. There was one particular "Persian Boy" (Malcolm's appellation – this was long before I'd read any Mary Renault) who played the flute and was incredibly lissom and sexy, with smooth dusky skin and beautifully regular features. He was probably half-caste. He was only fourteen when I was there and we seemed to indulge in a sort of mutual worship from afar: my feelings for him were pure lust, and he must have seen something in me too, for he would attend every gathering at which I performed and often make attempts at conversation. I would see his heavy stare in the audience and feel I was playing especially for him. The struggles I had with myself over what he might be thinking and whether he was "up for it" are recorded in my diary. I didn't fall in love with him the way I did with some later pupils, but there was a definite chemistry and I probably missed out on a lot of fun.

The most enjoyable teaching was with the younger classes from the junior school, aged eleven to thirteen. They responded far more naturally to my first bungling attempts to teach children and were bright, amusing and chirpy without being over-familiar. I knew then that this was the age group I most wanted to teach, even if it meant that the musical standards would be fairly rudimentary. Without becoming too analytical, I can say I envied them their spontaneity and wanted to be that age again myself. I suspect that part of me has never really grown up.

The school was also remarkably relaxed. Before staff meetings, the bar would be opened up and every master, there being very few women, would be drinking alcohol and many of them smoking as the headmaster entered the common room. Malcolm was almost never without his pipe, which he puffed at whenever he could, earning him the rather unkind nickname of Bogbreath. Despite this, he was much respected and the results he achieved were always excellent.

So, that spring term of 1980 was a success. There was only one class which gave me any sort of discipline trouble, the lowest streamed class of the third form, not malicious, just not at all bright and with zero ability to concentrate. I had told Kemp about them. Fortunately, the day he turned up for a surprise inspection, hoping to see me struggling with this class of half-wits, Malcolm and I had planned a clarinet demonstration: I would show them the instrument and play exciting fast music with Malcolm at the piano. With both him and Kemp in the room, their behaviour was excellent, much to Kemp's annoyance, and I was secretly pleased he hadn't witnessed some of my other classes.

The summer term back in Reading was dull by comparison and mostly consisted of written work. It was believed useful to send me to a speech therapist, as my voice was considered rather fuzzy and unclear, and thus a disadvantage when confronted by a large group of students. This had also come up in my last term at Bristol, when I was considering entering the profession, and I'd visited an ENT specialist in my home-town who concluded that my vocal chords might have become damaged in some way, as they were in fact bowed. The doctor thought this could have come about through misuse of the voice or even through emotional disturbance, and I was reminded of those awful first terms at Reed's at the time my voice was changing, when I was constantly being tormented about its perceived high pitch. My unusual voice has actually worked both ways, as some find it rather attractive. Gabriel said once, "Don't you dare try and change that sexy voice of yours." Like most of us, I hate hearing my recorded voice played back to me, as we all sound so different to ourselves. Part of the final assessment at Reading involved singing a song accompanied by a student, which I managed, but I have never been comfortable singing solos, and taking choirs was something I always found challenging.

There was quite a sharp lecturer at Reading who guided us through the philosophy and psychology of education in small groups, and I, along with others, often lit up a cigarette during these sessions. He used to allude to my voice too and, when he saw me smoke for the first time, remarked, "Ah, now I see, it's a smoker's voice!" He was a strong socialist and very against private schools, but we still got along well despite my background and intended career path. He made the group produce essays on often rather searching topics such as our ideal school, or sex education. A very intense girl forced me to state my position on abortion and would not let me off with a non-committal shrug and comment that I didn't really have an opinion either way. So, in an attempt to shut her up, I said that it was a woman's decision what to do with her body and I couldn't see why she should not terminate her own pregnancy. Unfortunately, this produced a storm of protest – I clearly had very firm opinions about the murder of an unborn child being OK, et cetera. She would not allow me my indifference on this very feminine topic.

Harder for someone who had spent the last few years concealing his real identity was an essay the lecturer asked us to compose about ourselves simply entitled "Me". It was not a subject I was prepared to write about openly then; it is difficult enough now. On rereading this again recently, I see that I spoke about myself as objectively as possible, almost as if I were writing about another person. The perceptive lecturer remarked that I had tried to put up a smoke screen, and he was right.

I did realise though that, with their extraordinary clarity of vision, children easily see through smoke screens and, while I might fool adults, it would not take long for pupils to see me for what I was. This was disturbing, though I hadn't reckoned on how they might or might not have the vocabulary to articulate precisely their feelings about someone they perceived as being attracted to them. In one comprehensive a cheeky girl had asked the teacher, "Are you a poof then, or what?" because he'd answered her questions, "Are you married?" and "Have you got a girlfriend?" both in the negative. I also knew from the Gathorne-Hardy book that many of the best teachers fancied their charges, and that, far from being a negative thing, it added a certain zest to the pupil-teacher relationship as long as the pupils didn't feel in any way threatened.

My term at Bearwood had also reassured me in this respect, and my first applications, all unsuccessful, were mostly to prep schools. Undeterred, I continued to scan *The Times Educational Supplement* every week for jobs in boys' boarding schools, preferably the low-age-group ones, but I included public schools with a junior department.

Eventually I landed what seemed to be the perfect job in St. Edmund's, a Catholic school in Hertfordshire, as assistant director of music to a man called Hugo Russell. At first glance he seemed an obvious queen with all the typical gay mannerisms. It might well have been that he fancied me rather than considered me the best person for the job, though the fact that I was an instrumentalist and he an organist and choir trainer helped too, as we would complement each other well. So I had made my first step on my, possibly ill-chosen, career path. It was not the ideal school. My initial impression had been that it was rather rough and Dickensian, but there was a new purpose-built music block and for the first time in my life I would be earning sensible money.

As preparation for learning to relate to children, I accepted an offer in the middle of the summer holiday to help for a week with a summer school run by a man from London who had an arrangement with Rosemead, the girls' school where my mother was a secretary-cum-senior administrator. It was an odd collection of boys and some girls, including some quite-rough London lads who had little respect for adults of any sort and kept talking of porn films with "lezzies" in. They were expressly anti-homosexual, and one of them was extremely rude to me when I dropped a catch during a cricket game, something I was simply able to ignore. I remember clearly, and with more pleasure, a needy French boy of about ten who insisted on kissing and hugging me, and any other adult who would let him. Once I found him crying, and was about to try and console him when another young man beat me to it. He lifted him off the ground full of hugs and consoling noises, almost as if the boy were a baby – which I suspect the London lads thought he was. What would one do today? The hugs and kisses were natural and simply part of the way the boy had been taught to relate; to reject them would be to reject and hurt him, and maybe leave him wondering what was wrong with him.

Late in that summer holiday I bought an overpriced clapped-out old mini from, I learned later, the meanest member of staff at Rosemead. It was not a good choice as it happened, and when I set out with some trepidation on that first long journey north to join the staff at St. Edmund's and start a new unknown life in the autumn term of 1980, along with several other callow young people fresh from university, the thing broke down somewhere near the old London orbital road. I finally arrived very late in the evening, and felt this was an inauspicious start to my new career.

In many ways, however, it turned out to be fine as a first post. The staff were welcoming, and there were parties and plenty of boozing, one of the more delightful traits of Catholics in my experience, in the few days leading up to that first day when I would be facing my new pupils for the first time. I also discovered that every Wednesday evening there was a special staff meal with several courses and unlimited wine – always a pleasant highlight in the week. After the sumptuous feast, one would repair to someone's room and drink spirits or excellent matured port, or both, supplied by a local merchant who gave regular tastings. There was often a good TV series to be caught as well, and so it was that I saw week by week the wonderful adaptation of Delderfield's novel *To Serve Them All My Days*. This would soon be followed by the equally excellent *Brideshead Revisited*, which a master would record on his video recorder – one of the first I ever saw.

My timetable was light, and I was given a whole day off each week, but, despite the school's status among colleges, my first impressions had been correct: everything was rather scruffy and primitive and the boys turned out to be far less friendly than those I'd encountered at Bearwood. There were certain pretentions too, like staff being expected to wear gowns, which I did for a short while until it was clear that most younger staff ignored this unspoken rule. The best aspect of the place was the local pub where the landlord, Len, sold the most wonderful local beer. The staff too, were an affable crowd, and it was clear that many of them, including several of the resident priests, were also into boys, though the topic was never discussed openly.

There were a fair amount of eccentric characters amongst the teachers whom, in my wicked way, I found I could imitate easily, and I used to entertain a small select group of cronies with my impressions. There was Father Pinot, head of one of the junior houses, who greeted all remarks with an affable false laugh, and Duncan Gallie, senior master in the other junior section, called St. Hugh's, who became a good friend, but had an abrupt manner and loud, barking voice. Several of the resident priests were alcoholics and would sometimes disappear to be "dried out". Father Le Flamant had a very good thing going with a pair of delicious-looking, sandy-haired brothers whose parents lived in the Cayman Islands, and he spent many holidays with them. There was the effete George Keeper, who always had a room full of boys in his free time and was forever talking about the latest antics of his favourites, and the creepy Bob Home who also filled his room with boys and kept very quiet about it. I was once very nearly beaten up by a great loud-mouthed bull of a man called John Wood, in charge of rugby, who never spoke in less than a shout. He literally charged at me one morning in the public bathroom when, my own room having no washing facilities, we found ourselves alone there together, for my perceived cheek of him in the dining room the previous evening. I left the bathroom hurriedly.

One person to whom I related very well was a student teacher whom I nicknamed Bunny. We were clearly kindred spirits and, without talking overtly about the beauty of boys, were able to communicate our feelings discreetly to each other through "serious" jokes which established our unspoken understanding of each other. I spent many happy hours in Bunny's company, including two retreats in a monastery near Gloucester, Prinknash Abbey, from where we, rather disgracefully, made day trips and went off to the pub each evening. He was one of the first people I knew to express the opinion that sex with boys was a good thing, and he hoped to work in a prep school where he would at least have plenty of chances of seeing his pupils naked. He'd been at Cambridge and had many stories about the naughty behaviour of boys in a school called St Faith's. This behaviour had clearly extended to the masters, because one of my friends from Reading had secured a post there and we kept in touch. He told me, with some embarrassment, that his predecessor had been asked to leave for having sex with his pupils – "clearly mad" was his judgement. As he was so obviously straight himself, I could only agree.

I made quite a few visits to Prinknash by myself too. I got to know many of the monks, who were a pleasant, earthy bunch. One in particular, Brother John, was a friend of Gabriel Strider and, from our conversations, he clearly realised that our relationship may not have been strictly platonic. Whilst dutifully attending the morning and evening masses, I would, during the day, take myself off to local swimming pools and made some extremely pleasant discoveries. Brother John, with a twinkle in his eye, would ask me if I'd seen anything nice when I was out, and I don't know to this day if he suspected my dangerous interest in watery places.

What I found most difficult about St. Ed.'s was the Catholicism. I hadn't appreciated until then just how different that mentality is. I considered myself freethinking, and here I was in an environment where I felt most people had been brainwashed from a very young age, even the most intelligent amongst the staff. The saying attributed to Saint Ignatius, the Jesuit founder, seemed most apt here: "Give me the boy until he is seven and I will give you the man." The level of indoctrination was very strong. Even to question holy writ would have been regarded as sinful, so I went along with it, pretending to be a Christian and half-heartedly accepting the attempts to convert me to the "one and only true faith". I did draw the line though when Duncan, with whom I usually got on very well, playing piano duets on Saturday afternoons and getting drunk together, asserted that my mother would burn in hell because she was divorced. I shouldn't have reacted so strongly to this, as Duncan was always saying that such and such a person would burn, and the highly eccentric matron in the junior department where he taught remarked that "he should pay more attention to his own soul", adding "there are things I could tell you about *him* right enough!"

She was a classic, loud-mouthed, red-headed Irish woman with opinions on everything, and forever slagging others off as well. I soon learned to imitate her accent and tone perfectly and provided her with a nickname which stuck, Bibol (pronounced Bible), as she'd constantly referred to one of her colleagues as "the biggest bitch on legs". According to Duncan, who was always present at shower time, lucky man, she used to don waterproofs – a sou'wester and heavy raincoat – and, armed with a riding crop, beat the boys on their bare buttocks for no apparent reason. One day, in revenge, they all decided they would confront her with erections to put her off her stride, and she backed off yelling, "You filthy, *filthy* beasts!"

With that image in your mind, let's return to more everyday matters. By pretending to be a Christian, it seemed there might just be some hope for me in the afterlife, even if I stubbornly remained Protestant. More importantly though, there might be more chance of a position in one of the two junior schools on the premises – gosh, I might even get to witness the antics of Bibol in St Hugh's at first hand.

The trouble was, try as I might, I just couldn't relate easily to the pupils in the school the way I could to the non-Catholic boys of Bearwood: the mentality just seemed too strange. Also, the organisation in the music department left something to be desired. I was given little guidance as to what was required of me beyond teaching the small number of class lessons I had each week, which I did not particularly enjoy. I have always been rather lazy by temperament, very content to have empty days ahead of me which I can easily fill with reading, playing or listening to music, travelling or whatever. Even writing this is proving something of an effort, and might well have been abandoned were I not receiving considerable encouragement from Edmund.

I was developing in other ways though, and, with a view to my future as a possible peripatetic wind teacher, started playing the flute, oboe and, most importantly, the bassoon, which I took to easily. I had always been attracted to this instrument, but had never been able to afford one, and of course my own public school had not possessed one either. I soon obtained my grade 8 distinction, switched from viola to bassoon in the reasonably competent Hertford Symphony Orchestra, and was given the only boy in the school who learned the instrument as a pupil. He was great fun and we got along very well, as I did with many there on a one-to-one basis. The exception here was a black piano student in the sixth form called Mark de Brito who was exceptionally talented, but possessed a soul of ice. Whilst our relations were not *un*friendly, I found him quite difficult as, although he played with technical skill, he denied that music had any meaning and could not relate to the tunefulness of the Dvořák 'cello concerto which he was studying for A level. One day, as an aside, he showed me a book of Latin excerpts with translations which spoke of men's love of boys and smirked knowingly. Nothing was said and I'm still not sure whether he was telling me that he fancied boys or whether he knew I did.

There was, however, a distinct "us and them" feel between boys and masters, which could be unpleasant and malicious. I saw it clearly in my first week, when someone had scrawled "Russell's a Poof" on the music room blackboard, and Hugo Russell rubbed it off in great agitation: "Oh dearie dearie *me*." I did a passable imitation of him too, and was told I should be on stage by the rather shy John Hayes, my closest friend there. Instead of "boys", Russell would refer to "bays": "Dearie me, these bays are a bit *too* much sometimes!" When he'd drunk a little over the eight at any one of the many staff parties held in the master's common room, people would urge him to do his teapot impression: "I'm a little teapot, short and stout, here is my handle (hand on waist, arm curved), here is my spout (other arm held out drooping at the wrist)." Did Russell realise just why everyone was laughing so uproariously and urging him on?

My fuzzy voice (that again!) seemed to provide amusement for certain older boys, who used to croak crude imitations of it through windows when they thought they could not be seen. It was intended to wound, and did so, but not in the way it had just ten years before, when I'd started at Reed's. I found it odd more than anything, as they were mostly boys I didn't know and hadn't taught.

So, I muddled along and began to make positive use of all the free time I was given. My day off, always a Tuesday, was often spent in London and I joined the British Museum reading room library. This was easier than I'd imagined: I simply claimed I was writing a book on Forrest Reid and a ticket arrived in the post a few days later. I would dutifully turn up quite early, choose a desk and pre-order all the Reid books I hadn't read, along with critical commentaries to be found in obscure literary books and arts magazines. I would then go to a local café and eat a large omelette with coffee, which cost about £3. When I returned to the reading room, all the books would be waiting for me at my selected desk. Thus was I able to enjoy for the first time that elusive second novel, *The Garden God*, which I found so charming that I had it gradually copied each week: twenty pages a time was all that was allowed. One holiday, I had the pages bound into a book which I handled with great joy: in those days it was such a rare item.

During my trips to London I also got to know all the best second-hand dealers and paid enormous sums for first editions of Reid's books and then for those of other writers I'd discovered through investigations in the British Library. I gradually became bolder and bolder and started ordering books which addressed my sexuality directly and made some groundbreaking discoveries.

I once went to London with Father Dickie, who might best have been described as a Rabelaisian priest: a heavy drinker, forever swearing and getting into trouble with the headmaster. He would hear boys' confessions and, when they told him about their masturbation, he would dismiss it airily: "Ah, that's not a sin, I do it meself!" We saw a film called *Absolution* which starred Richard Burton, Billy Connelly and David Bradley, with the plot centring around the Seal of the Confessional: the absolute duty of priests not to disclose anything that they learn from penitents. Even Father Dickie was shocked at the brutal murder committed by the priest near the end.

I also discovered swimming pools during this time. I remembered that way back, during one of my stays with Williamson and his mother, we went to a pool in Crawley and I noticed that in the open changing room nearly all boys unselfconsciously stripped naked, often before entering the pool and nearly always afterwards. They would revel in their nudity, having towel fights, throwing their trunks around, and suchlike. One Saturday afternoon, en route back home to the south coast, I rather nervously visited this very same pool, hardly daring to imagine that the layout and behaviour would be the same. In the event, I was utterly overwhelmed by the sheer quantity of naked boys one was able to see. What had I been missing since leaving school? Well, I soon made up for lost time and made a point of going to every pool I could discover. I made a list of them, indicating how "good" they were and how many times I went there, as I didn't want to get too well-known in any one place. There was still an amazing innocence in those pre-internet days. We might all be more knowledgeable now, but boy, have we paid the price for it.

The British Library proved useful here too, as there was a book on display listing every pool and leisure centre in the country. Leisure centres then always had pools which often shared the changing rooms with other sports, after playing which boys would sometimes shower naked too – the one thing that most swimmers didn't do.

Once you had your British Library ticket, you could look at any book in the library you wanted to, so I soon became much bolder in my requests and discovered a whole raft of material which addressed the subject of boy-love more directly than anything I had hitherto managed to find. The closest before had been the book *Lord Dismiss Us* by Michael Campbell, which I'd read in my first term in St. Edmund's, and the film of *Death in Venice*, which knocked me for six when I first saw it on our small black-and-white television at home. I found, for example, all the issues of *Magpie*, that rather makeshift magazine produced by the members of PIE: a "subversive" group which had been much in the news during my time at university. Apart from amusing articles by their treasurer, Charles Napier, with such titles as "chicken farming", there were serious reviews of books with titles like *Love in Earnest* by Timothy d'Arch Smith, and *The Death of Narcissus* by Morris Fraser. The latter contained excellent material on Forrest Reid amongst other select writers. There were also pornographic items which could only be viewed in a special room under greater, though not intrusive, supervision.

I made a long list of books I wanted to read, and discovered to my joy and amazement that my local library in Worthing had many of them in "reserve stock" – books not on the shelves but deemed to be worth keeping. Thus I was, in the comfort of my own home, and often in bed, able to devour such items as Angus Stewart's *Sandel*, *The Erl-King* by French writer Michel Tournier, and Michael Davidson's *The World, the Flesh and Myself*. I was slightly disconcerted to see that someone had scribbled at the end of that book: "this man should be permanently incarcerated" – this only reinforced just how dangerous my tastes were.

Michael Davidson's second book, *Some Boys*, proved far more elusive. I eventually tracked it down to a library in Stevenage, where there was an excellent swimming pool; amazingly, I was permitted to borrow it "on trust". That is to say, no ID or library membership was required: it was my word as a gentleman that I would return that book, which I duly did after copying and binding it in much the same way I did the short Forrest Reid book. The journey from Worthing to Stevenage and back, for it was the holidays, yielded another swimming pool discovery, Farnborough, which was duly noted in my large ledger: "visits: 1; attendance: extremely busy; behaviour of boys: excellent". I was to pay that pool quite a few subsequent visits, one of them nearly proving fatal.

After reading d'Arch Smith's exhaustive study of the "Uranian" poets, also in my local library, my wants list increased considerably and I wrote off to various booksearch companies. One afternoon in Heffer's bookshop in Cambridge, I asked if they could find me something called *The Asbestos Diary* by the oddly-named author Casimir Dukahz. They calmly said they could, though no other bookshop had been able to. Within a fortnight it had arrived, along with a limited edition of *The Venice Letters* by the eccentrically self-named Baron Corvo. I used to visit Cambridge as a pleasant alternative to London, rounding off the day in King's College Chapel for evensong: musically, spiritually and of course visually stimulating.

The purchase of *The Asbestos Diary* proved especially fruitful, as I immediately noticed that it was published by a small company in Amsterdam called the Coltsfoot Press. At the back was a long list of all their other books with prices in Dutch guilders. I promptly, and somewhat impetuously, ordered a huge amount of these to be delivered to my address in Worthing, changing the equivalent amount of sterling into high-denomination Dutch notes and stuffing them into an envelope along with my order. To my astonishment, every book arrived without having being opened by customs, apart from something in two volumes called *The International Journal of Greek Love*, which looked far too scholarly to attract interest. My guardian angel was protecting me: not only was this an honest firm, but I'd got away with an act of foolish recklessness. The bassoon reeds I ordered from Germany were frequently opened for inspection, and I hadn't paused to think. My mother did ask me what those "funny little packages" which kept arriving were, and I airily replied: "Oh, just books."

"But what books?"

"Rare and valuable ones for my collection."

Not a direct lie, but a horrible deception. If there had been a problem with their import, it would have been she who would have received a nasty visit. I later learned that many others had indeed had enormous trouble through the import of Coltsfoot Press material, and I resolved that, if I ever wanted more, I would go to Amsterdam and buy them personally. Also, according to many of the articles I read, the Netherlands still had a reputation for tolerance towards boy-love.

Through the Hertford Symphony Orchestra, I discovered the Dartington summer music school then run by Peter Maxwell Davies who, along with Michael Tippett, was one of my favourite modern composers. I spent five summers there and rubbed shoulders with many famous musicians I admired. I also made friends with a charming American viola player called Barbara-Sue White from Princeton, who later invited me over to stay with her and her family. She had a rather shy fourteen-year-old son, Kevin, who asked me to play chess with him. He was clearly too good for stupid old me who had never learned to play the game properly, so I politely refused. One Dartington highlight was when Michael Tippett was resident with his lover and biographer Meirion Bowen, and Kevin was there with his mother. I spontaneously asked Michael if he would like a game of croquet. He, then a youthful eighty-four years old, leapt at the chance and partnered Kevin, whilst I was stuck with an extremely camp man from Tippett's publisher, Schott, who kept making annoying lewd comments about composers and young boys which I fielded with aplomb. I wrote to Michael Tippett after that summer, and still have his gracious and amusing hand-written reply.

Another highlight from this period was discovering Brockwood Park in Hampshire, one of the special schools which Jiddu Krishnamurti had founded around the world. I was privileged in 1984 to attend, with my mother, a series of talks he gave there to a packed audience in a huge marquee. Aged nearly ninety and a slight diminutive figure physically, his sheer presence seemed to fill the whole space when he slowly mounted the steps to the platform and settled himself onto a small upright chair. He would wait several minutes before beginning his always-unprepared talk. There would not be a sound from the crowd who were awed by a sense of his greatness and spiritual fragrance. He would then speak for about ninety minutes on matters concerning everyday life and its challenges, as well as deeper subjects such as the difference between a religious mind and the dulling effect of blindly following organised religious systems.

I felt blessed when I was able to shake his hand to thank him for all his selfless good work over the years. Ordinary people approached him to offer gratitude for all he had done to help them; this wasn't a place for drop-outs or religious freaks. I became more aware than ever that whatever troubles my secret sexuality might cause me, everyone seemed to have their own cross to bear, their own agonies and doubts which would seem so insignificant in the face of death. "Die every moment" seemed to be one of his messages, and he certainly provided me with an inner strength which has helped me through many a personal crisis by awakening something inside me which transcends ego or the vacillations of feeling we all experience. I have shared the insights Krishnamurti kindled within me with only a handful of people, one of them an astonishingly gifted pupil aged twelve who was suffering enormous depression, and who discovered a similar inner strength through an intuitive non-verbal under-standing of Krishnamurti's core being.

Thus did my new double life unfold over a period of about four years. I found all sorts of opportunities to sneak out of St. Edmund's during the afternoon and discover new pools, sometimes arriving back late for an individual lesson, slightly flustered and with wet hair. When at the school, I kept my behaviour as impeccable as I possibly could, though, to be honest, there were few temptations. I wasn't offered a place in either of the junior houses, but a job as assistant housemaster in a senior house instead. I performed my duties as such punctiliously, even having groups of seniors in my room for "coffee evenings" and showing them films on my newly-acquired, very expensive VHS recorder (a must after seeing what they could do), which made me very popular for a time. My cover as a monastic teacher, interested only in booze and music, was partially blown by the incident which I will call "the shower-room window".

When in the music block early one summer evening, intending to practise the bassoon for the grade 8 exam I had entered myself for, I happened, without at first realising it, to be in the one practice room which was opposite the shower room of one of the boarding houses. The latter room's frosted-glass window had always remained shut during the colder winter and spring terms, and I didn't even know if it was ever opened or indeed what the room was.

To my curious surprise and delight, I noticed that this window had now been opened and that it looked right onto an empty row of showers. One was close enough to see anything that might or might not take place there. Forgoing the pub for once, I remained in the practice room, practising less diligently than usual and hoping, but little dreaming, that the window would remain open when the boys performed their evening's ablutions. Sex has always beaten booze for me, even if it be, of necessity, furtive and voyeuristic.

Amazingly, that evening my dreams came true. A host of boys, some of whom I had been curious about, appeared naked before my eyes. It started with the juniors of the house and, as the evening progressed, the seniors also took their showers. The strange thing here was that some of the bigger boys wore swimming trunks, but it was a minority, and all through the proceedings I felt that rush of exultation Michael Davidson so wonderfully describes when he sees a boy naked for the first time. "Who next?" I was wondering, "surely not the lovely blond Johnson." I almost fainted when he did appear and turned out to have a memorable whopper. Fortunately, at that hour there was nobody else in the music block, and I was able to return to my room, head full of wonderful images, and … (here I will draw a veil). It would now be rather fun to see these same boys dressed in their drab uniforms and know, without them knowing, more about them than they suspected.

This magnificent discovery became something of an addiction, and I would always make a point of checking whether the window was open and wonder who I would see – Johnson, to my delight, was a regular. I was nearly caught out by dear Hugo Russell on one occasion, but I'd heard the footsteps downstairs and rapidly decamped to the next practice room. I'm not sure whether he had made the same discovery, but, being a keyboard player, he would have had no earthly reason to be standing in that room.

My luck held for some weeks until the boys themselves must have begun to realise one day that the window was overlooked, though this was far from obvious, and then set a sort of trap. I returned from my orchestral rehearsal one evening and saw that the window was open, which it hadn't been for some time – so what was it going to be, pub or practice room? No contest. I eagerly rushed into the room and pretended to be playing the viola only to see heads poking from the window and jeering voices. In as dignified a way as I could, I continued to "practise" with my head turned away and, after a reasonably respectable interval, put the instrument away and left.

It was the last time the window was ever opened, and I deduced from odd remarks by certain staff and senior boys that my voyeuristic antics had been registered. As there had been no other "misbehaviour", there was nothing anyone could do about it, but there was no getting away from the fact that on that final occasion the window had been left open as a sort of honey trap. Would Mr. Nicholson go to the pub, as usual after his return in the middle of the evening, or to the practice room despite having already spent three hours practising with a full orchestra?

I was by this time anyway seriously looking around for a new post, and attending quite a few interviews in prep schools, as well as one public school which seemed good. A new master, Graham P., had taught in it before moving to Stowe and then to St. Edmund's and had many positive stories to tell about it. Despite being a Catholic, he too disliked the atmosphere of St. Edmund's and was very supportive of me in my efforts to find something more congenial. He returned to his old job in Stowe quite soon after taking up his post at St. Edmund's – they hadn't wanted him to leave, such was his popularity – and I spent many a pleasant weekend at Stowe in the company of well-balanced, civilised boys in the house where Graham was assistant housemaster. Such a difference in atmosphere.

I was offered a job in a prep school in Surrey, but after seeing the behaviour of the boys and the disrespect shown to the struggling music teacher, I turned it down. Soon after this there was a vacancy at a much better school nearby for a newly created post of Assistant Director of Music. This was a school of 120 boys called Feltonfleet. I applied for this post and had an extremely positive interview with the headmaster and a far less positive one with the brash young woman who was the current holder of the Director's position. I decided I would, however, definitely accept this job if offered it, as the place was clearly well-run and the boys seemed happy and polite. One of the head's questions was "Do you prefer boys or girls?" – a question I had no hesitation in answering truthfully in those less aware times. As it turned out, the young woman, very likely intuiting my liking for boys, chose a younger, inexperienced man against the wishes of the headmaster. Probably she realised my lack of interest in her; I learned later that she made almost a nuisance of herself with the bachelor staff, accusing all those who did not wish to bed her of sexual inadequacy.

To my surprise, however, during the summer holiday of 1984, the head contacted me with an offer – not of Assistant Director of Music, but the top job. There had clearly been some sort of row between him and the woman, Marlene James, who had resigned in a huff, expecting her resignation not to be accepted, but her bluff had been called. I was given a week to decide and was at the time touring the West Country in my car. I dithered for a while – I had no ambitions as an administrator; being Assistant, with no ultimate responsibility, suited me fine. But then I was also applying for jobs at bigger schools where I would be on my own. On the third day, I called the headmaster and accepted the post, which would begin in January 1985 – a glorious new phase of my life in which all sorts of new doors were opened for me.

INTERLUDE

Before continuing with the story of my career and describing the hazardous way in which I finally found a way into the rather secret world of active boy-love, meeting many new wonderful and interesting people, and some less than savoury ones, I will pause here to present three short cameos which illustrate just how boys have changed since the 1980s. All of them took place before my sex life had truly begun and might be regarded as "missed opportunities" by those less green than I.

1) Boy in woods near St. Edmund's.

I often would walk in the pleasant green area of woodland adjoining the school. It was peaceful and in the middle of a weekday afternoon one rarely encountered anyone else. Inspiration for simple orchestral pieces often came to me whilst strolling here, which were later used with some success with the mediocre school orchestras one was always trying to find material for.

One afternoon whilst I was thus happily occupied, a boy of about eleven was sauntering towards me from the opposite direction, dressed in school uniform and carrying quite a large satchel. He was easy on the eye, and I automatically smiled at him.

He beamed back and asked me to walk with him back to his house, chatting idly all the while.

"So where are you from then?" he asked me.

"From the college up the road."

"Aren't you just a bit old to be still at school?"

"Yes, of course. I'm not a boy. I teach there."

"Oh, cool!" … "Hey, you'll never guess what happened to me in the showers this afternoon."

"I dread to think! What?"

Giggle from boy. "I slipped on the soap and fell right over on me bum – it didn't half hurt!"

"Oh dear!"

After more idle chat …

"Well, here we are nearly at my house. It's just down there. Why don't you come in with me? My mum's never back until much later."

"Well, I don't know."

"Oh go on, please, it would be nice."

"I'm sorry. I must really be getting back – perhaps another time."

"OK. Tara then."

And he disappeared down the path as I cursed my timidity. I often walked that way again, hoping to see him, but I never did.

2) Boy on Newhaven/Dieppe cross-channel ferry.

Quite often in the holidays my mother and various friends of hers would make a day trip to Dieppe. It was absurdly cheap and, if one set off very early in the morning, one would be in time for an excellent meal at a French café. There would then be plenty of time in the afternoon to go shopping to stock up on wine, cheese et cetera before the tedious four-hour journey back.

On this occasion, I was travelling with my mother and Mary, the girl my mother had raised and who was then living in Worthing. As usual, I wandered off to explore the large boat on my own.

It was not at all busy and I found myself in a large deserted area with wooden seats fixed to the floor, extremely close together. At first I thought I was alone. Then I caught sight of a mop of fair hair in the middle of one of the rows.

The mop turned, revealing the handsome smiling face of a boy of about twelve. I had scarcely time to react before he addressed me in a beguilingly friendly West Country accent.

"Hello! You on your own then?"

"Er, no, not exactly!"

"Why don't you come and sit down for a while next to me?"

"Oh, OK."

As the absurdly small seats were so close together, I moved into the row and sat down leaving a chair between him and myself.

"'Ere, what you doin'? I said *next* to me. Cummon!"

I needed no further encouragement, although this meant that our bodies were touching, something the boy seemed to like, as did I of course.

"So, I'm Tom. What's your name then?"

"Stephen." After a slight pause I added: "Where are your parents?"

"Oh they're asleep upstairs. It gets so borin'.'"

"What do they do?"

"They're teachers!"

He then looked up at me with a cheeky smile on his face. "Hey, have you got a guuuurlfriend then?"

"Er, no!"

"Neither have I, guuurls are borin'!"

There followed some more idle chatter, during which the sides of our legs and bodies remained in close contact. Was it my imagination or was the boy actively pressing against me? And was I being rather bold and doing the same? Whatever, it felt very good and I loved his company and sparkle. About fifteen minutes must have passed before the spell was broken by other passengers entering the area.

I can't recall who moved first, but there was reluctance on both sides. We eventually parted with a non-committal "See you again then", which of course neither of us ever did.

Before relating my final encounter from the early eighties, I should add here that boys' behaviour in swimming pools was often pleasantly exhibitionistic and friendly. Not only did they quite happily take all their clothes off, but sometimes they would disappear together behind a locker and indulge in some surreptitious masturbation with a friend or two – something I also observed on the local beach on many a happy occasion. In the pool itself one would sometimes be accosted by a lone boy wanting to race you or simply play for a while. In the changing room, if a pair of trunks were too tight to put on because the drawstring had become knotted, a boy might ask you to undo it for him, happily standing there fully nude in front of you whilst you dealt with the offending garment – none too hastily, I might add.

I'm sure, as with the final story from this period, one could have easily struck up a friendship with many a boy in a swimming pool, but where could it go? Could one walk back to his house and greet his parents as the man their son has just picked up in the pool? Amazingly, this did happen to me later in another country, but in earlier days I felt it was safer to enjoy such sights as I could and be grateful for them.

Such sights are long gone now, of course.

3) Boy in amusement arcade.

When I was with Bunny, we would often go to pubs which had Space Invader machines. They were rather simple given the high degree of sophistication now achievable with computer animation, but fun to play nevertheless, and I became quite good at them.

Often in the seafront arcades a boy would latch on to me when I was playing one of these machines by myself. "Give you a game, mate?"

"Yeah, sure!" But that would be it and the boy would saunter off once the game was over.

Once, however, after finishing two or three games with me, a pleasant slightly older lad of thirteen or so turned to me and said, "Where shall we go now?"

"How about the pier, there's some good amusements there."

"OK, great."

After half an hour or so on the slot machines, he turned to me again with a similar question: "So what shall we do now?"

"What about a coffee, or coke and hamburger at the café?"

Same response, and plenty of idle friendly chatter, almost as if we had known each other for years. At one point he said, "I wish you was me dad. It's much more fun with you than it is at home!"

After a thoroughly enjoyable afternoon spent innocently in each other's company the time came to part. Sex hadn't been mentioned and maybe he'd have run a mile if in response to "So, what next then?" I'd said, "How about we go into that toilet there and have some fun?"

That would have spoiled a delightful afternoon, but I still wonder if he might have said: "Now you're talking. I thought you'd never get round to it!"

If the law, even back then, hadn't been so draconian, I might have been less timid, as these were all boys who had voluntarily attached themselves to me and, had they been willing to indulge in some hanky-panky, I would not have felt I was betraying anyone's trust.

This would have been a different situation from my role as a teacher. Also, alas, from the rare times I was asked to look after a boy.

A final indulgence before continuing is my memory of a French boy, Jérôme.

As my timetable was so light at St. Ed.'s, I agreed to teach some French in the prep school, St Hugh's, and thought it would be a good idea to spend time with a French family before starting my French classes the following summer term. I could be very specific with the agency which found suitable families, and I made it very clear that I wanted a family with young boys in it – not girls.

They told me that this family had a boy of ten and a boy of fourteen. Fine, but when I arrived, the ten-year-old was not there, though the fourteen-year-old was. He was a handsome mischievous boy who, remarkably, was still being washed by his mother every morning. This happened, agonisingly, in the small bathroom which adjoined my bedroom and I would hear the splashes of water and the mother shrieking for him to behave: "Jérôme, arrête!" It took all my powers of self-restraint not to go into the bathroom and ask if I could be of assistance …

The following summer, he was staying in Littlehampton with a family who spoke no French and with whom he was far from happy. His father rang from Paris and asked if I would take Jérôme out for the day. This was at a time my mother was away, so I had the flat to myself.

Of course! Bien sûr!

I arrived at the dingy house where he was staying, and was greeted by a rather common woman who evidently took in French children just for the money and seemingly had little interest in them or what they did. As no one spoke French (perhaps something his father desired, to force him to use what poor English he had), Jérôme had clearly been bored and was delighted to see me.

I took him back to Worthing and we had some fun with all the seafront amusements described above. We had lunch at a small restaurant, after which he came back to the flat. I was able to entertain him with videos of things like Monty Python, which was visual enough for him to find funny, and we played some board games. He was a very physical boy and would spontaneously hold my hand when we were out and, at one stage, was happy for me to put my arm around him.

All the while I was remembering the noisy showers he took, with his mother attempting to scrub him, and only just held back from suggesting that as it was rather hot and we were both a little sweaty … how about … I did not have the slightest doubt that he would have thrown off his clothes and jumped into the shower with me like a shot, had I suggested it, and who knows what this might have led to with such an extrovert and vivacious boy, but again that voice of caution held me back. Suppose he told his father who had entrusted his son to my care for the day? There might be no problem about it, though I felt it might have been going rather beyond what he had in mind when he asked me to look after Jérôme.

So the boy was delivered back to Littlehampton on time, unwashed and unmolested. Sadly I never saw him again.

VI. Second Job and Branching Out

In chapter four I talked of my discovery of various authors who altered my whole way of looking at the world. Of these, Colin Wilson explored the broadest range of subject matters. In fact, there was nothing he didn't cover in the same spirit of open-minded investigation, recognising that the world is so vast that, despite all the amazing progress over the years, there is still so much we don't know about it. One lifetime is woefully insufficient to even begin to answer the fundamental questions of how and why we come to be on this small piece of revolving rock, and whether we have any purpose beyond staying alive as long as possible on it and trying to make it a better place for ourselves, others and future generations.

I have always been fairly sceptical about questions concerning the occult, though never, bearing in mind the famous quotation about Horatio, prepared to dismiss it all as complete nonsense. After my mother and I moved to Worthing in 1980, the Littlehampton house remained empty throughout the summer holiday before I went to Reading, and two close friends, John and Nigel came down to stay, being able to sleep at Rosemead. One thing they were anxious to try was a Ouija board, a simple set-up involving letters, numbers 0 to 9, and YES and NO being placed in a circle round a smooth table top. Then fingers would be placed on an inverted glass and questions asked, the first inevitably being, "Is there anybody there?"

The first time we tried this, we received the answer "YES" and went on to ask who it was. The glass, certainly seeming to be moving of its own accord (as we were far too serious about it all to mess around), spelled out the word D-E-V-I-L and John immediately picked it up in some panic and shouted out: "In the name of Jesus Christ be gone!"

The second time we seemed to have trapped a more friendly spirit who chatted away quite happily, but most of it was inconsequential nonsense. Over a period of several days, we must have tried contacting spirits in this way well over twenty times. Though the glass always moved and often seemed to give useful information, it turned out to be false whenever we could verify it. An example of this comes from Nigel, whose father had simply walked out on his mother when he was very young, and nothing more had ever been heard of him.

"Is my father still alive?"

"Yes!"

"Where is he living?"

"New York."

"What name does he go by?" followed by "What's his address?" and then "What's his telephone number?"

The glass provided credible answers to these last three questions, including a feasible New York address complete with postcode, and a telephone number with the correct area code and number of digits which none of us would have been aware of. When Nigel checked it all out later, none of the information related to anything real in New York.

It was clear though that *something* was going on, and that it was something probably best left alone. When at university, I'd read Wilson's two large books on occult subjects, the first simply called *The Occult* and the second *Mysteries*, and, later on, one called *Afterlife*. I was impressed by the scientific way he explored the various topics – neither as a believer nor as a complete sceptic, but as one prepared to look at the evidence and draw his own conclusions. Through Wilson, I discovered the I Ching and the works of Carl Jung, who was not only an avid user of the I Ching but also an adept at astrology, which he would use to help his patients. Jung's *Memories, Dreams, Reflections* blew my mind at this time.

Until comparatively recently, I have always had a copy of the I Ching to hand and, at important times, consulted it using the coin method. I also dipped into it as a simple reading book containing much ancient Chinese wisdom with its numerous contributions from Confucius, who formulated his own insightful interpretations of the sixty-four hexagrams.

"Where on earth are you going with all this Stephen?" I hear the reader ask impatiently, if indeed he is still with me. "What's happened to all those fun stories about boys? I'm jolly well going to stop reading right now unless you bloody well get on with it!"

OK, OK, just be patient, there *is* a point to this diversion. Now, where was I before being so rudely interrupted – ah yes.

In *The Occult*, Wilson said he'd only once ever had six unbroken lines when consulting the I Ching, unambiguously meaning great success and good fortune, and that was when he asked it about his future career as a writer. Before going to Feltonfleet, I asked it the question, "Will this be a good move for me?" and also received six unbroken lines, the only time ever for me too. Unlike the car breaking down on the way to St. Ed.'s, I felt that this was at least a good omen.

Indeed, as soon as I arrived at the school, it felt right. The atmosphere was good, I had a wonderful room in a staff house with a lovely friendly cleaner provided, who looked after everything, including my washing. It wasn't all going to be plain sailing by any means – life rarely is – but I knew in my bones that I'd landed on my feet and all would be well.

The first problem I'd have to deal with was the Marlene James cult. She had been extremely popular with certain boys, and also her assistant, Philip Lloyd, who clearly didn't like me from the start and whose supercilious face wore a permanent sneer. He was a fine musician though and we did find a way of working together, until he himself thankfully decided to resign at the end of the summer term and become a private peripatetic teacher. To my later regret, I allowed him to come back and teach private piano lessons, so that his own pupils would have continuity: something he hadn't asked me about directly, but had requested through the head. It would have been better to have a clean break from him and his first boss. Marlene James was always "popping back"; as she'd left without securing a job, she hoped the boys would beg her to return, saying how awful it had been since she left and how useless I was. Mercifully this didn't happen, and I soon found myself, to my surprise and delight, becoming popular with these well-brought-up, sensitive and intelligent boys. There was also a fair amount of support from the other staff, who, to put it bluntly, had found her overbearing attitude something of a pain.

The very first day was memorable for two reasons.

1) It had snowed heavily in the night and the ground was thick with it.

2) Despite this, games happened as normal and, as Monday was my "duty day", I got to see every boy in the school naked.

All the juniors did a "run and swim", which I was shown how to supervise by the much feared and respected second master. The seniors changed into games clothes after lunch, then showered later on, supervised by one of the duty masters. The duties for the day were evenly divided up between the two members of staff and, if both were males, they could decide together who would take the showers – the female staff were not allowed to perform this task. Rather boldly, I made it quite plain that I would be happy to do the "grisly" shower duty, and this met with no resistance from dear Simon S., who was in charge of the scouts. No more sneaking up to practice rooms hoping to find a window open at any rate …

I wasn't quite as bold as the art master, Samuel M., who made a point of volunteering for extra shower duties whenever he could, after, for example, such events as dramatic productions. He would also often come into the changing room when another member of staff was taking showers, on the pretext of wishing to speak to a particular boy about some pressing matter. As he was a good teacher and liked by the boys, this was tolerated, though I don't think anyone was fooled when he spoke of "my girlfriend Dorothy" who lived up in York and whom he could, sadly, only see in the holidays. I had recently heard the phrase "friend of Dorothy" but didn't want to rock the boat by saying to him, "Oh, so you're a friend of Dorothy, are you Samuel?"

Early in that first term, the headmaster told me of the Music Director before Marlene. He had had to dismiss him for incompetence, and he was anyway nearing retirement age. I had met this man, who was a good friend of Samuel, they going to the pub together every Monday evening, and he'd seemed pleasant enough and certainly not that geriatric or superannuated. Now I was told the truth. The head didn't want me to associate with this man because he was a "queer" and there had been certain "rumours".

"Oh dear, Headmaster, how terrible!"

"Yes, well, Stephen, I just felt you ought to know."

I wondered if Samuel knew of this and, if so, why he so happily and openly managed to maintain his friendship with him. For me it was a pity, as I would have liked to get to know him too.

I didn't need to inquire much further about him though, for certain extremely attractive boys told me of how Mr. Taylor had behaved with them, especially when they were in games clothes, of which the shorts were very short. There was one extremely sexy boy who must have sensed my attraction to him and would often, almost without realising, play up to it. He once nestled himself next to me during a private lesson and said, "Mr. Taylor used to do *this*, Sir" and started massaging his bare thigh, moving up and down it sensually with his right hand and, at the same time, looking at me intently to gauge my reaction.

"Oh really, Rory, that's interesting. Now how about we try from bar 52 again?"

It was the gentlest of rejections, but oh how much it cost me not to answer properly what I perceived as a need in the boy. And, let's not beat about the bush, a need in myself too, and one I'd repressed for far too long.

So, all in all, I had two extremely successful terms and seemed to be liked by both boys and their parents, who were invited each Wednesday evening to participate in various activities. There was a very keen group of mothers, and a few fathers, who, along with some of the boys, were eager to put on a musical production in the two winter terms. This was something Marlene had excelled at: people were still talking about her wonderful production of *Cats* and all the marvellous costumes, backdrops et cetera provided by her special group of adult friends (with whom I did not get on so well). Fortunately, with the taciturn help of Philip Lloyd, we were able to do a passable production of *Jesus Christ Superstar*. I also managed to start a school orchestra, something which the head was particularly keen on, as there had been nothing before. He had remarked that Marlene only played the recorder and, "You can't get very excited about that!"

Another highlight of that first term was when the school choir merged with forces from Reed's, just round the corner, to perform Mendelssohn's *Elijah*. It was the same Director of Music as when I'd been there, but we swallowed our differences and he proved very helpful in recommending material and lending me music and instruments for various projects. In the actual performance, I played the second bassoon in a large orchestra amassed for the occasion at Reed's, and sat next to an amusing and beautiful young female bassoonist with whom I was able to flirt rather enjoyably. This didn't go unnoticed by the boys and did my reputation no harm whatsoever.

I had a sense of good things in my past bearing fruit. One of the first pieces I did with the choir was an anthem by Gabriel Strider, which went down well. I also received an emergency phone call from the Woking Symphony Orchestra, whose first clarinettist had let them down on the day of a big concert, asking me to step in at the last minute. I played the music by sight, attending only the final afternoon rehearsal. It wasn't too taxing, and as a result they all but begged me to stay and play for them permanently which I did, even though I'd already joined the far more prestigious Surrey Philharmonic on bassoon.

I had a pleasant surprise that day, for on the first desk of the cello section, also brought in along with a few other pros to bolster the string section, was none other than Miriam, and we resumed our friendship which continued for a good few more years after that. The following term, I took a group of boys to the Woking concert in the minivan, and Miriam was again playing and joined us in the van after eating supper with me at the school. It was assumed she was my girlfriend, especially as she'd been to visit a few times already.

I still adored her, but she already had a boyfriend and even expressed slight disapproval of my working with boys when she knew "all about me". I found this curious, for men who fancy women happily work together and are not considered to be predators or rapists. But it wasn't a huge problem for her, and there certainly wasn't the sort of universal demonisation of boy-lovers which exists today. There were signs of it starting though, and so being perceived as "normal" was certainly useful, even if a few people were not fooled.

I knew of Philip Lloyd's resignation about two thirds of the way through the summer term, typically not from him but from the head, who was keen that I should meet all the applicants for his replacement. In answer to one of my questions, the head said he'd prefer a single man, but suitability for the job was the main criterion. It being late in the year, there were not a great deal of applicants, and the person who proved the least unsuitable was a strikingly ugly young woman who was applying from a school near Liverpool which was closing down. She had glowing references, wore a stiff suit and did her best to assume command. She answered all questions in a trill Liverpudlian accent, with an assurance and confidence which seemed rather forced, and even got out her fags when the time came for a coffee break. This was something else which had not yet been universally demonised in those more liberally-minded days.

Despite her bossy manner and unappealing appearance, we did seem to be compatible as far as our skills went. She was happy to take the choir, with me at the piano, she being a very poor pianist. She also enjoyed class teaching and wanted to do as many class lessons as possible – again I was very pleased that she was keen to do the parts of the job I found least enjoyable, as had Philip Lloyd.

Stephen (on the right) with the choir at Feltonfleet

So, at the beginning of the following autumn term, Karen S. joined the school. She turned out to have an extraordinary mixture of qualities, being personally very insecure on account of her looks and musical abilities, but possessed of a heart of gold and a determination to succeed, as well as a sense of humour almost as wicked as mine. On many occasions during those first few weeks, I would be in her room while she cried her eyes out, as she was missing Liverpool and couldn't relate to the southern mentality (which for me had been a homecoming). The boys found her odd and she was not at first liked. They would complain about her constant smoking, even during private lessons, which made her breath bad, as well as her screeching, abrupt manner, but she had a gritty determination that refused to accept defeat.

Most evenings we would go down to the pub and discuss how things were going. I had made the mistake, on the very first day of showing her round, of putting a brotherly arm round her waist as we entered the swimming pool area, and she had responded with an ardour which I'd found rather alarming. It was the last time I touched her, mainly because she was so keen that I should. As she told me later, she had fallen in love with me that very first time we met for her interview. I had tripped and almost fallen when showing her round the grounds and she'd uttered a loud "Whoops!" which became a sort of catchword whenever anything went wrong. She timed her love for me from that moment.

It was another case of the wrong woman. I really could not have done anything sexual with her, and indeed a firmly heterosexual friend of mine expressed the same opinion when he met her, saying that he'd rather not think about what she might have between her legs. She also became fiercely jealous of anyone else I showed affection towards, be it boy or Miriam, who still came to visit me occasionally.

Despite all this, we established an excellent *modus vivendi*, and music in the school really began to flourish. She brought a new dimension to the end-of-term concerts with her popular percussion band, and was successful in establishing a junior orchestra. This made boys actually willing to be promoted to the main orchestra. Playing in an orchestra is not an easy or natural activity for boys, so there had been an element of coercion, with support from the head, when trying to get it established. I was also inspired to compose pieces for the orchestra to play, especially geared to the talent we had. The Woking Orchestra would obligingly play through them for me, so that I could record them and play them to the boys at the first rehearsal – it is always helpful when you know how a piece of music is supposed to sound.

I wrote out the individual parts in such a way that any junior group could play the pieces with whatever instruments they had available, and came close to getting them published. I even had a letter from my first bassoon pupil, who had moved on to Eton. He had gained a place in the Independent Association of Prep Schools orchestra course for the summer holiday, again much to the delight of the head, as this had been another of his dreams. One of my efforts had been selected for the IAPS orchestra to play – without my knowledge, as I'd hoped to establish some sort of copyright for them. It just happened to be the Woking conductor who was in charge of this group and he had kept copies for himself.

So, everything seemed to be going my way. I was truly happy for the first time since being sent away to school, and my social life was broadening. As London was a short train ride away, I would often go there on my half day, which was sacrosanct, resuming my studies in the British Library, visiting Miriam and often taking in a show or a concert. I also had a whole new raft of swimming pools to explore, which despite my happy new life still exercised a powerful magnetic force. It is impossible to explain that rush of adrenalin on entering a packed new pool with a good geographical layout.

This obsession was to prove my downfall and bring significant change to that rather unreal, privileged, yet not quite fulfilled existence I had been enjoying until the summer term of 1986.

I received a phone call from my highly distressed mother one lunchtime in the third week of that term, telling me that the police had been to the house in Worthing asking for me. To explain this I need to talk about something which had occurred during the previous holiday and which I thought I'd got away with. It led to weeks of agonised uncertainty, during which I existed in a state of unutterable dread. Horrible as this was at the time, it was eventually to prove a blessing in disguise, forcing me to face my essential nature full on and act out what had previously only existed in my perfervid imagination.

The spring term had had its hiccups, mainly brought about by the fact that when we got back from the pub Karen and I would stay up until the wee small hours playing snooker together on the boys' half-size table. I was a reasonably competent player and one of my extra-curricular activities was to organise a staff v. boys snooker tournament each term, which proved remarkably successful and popular. Karen clearly had more stamina than me and, as these very late nights began to catch up on me, I made a near-fatal blunder. We did not by then have enough boys taking Associated Board music exams to justify an examiner coming to the school, so we had to take small groups down to the local centre in Esher. Somehow I got the date wrong, as did Karen – unusually, since she was far better than me at such details – and we took them down a day early. No real damage was done as we were able to take them on the next day and the exams were successfully completed, with satisfying results. The whole matter would have been pardonable (and indeed had been pardoned by the headmaster) and quickly forgotten, had not one of the boys had a very influential parent who complained in the strongest terms. The result was a most unpleasant interview with the head and second master, which left me shattered. I felt my job was hanging by a thread: every perceived fault in my character and performance was thrown at me. Maybe I should follow Philip Lloyd and work as a peripatetic teacher? This was pretty near the end of term and I was still reeling from the effects of this harsh dressing-down when I went home.

It really did seem as if the gods had turned against me during this period, and I probably should have stayed at home in Worthing, reading and composing next term's piece for the school orchestra. However, I decided to spend an evening with John (he of the Ouija board) in Orpington. This was before he married, and we always had a fun boozy time together. On the way there, I stopped off at that excellent pool in Farnborough, discovered on my trip to Stevenage, in which the cubicles at the back of the room had had their locks changed, meaning that there were large peepholes where the old locks had been. None of the boys used them to change and one could sit invisibly inside to witness the orgy of naked frolics going on in the large open area. I'd spent many a happy afternoon there since discovering it on my trip to pick up *Some Boys*.

On this occasion there were not that many boys to be seen, but as soon as I emerged from the cubicle and went into the shower prior to a brief swim, two delightfully mischievous boys came out, and I could not resist going straight back into the cubicle to see what they would do. There had been a man on his own in the shower who, unbeknownst to me, had observed this – I was getting far too incautious, having had no trouble in pools since beginning the dangerous hobby four years previously. I stayed there for some time and was suddenly aware of the view from the peephole becoming blocked by a large male body. At first I thought nothing of this: somebody changing close by, no doubt.

After another ten minutes or so, I ventured to look again through the aperture and saw, to my horror, the same man from the showers standing further back and staring fixedly at my cubicle. I had been well and truly rumbled. Summoning as much self-possession as I could, I hurriedly got dressed. There was no sign of the man as I got out of the cubicle and left the leisure centre. Was he looking out for me? Had he followed me out? I quickly found my car and drove off, relieved to be away from a potentially dangerous situation, and spent a happy evening with John.

Stephen – hadn't there been enough portents that the powers which look over us were determined to teach you a lesson, were displeased at your complacent happiness and determined to shake you out of it?

Why oh why, oh foolish callow youth, could you not have then exercised some basic caution and forsaken this silly otiose activity which, though extremely titillating, offered thrills which could prove to be far too expensive?

But I didn't listen to that small inner voice of reason and, on the way back from John's, stopped off at another favourite pool from the past in Tunbridge Wells. It was magnificent! So magnificent that I completely lost any sense of risk or danger in what I was doing, lingering for a long time in a small open changing-room mostly full of boys of all ages happily revelling in their nakedness. A group of twelve- to thirteen-year-olds were chatting nude together and comparing sizes; one of them remarked, "I charge the girls at school 10p. each to have a look and make a lot more than me dad gives me for pocket money!"

Gradually I became aware of a hairy man regarding me with huge suspicion. He was built like a lorry driver and was definitely not someone you would want to mess with – fortunately he then left the changing room. Whoops! Time to go, Stephen.

I started dressing as casually as I could, but the man returned with a young attendant who looked extremely flustered and pretended to be checking lockers. Oh fuck, rumbled again, twice in as many days, act calm!

Instead of leaving immediately, I decided to play it cool and went to the café for a coffee before returning to my car. Nothing happened. Good, they had nothing they could accuse me of; I hadn't been challenged. When I got back to the car I spent a little time inside it reading, then sorting things out (mustn't seem agitated, Stephen), before finally starting to drive away and getting caught in a long line of cars leaving. It was then that I noticed the "lorry driver" and the attendant at the window of the centre, and the attendant was writing something down …

I felt sick inside all the way home, and a terrible sense of foreboding. Mother was going out to play bridge that evening and had cooked one of my favourite meals for me to eat while she was out, but the food turned to ashes in my mouth and I was physically sick into the lavatory bowl – a most unusual occurrence. However, nothing untoward resulted during the three remaining weeks of that holiday, two of which were spent in New York visiting Barbara-Sue and her family and having a wonderful "normal" time.

One memorable part of my New York stay was a trip to Atlantic City by bus where, instead of buying a ticket, you were paid

$30 in cash to lure you into the gambling dens. We were not lured, and I brought back many fun souvenirs from that holiday, including an oversize Budweiser mug (Budweiser being then my favourite tipple in the local pub) and a working model fruit machine, both of which I have only recently given away. I also played professionally for a bar mitzvah, for which I was well paid, and can vividly remember the attractive Jewish boy undertaking his coming-of-age ritual. I still have the photos of me playing in Barbara-Sue's Princeton group. So, it was an altogether happy trip.

With those two narrow squeaks, I had firmly resolved to give the pools a rest for a while. I seemed to have got the message in time: it had been nearly six weeks since that drive to John's flat in Orpington, and so I must have got away with it – surely.

In retrospect there were many things which were lucky about that fateful Saturday lunchtime when I received the phone call from my mother, the fact that I hadn't had the car registered at my school address being top of the list. Mr. Plod coming to the school to interview me about indecency in a public place would have ended my career there and then – "curtains", as Gabriel Strider later put it.

In addition:

It was lucky that I had a rare free afternoon that day, with no Sunday morning service to attend.

It was lucky that the weather was good and remained so for another week (to be explained).

It was lucky that the same two policemen who had come to visit my mother were still on duty in the police station when I arrived there some hours later.

I still had my lovely collection of Coltsfoot Press books and Pan magazines as well as some slightly more racy German photo albums which I'd seen advertised in Pan and bought sending DM in an envelope (and which also hadn't been opened by customs - more recklessness). These were kept in a locked suitcase in my room, and I knew that the first thing police did if there was "boy" trouble was to raid your home looking for corroborative material. In my panic I seized the case and, on the way down to the south coast, entered a large woodland area where I deposited it, with a heavy heart, under a tree and covered it over with as much bracken, leaves, earth and such like as I could.

I arrived home to find mother extremely anxious. She said the police wanted to question me about an incident in a swimming pool, and she referred back to the conversation we'd had when I was unhappy at university, when I'd said I *might* be gay, and asked me precisely what my feelings were.

"Um, I rather like boys."

"And have you done this before, gone to swimming pools to be near them?"

"Erm, once or twice."

The interview at the station would not be so easy, though considerably more so than it would be these days.

The sergeant in charge said he was pleased I'd turned up, as that meant the paperwork involved in referring the case to Surrey would be prevented.

They had a whole raft of pre-prepared questions, and a constable was called into the interview room to write down my answers; this was even before cassette recorders were used for such a process.

I was still too green to realise that "no comment" would have been far the best way to answer every question, and anyway they started off innocently enough: name address, occupation and so on.

Then, "Are you married?"

"No."

"Do you have a girlfriend?"

"Sort of."

"Huh! Are you attracted to men?"

Confidently, "No!"

"Are you attracted to boys?"

Less confidently: "Um, no …"

"Do you masturbate?"

"Sometimes, doesn't everybody?"

"Were you at Tunbridge Wells swimming pool on 11th March this year."

"Um, maybe, I can't quite remember. Yes, I think so."

"Did you get an erection in the changing-rooms?"

And so it went on. I had been accused of wanking over boys under my towel, which I may well have been doing, though that particular technique had never been consciously worked out at this stage. On the erection question, I'd remarked that sometimes it happens when you don't want it to, and this caused some dry merriment with the fifty-year-old cop retorting, "Yes, and sometimes it doesn't happen when you do – ho ho ho!"

I somewhat stupidly said at one point, "Why would I go to a pool to look at naked boys when I see them most days in my job?"

This provoked anger: "You shouldn't be doing that job, sonny! If I had my way, I'd make sure you weren't!"

The older cop finished by telling me he had a nose for "that sort of thing" and could tell that I was guilty. Previously he'd cajoled me by saying "Come on, son, it's not considered so bad to be homosexual these days, is it?"

I was made to read through my statement, full of spelling errors, and sign it. I was then told I could expect a letter sometime in the next few weeks, after they had decided whether or not to take the matter further.

After a poor night's sleep in Worthing, I returned to my job in a chastened and distraught frame of mind.

Karen was full of questions which I would not answer. For example: "You were as white as a sheet after that phone call. Have you had some bad news about medical test results?"

"No. I'll tell you about it when I can."

I performed my duties mechanically, aware that I was already under some sort of ultimatum from last term's blunder. Gradually, I managed to return to a reasonably calm frame of mind and considered the worst possible case, and what I would do if the whole business came into the open.

The first consideration was the suitcase in the woods. The police hadn't raided me, and the element of surprise necessary for them to hope they would find something was no longer there. The matter was being dealt with by Sussex police anyway. The weather had remained fine all week and the following weekend I drove back down to the woods, located the spot and to my relief found the case was still there, unopened and dry.

I phoned Gabriel Strider in Bristol and explained my predicament briefly, asking if I could deposit the suitcase with him. He agreed. On my next half day, I drove straight to his Bristol flat, was greeted with a huge healing hug, and told him everything.

He listened uncensoriously and confirmed he *would* look after the suitcase, but had a bad feeling about it. Shouldn't I destroy everything in it?

"No, I couldn't possibly do that."

"Well, at least give up this swimming pool nonsense".

"You don't need to tell me that!"

It was a magical afternoon – just being with him made me feel better. He promised to put me in touch with a gay priest he knew in London, Kenneth Davies from St. Dunstan's, who had many contacts and who, he was sure, would be able to help me. He also, at my request, agreed to phone my mother and try to reassure her that all would be well, which bless him he did! My mother later told me she'd gone into a church and prayed, and received an overwhelmingly blessed sense that everything would be fine.

This was still the time when a great distinction between boy-love and gay homosexuality was not really made, and I was to visit dear Kenneth in his church office every Tuesday afternoon. He was first of the opinion that I needed a gay relationship such as he had, but was not condemnatory, and finally agreed that if men were no use to me, I must find a real boy.

"Any boy would do!" I said

"Not any boy. You don't want a big fat Billy Bunter, do you?"

"No!"

He told me one day of a bulky builder he'd observed outside his house befriending boys and giving them sweets, and amusingly had thought of me. Previously, he had not been so aware of the phenomenon, but now he was observing it more and more. Each session would end with a long hug, and no mention was ever made of God in all the times I went to see him.

Kenneth did indeed know many people, including a teacher, Adam, who'd been imprisoned in the seventies for sex with boys and who was now living in Thailand and enjoying a fulfilled life with no fear of arrest. On his release from prison in England, he'd been too terrified to even look at boys, but he had met an extremely youthful-looking gay man he was to say "looked about fifteen even though he was twenty-two" and there had been instant mutual attraction. They'd had an affair which matured into a warm friendship which they still maintained, and do to this day. Adam's friend was called Oliver and worked in London; Kenneth would see if he could put me in touch with him, with a possible view to meeting Adam in Bangkok. Adam knew someone called John Stamford, who was involved with the Spartacus gay guides produced in Amsterdam. This man would often ask Adam to show people the ropes in both Bangkok and Pattaya, which he happily did. All Adam asked in return was to be taken out to a decent restaurant.

This was exciting. I knew of Stamford from the *Pan* magazine – if only something might come of this.

I had seven long weeks of waiting, the beginning of which coincided with the Chernobyl disaster. This symbolised my inner turmoil, but I somehow kept going normally. I even took to having a late-night swim each evening in the school pool, which was considered rather out of character, but would at least make my having been in public pools in the holidays a little more plausible, should the story come out. Karen was as bemused as ever, especially as I stopped socialising with her so much. She clearly wondered if she had done something to offend me, but it was mainly to avoid her questioning. I kept receiving special notes and assurances of love and friendship which were well-intended, but which I'd have preferred, on balance, not to receive.

On one half day I was in Epsom, and in the market saw a person advertising palm readings. I was tempted by this, but managed to alienate the man by suggesting I pay him "on results", something which didn't go down at all well! I mentioned this as something amusing to Karen who, in typical fashion, went there on her next free afternoon and had a reading done which was eerily accurate. She showed me the paper on which the chiromancer had written everything down – my initials, the fact she was in love with me, and my being in trouble; trouble relating to some form of indecency about which I may or may not have been aware. He also predicted a happy outcome though, which was rather cheering. Karen and I were in some ways telepathically linked, and she always seemed to know far more about me than I ever told her. There were to be some even more spooky events later on, before I finally left the school under something of a cloud.

Meanwhile I successfully contacted Oliver, who was still a good-looking young man. He spoke extremely softly: one had to lower one's head towards him and strain one's ears if in a public place, or it would be impossible to catch anything he said. We hit it off fairly well, and used to meet most Tuesday evenings for a meal out – often in one of the few Thai restaurants which were beginning to establish themselves in London. I was completely open with him, and he was entirely sympathetic and very positive that everyone should find sexual partners to suit their particular focus and ages of attraction. He'd recently returned from Thailand and spoke enticingly of how sexy the boys were, both in looks and behaviour. He was happy to contact Adam on my behalf, with a view to my visiting him in the summer holiday. One proviso of Adam's would be that there weren't any current serious boy problems; Oliver seemed to regard the Tunbridge Wells matter as rather trivial, which was encouraging. By serious, Adam meant accusations of buggery, which was what he'd faced.

Oliver would later introduce me to the gay scene in Earl's Court and to noisy bars with names like Heaven, where he would often pick up men.

Eventually, one memorable morning just before half term, which was always late in the summer term, occurring two thirds of the way through, a letter was sent to the school. It was inaccurately addressed and my name was so misspelled as to be almost unrecognisable. It was something of a miracle that it arrived, that I was one of the first to see it on the chest in the school hall that morning and that I realised what it must be, otherwise it might well have been opened by the school secretary and that, as the saying goes, would have been that. I wonder to this day if that sergeant, in view of his comments to me, hadn't done this deliberately, not wanting me to escape scot-free. Anyway, the contents of the letter were brief and to the point:

Address of Police station …

My name …

On Tuesday March 11th this year, you were accused of an act of indecency at a swimming pool in Tunbridge Wells.

This case has now been fully investigated and no further action will be taken.

Signed et cetera.

The relief was of course indescribable.

After all the celebrations (Karen was also overjoyed, bless her) and telephone calls, I was able to enjoy a week's break without the sword of Damocles hanging over me. As well as spending some time in Worthing, I was invited to Kenneth's house to meet his long-time partner (whom I believe he is still with after all these years), and I passed an enjoyable evening in Oliver's flat with him and his latest boyfriend.

Those final four weeks of term passed in a haze of unmitigated joy, as well as excitement about my forthcoming trip. All my subsidiary plans if the case had been pursued, as it surely would be nowadays, were now unnecessary. I appreciated my situation all the more, being in a place surrounded by mostly beautiful, if untouchable, boys doing work I found congenial. I soon paid another visit to Gabriel Strider in Bristol to pick up the suitcase, and he again expressed misgivings about me owning such material but didn't harp on too much about it. I showed him some of the music I had written for the school orchestra and played him the recordings of the Woking Symphony Orchestra performances. He was surprisingly encouraging about it, not being one to offer false praise.

The main business now was to get a good flight booked to Bangkok at a reasonable price. I toured the London "bucket shops" until I found one, deciding I would fly after my customary stay in Dartington in late July/early August. I was now communicating directly with Adam by letter, who told me much about how things were. He sounded a small note of caution that after experiencing complete liberation where he lived, I might find it less easy to keep my hands to myself when I got back to the UK. On learning that I would be flying Royal Jordanian with a stopover in Amman on the way back, he helpfully suggested some places where I might find boys there. The date of my flight was to be the 17th August, and I made no secret of the fact I was going there, which prompted a rather silly letter from Karen with the obvious pun on Bangkok (which she spelled Bangcoc). My mother expressed uneasiness about my going, but when she realised that nothing would dissuade me from it, passed on her camera and told me to make sure I got some good snaps.

My feeling about the whole trip was immensely positive: this would be an adventure and one which would change my life.

VII. Further Journeys into Self-Discovery

Each man had only one genuine vocation – to find the way to himself ... His task was to discover his own destiny – not an arbitrary one – and to live it out wholly and resolutely within himself. Everything else was only a would-be existence, an attempt at evasion, a flight back to the ideals of the masses, conformity and fear of one's own inwardness.
HERMAN HESSE, *Demian*

I prepared for the trip as well as I could, reading regular guidebooks as well as books on Buddhism. I had a useful phrase book with both Thai script and transliteration, and felt as ready as I'd ever be when the time came. As I was flying from Heathrow, I spent the night before with Oliver, whose flat was close to Barons Court tube station and we had a farewell Thai meal out together.

I enjoyed the flight, and even the short stopover in Amman was new and fascinating. I recalled how Graham P. at St. Ed.'s had spent a holiday in Jordan and had spoken of having been propositioned by many young boys, which led to one or two other staff taking an interest in going there. In the transfer lounge was a large group of Arab boys, dressed in their gleaming white dishdashas, whom I automatically gravitated towards. They returned my smiles with beaming ones of their own, revealing gleaming white teeth, and becoming most excited that this foreign man was showing an interest in them. They gradually surrounded me, some pressing against me with no awareness of body space, and asked me many questions in broken English – it was all rather delightful and boded well for the holiday.

Adam and his current live-in, Lorn, duly met me at Don Meuang International Airport, rather a small ramshackle affair, but which was soon to be completely refurbished. He drove me back to his impressive triplex apartment in Soi Sala Daeng, the same street where, I learned later, the infamous murderer Charles Sobhraj had also lived, in Kanit house. En route, Adam pointed out various sights, including the policemen whose uniform was so different from those of England, and to my eye far less threatening. The first evening was mainly spent chatting, though I do recall Adam chastising Lorn later on, as he was forever doing, and his walking around the place naked. I was thus able to confirm what Oliver had told me about the unusual size of Adam's weapon – how on earth had he fitted *that* up the bums of the eleven-year-olds he'd been convicted for in Gray Britain!?

Although I suffered some jet lag, Adam seemed to think I should be initiated as soon as possible, and had arranged a meeting with the then notorious Madame Cécile, an elderly Vietnamese procuress who had supplied boys to many over the years, including some film stars apparently. I recently learned from a friend I shall simply call CE that she would meet him at the airport on his visits there, always with a boy whom she knew would be his type. This presumably was Adam's thinking, rather than simply taking me round the corner to Robinson's supermarket on Silom Road, outside which, at almost any time of day or night, willing boys would be found. Adam sometimes had as many as four or five of these in his house for some fun on the side, whilst retaining Lorn as his then special boy. Lorn being half *farang* (Caucasian), he could and would try and pass him off as his son when we were out and about.

To reach Madame Cécile's place, one could only drive a certain distance, as there was no proper road for the last few hundred metres, and barely a pavement. One negotiated a huge jumble of tiny houses with open fronts containing many large families squatting down in what appeared to be a single room. It was extremely hot and muggy, and I had certainly never witnessed such poverty before, so it was all something of a culture shock. However, the people did not seem unhappy and waved and shouted out to Adam, who cheerfully replied in his limited Thai.

Mme. Cécile clearly commanded huge respect and Adam waied her and bade me do the same. He spoke to her in Thai, and I was happily able to converse with her in French. We sipped tea from a glass as we waited for the boys she had sent for to be produced. Eventually they arrived, rather a large confident-looking one and a much smaller nervous-looking lad. Apparently, Adam had only wanted the one small boy for me, but he would not come on his own and so his larger friend was there to accompany and reassure him. This young, frightened and surprisingly light-skinned boy was to be my first sexual encounter since those happy days at prep school, and judging by how apprehensive he seemed, I was to be his first ever sexual partner, unless he'd had a previous bad experience. My heart went out to him.

Whilst not exactly a failure, sex with my first boy for sixteen years was not the amazing event that might have been hoped for. Once Adam had disappeared into his bedroom, the boy became extremely uneasy and only by the gentlest of persuasion could he be persuaded to remove his clothing. He required much cuddling and comforting cooing noises before he would relax at all. The sex was of the gentlest and neither of us reached orgasm, though he did definitely cheer up – he'd probably been expecting the worst in the form of an unwanted prick forced up his backside. As this was clearly not desired, I did not even attempt it.

Adam was rather cross that the boy had proven so unwilling and was all for complaining to Mme. Cécile, but I dissuaded him from this. She'd delivered what he'd asked for.

Later that week we would be visiting Pattaya but, before that, Adam felt I should experience all the different types of bar to be found in Patpong; I would thus also be able to describe realistically the girlie places should anyone be curious about how I'd got on in what was, wrongly in my view, reputed to be one of the most lubricious cities in the world. So we went to gay bars where simpering seventeen-year-olds sidled up to you and called you "velly handsome man", adding "you go with I, short tie', long tie', whatever you want!" One bar, called the Super A, was particularly outrageous: it featured naked dancing by quite young boys, culminating in a fucking show where two older boys performed together to extremely loud and pulsating music.

The girlie bars were also as I'd been led to expect, with teenagers barely more than sixteen performing supposedly provocative naked dances. I also witnessed the famous ping pong ball act, whereby an astonishing number of these items were stuffed up a girl's cunt and made to pop out in a controlled way, being aimed at various parts of the room.

I also dutifully did the regular tourist stuff, visiting various impressive *wats* and taking photos. I went to a snake farm and had a picture taken of me with a large python curled around me.

Before our trip down to Pattaya on the following Friday, I'd also befriended Lorn, who, at fourteen and very experienced, was a much better proposition than the poor frightened wretch found for me by Mme. Cécile. When Adam was at work the next day, Lorn had gone into the bathroom and not locked the door, so I naturally followed him in. After a token pretence at modesty, with one hand covering a respectably-sized member with a few whisps of hair, my ideal in many ways, he allowed me to join him and much watery fun was had. This led to more earnest explorations, and finally I had my first orgasm with a boy after many years.

Whilst at the British Library, I'd read one or two articles about sex with boys and what they liked most, listing many erogenous zones apart from obvious ones, including the ears, nipples and nape of the neck. With Adam's blessing, and to Lorn's apparent delight, I explored these zones thoroughly over the next few days, and found that he most enjoyed having his ear nibbled, something he would do to me in return. I used to have video footage of this holiday, taken by Adam, in which, on a day trip to Ayutthaya, ancient capital city of Siam, Lorn kept on nibbling my ears!

So, on the Friday afternoon we went down to Pattaya, once a peaceful fishing village until the Americans came whilst on leave from Vietnam. It soon grew into a lurid town full of bars and restaurants and a place where any taste could be accommodated. The plan was that Adam would show me everything and leave me there when he returned for work on Sunday night. He had the use of one of his firm's bungalows situated some way out of the town, and we stayed in that. It was fine except for the lack of air conditioning, though there were powerful fans. I was shown the infamous Siren Bar where, at that time, peds could find boys of a wide variety of ages who came to the town for the purpose of meeting men. This, I was to discover, was not nearly so sleazy and money-driven as it may sound, as many of them were hoping for a sort of sugar daddy or someone who would care for them, and partings could be quite emotional. The boys were cared for by a young woman nicknamed Nit, who served in the bar and who would know exactly who the good and bad *farang* were and advise the boys accordingly. Likewise she would inform the *farang* if a boy was difficult and dishonest, or diseased. Once, on a later trip, she was very shocked when a beautiful boy with Aids was picked up by a friend of mine who, in the event, only wanted to take pictures.

For the Friday and Saturday nights I had two different boys to share my bed with, as did Adam, with Lorn away on a trip of his own. During the day we returned the boys back to the Siren Bar and explored other parts of the town, where young women would cry out to us from behind open-air bars:

"You come with I."

"No sorry, I only like boys!"

"What, you like boy. I cry!"

There was the pleasant Jomtien beach where *farang* would relax with their boys. During the day, boys were also to be seen wandering around the town, maybe selling chewing gum or cigarette lighters, and often making eye contact to show availability. One character I first met then, but never had, was nicknamed big silly Kai, a strikingly good-looking, sunny-natured boy, who was forever giggling and making jokes. On later visits, he would visit my room, drink coke and watch *nang pi* (ghost films), but, for whatever reason, I never wanted sex with him, and not for lack of him offering. I simply saw him as a friend and fun to be with.

The biggest mistake Adam made was suggesting I rent a small motor scooter so that I could continue using the bungalow while he was back in Bangkok. Had I known you could stay in a comfortable little hotel near the Siren Bar, with air con, for the equivalent of £10 a night, I would certainly not have rented this cheap, but much more inconvenient, scooter. It did work well for the first night but, on the second, disaster struck. I met an Englishman in the Siren Bar, small in stature and with short curly greyish hair who looked to be in his late fifties; he was rather gaudily dressed with items of bling jewellery on his person and an air of decadence about him. He suddenly came over to where I was sitting and addressed me in an uncomfortably forthright manner. I was still in a state of mild culture shock and felt tremendous tenderness towards many of these boys, who were happy to sleep with you for a hundred baht a night or less if it was late and they hadn't been claimed.

Imagine a rather common gruff Essex accent:

"'Ello!" he shouted above the noise of the Thai boxing and loud music.

"Oh, hello."

"Yew 'ere for the boys then?!" he asked in an equally stentorian voice. Why not get a megaphone?

"Er, well …"

"Oh, come on, don't be so bloody British abart it. I am, been coming 'ere for years!"

"Oh right!"

"Oi'll give you a tip!"

"Right, thanks!" Please don't, I thought.

"See, the thing to do is not try and fuck 'em while they're on their tummies, much too 'ard!"

"Oh, I see," I said, cringing inside.

"Nah, wot yew should do is lie 'em on their backs, then grab their legs and pull 'em *right* over their body. Then it's much easier to get in, yer see! Try it next time …"

"Well thanks awfully, must be going now."

This was my introduction to Roy Hardy, sometimes known to others as Legs Over Roy and, later on I discovered, BOF (boring old fart) Roy. I was to meet him a few more times on that first trip. As he didn't live too far away from the school, he gave me his phone number and suggested I call him up when I got back to England. He had "masses of porn" he could show me, and knew some interesting people. I vaguely promised I would.

A little later I found not one, but two delightful-looking boys who would be happy to come back to the bungalow with me. I thought I'd just about mastered the scooter, and the night before had managed to drive off quite easily with only one boy on the back. Two, however, turned out to be an altogether different proposition.

The area was always thick with traffic and, as soon as I saw a gap, I accelerated quickly out in the road, only for the small bike to tip up alarmingly at the front like a frightened horse, throwing me and the boys into the road whilst the scooter careered across the road, colliding with an expensive new-looking Mercedes driven by a posh Thai lady who, I discovered later, spoke reasonable English. She was extremely irate about the damage done to her car and promptly summoned the police. I was more concerned about the boys, who, mercifully, had scuttled off quickly, seemingly unharmed.

After three tedious hours during which I had to phone Adam to explain my predicament, and someone was called to assess the damage to the Mercedes – a staggering 20,000 baht, it was finally agreed that I would return to the police station at the weekend and pay over the money. In the meantime, they would keep my passport until the cash was handed over, and we had to drive to the bungalow to pick it up. After this major blip, I found to my astonishment that the bike was still in working order, though parts of it were rather bent out of shape. I went back into the Siren Bar to see who, if anyone, was still there. To my further amazement, the same pair had waited for me and immediately skipped over as I entered, once again mounting the bike with seemingly few qualms.

Taking things much more steadily, we arrived safely back at the bungalow and passed a most enjoyable night of fun sex – my first threesome! They found my phrasebook and, with great merriment, kept pointing at Thai words and expressions which translated as "be careful", "go slowly", "take it easy" and so on. Fortunately I was able to get the damage to the bike repaired for just a few hundred baht and, when I finally returned it, there were no problems.

It soon spread how much my little accident was going to cost, and I learned the Thai for 20,000 long before I had mastered all the smaller numbers. Even on subsequent trips, I was remembered as the *farang* who had had the expensive accident. To me, it was worth the money knowing that everyone was safe and that the matter was completely closed, which it was. It also gave me something to talk about with curious staff when I returned next term.

Needless to say, I did not immediately follow Roy's advice and was happy doing whatever the boys were relaxed with, which was far more than Mme. Cécile's offering. One boy, for example, was lying on the bed naked, and I started with his feet, planning to travel all round his body and leave the most interesting part until last. "*Mai dai!*" he exclaimed, which I knew meant "Not permitted!", and I inwardly groaned, thinking this might be another "You can look, but don't touch" scenario. However, all other parts of the body were met with a happy "Dai". How foolish of me to forget that Thais consider their feet dirty, and not generally something to be touched!

My emotions were all over the place too. Whilst it was extraordinary that such a scene should exist at all, I could not but admire and respect these young tender creatures who so trustingly gave themselves to strangers. Maybe they developed an instinct about who was safe, and I never heard of any of them getting hurt. My final night alone in the bungalow was the most touching of all. I'd decided that I wanted a night on my own and gently turned down all offers, as I had my evening drink of chilled Singha beer, or maybe Kloster, the slightly posher alternative then available. I was about to leave when a pleasant-looking boy who looked no older than ten pleaded with me to take him back for the night, and kept saying "No money!" "Pliz pliz!" "I come with you – plizzzz!"

Well, only a heart of stone would have resisted such an appeal, and it was delightful simply watching him pad around the place naked (his idea), gratefully eating food, making sure he washed and even cleaning his teeth with a spare brush I'd brought along with me. My feelings were wholly paternal, and all I wanted was to put him in my suitcase and take him back home and bring him up in a decent home and show him all the love I felt I had inside me. He lay with me in bed cuddled up close, with his arms around me and slept soundly and silently and, as with big silly Kai, but for entirely different reasons, I had no wish to have any sort of sex with him.

He of course received some money, and we parted amiably enough the next day, though he clearly wanted me to carry on seeing him, but Adam was returning and we had other trips planned.

I'll finish this account of the holiday with a few random memories.

My hair was long and Adam took me to have it cut by what I thought was a woman, to his great amusement; it was in fact a "ladyboy", or *kathoey*, as they are commonly known. My guidebook translated the word as homosexual but, as transvestites are normally not androphilic, I wasn't sure about this. Unlike transvestites, *kathoey* clearly made as much effort as possible to look and sound as feminine. Perhaps, if the custom still exists, many of them now make the full leap and become fully transgender, which is these days so much more common – even, dare I say, politically correct.

I met quite a few other peds, and had some enjoyable conversations, but none of them lived close to me as Roy did. He became more affable on subsequent meetings and had a fund of stories about Thailand and other places where he'd had boys. He was married with a daughter, but effectively separated though not divorced. It was Roy who told me that the actor Roger Moore used to come to Thailand for the boys, though I forget on what authority he had this information. There was also a collection of public-school teachers from a very well-known school I soon learned was Hurstpierpoint, who kept within their circle and did not seek the company of other *farang*. One of my first memories of this group was being in Siren Bar and noticing them sitting slightly apart, as they assessed the talent available. One of them exclaimed loudly in a rather hoity-toity accent, "It's all pretty second eleven stuff here this evening!"

I did many more normal touristy things and took plenty of photos of the boys I'd had as well as of the places we visited, and made sure I didn't get them mixed up when later showing people my snaps back home. Lorn, as well as being the boy who'd really initiated me into sex, also showed me round places in Bangkok such as the local swimming pool, and, more surprisingly, local schools. We were simply able to wander into any government school and watch lessons being taught without being challenged in any way; I doubt very much whether that would be the case now.

All too soon it was time to return to drab old England. I vowed that when I returned to Thailand my Thai would be at least as good as Adam's, as he was forever saying things I could not understand to Lorn and others. I also wanted to be able to communicate decently with all Thai people, but, of course, especially with the boys.

My journey back to the UK was uneventful, and I was pleased to have the stopover in Amman, though I had no wish to start searching for these clubs Adam had told me about. I was still in a daze with all I'd seen and done, and knew that if I could have afforded it, I'd have been tempted to move permanently to Thailand the next week. I still had my job though, which paid well and which I adored. I'd be a fool to throw up all that on the basis of one dazzling visit to a different culture. On the final leg of the journey, the train down from Victoria to Worthing, I had a delightful encounter which I'll briefly relate, as it again illustrates how different Britain now is.

I found myself sitting opposite an attractive blond boy of about eleven who beamed at me and, on seeing my cases, starting chatting: "You've got a lot of luggage. Have you come a long way?"

"Yes, I've just travelled from Thailand."

"That's pretty far isn't it, but not as far as I've come."

"And where would that be?"

"Sydney Australia, all on my own!"

"Gosh, that is impressive. Don't your parents worry about you travelling alone?"

"Nah, they think it's good for me, and they encourage me to meet new people and talk to them. I live in Angmering. What about you?"

And so the time passed and I discovered where he went to school, his hobbies and much else besides, and though he also expressed a hope that we'd meet again, I did not make any attempt to write down his phone number or contact him. I was back in England: boys, even friendly ones, could lead to trouble and I'd now discovered Thailand. I do wonder even now, however, if his parents were as liberally-minded as he suggested, and whether a friendship might have been possible.

On returning to work, I was able to give an edited, but still detailed, version of my holiday to interested staff. The headmaster was concerned whether the bike incident hadn't led to any sort of court case, and when I casually mentioned to the much-feared deputy head that fourteen-year-old girls were readily available, he simply remarked, "Bring *me* back a few!" Whatever people thought privately, they accepted my holiday stories and I think were less suspicious than they might have been if I'd not been prepared to chat about my visit to distant climes. Such journeys were then far less common and much more expensive than nowadays, and holidays in the Far East still had an exotic feel about them, which has all but vanished.

As well as getting back into school routine, I made a point of learning all I could about the Thai language and culture in preparation for my next visit. I discovered the large temple in Wimbledon, where a saint of a man gave free Thai lessons, and went there every Sunday afternoon. There were also many young people hanging around while their parents attended other activities, who were extremely friendly. In addition to the group lesson once a week, I worked my way through the Thai Linguaphone course, and discovered a shop in Earl's Court where you could rent out a large collection of Thai movies, some of which were very sweet. I discovered that there was a flourishing Thai community in London and, being readily accepted, went along to their gatherings, put up with the noisy music that was often played and sometimes taxied chatty young women in my car. On one such ride I had the Linguaphone tape at a place where I simply couldn't catch what was being said at the end of a long description of an area of Bangkok. I put on the tape and, when we reached this part, the women all hooted with laughter, but I never found out what it meant!

I continued to see Oliver regularly and, after meals out at a variety of places, I would accompany him to his gay clubs, from where he often dragged back a new man for the night. One rather ugly man collapsed drunk on the doorstep; he was fine the following morning and quite polite. I later asked Oliver what he could see in him, and he replied: "He had a wonderful cock!" We also went regularly to the cinema and I saw many new releases on the big screen, including *Crocodile Dundee*. At the theatre in Hammersmith we saw a play about a man who'd been a friend of a family and had also been having sex with their twelve-year-old son, and the consequences of the discovery two years later. It was all rather melodramatic, but did at least address the topic honestly, if from a typically biased British viewpoint.

After some deep reflection, I decided to contact Roy, who lived in a mobile home near Ashford. He clearly knew quite a few people, including Francis Canning, whom I'd heard of from my reading of *Magpie* magazine in the British Library. Roy told me quite a lot about Francis, who lived very close to my school: "'E always 'as boys rarnd 'is 'ouse, and some of them are bloody gorgeous!"

He agreed to phone Francis on my behalf, but the first time he was out and Roy spoke with a fourteen-year-old called Sam, whom I met later and who was indeed gorgeous.

Immediately Roy's voice softened, he almost simpered: "Oh it's you, Sam. How are you? What are you doing now?" et cetera.

As promised, Roy showed me some of his porn, including many of the hard "Golden Boy" tapes which had been filmed in Baltimore in the seventies. Later I met people involved in the making of these movies, which were openly on sale in Copenhagen and brought back by determined travellers in their luggage. These films all followed a routine with sometimes a little story which ended up with two or more boys fucking. In one, a boy was stimulating his anus with a large carrot, prior to being fucked. I wasn't sure what to make of such blatant in-your-face sex, and it did little to arouse erotic feelings whilst sitting in a grubby mobile home, when Roy said, "Ugh, oi wouln't loike to eat that carrot! Would you?"

"No."

Kindly, he later allowed me to borrow some tapes once he began to trust me, and I was able to copy them. Watching them alone in the privacy of my room was definitely preferable!

He succeeded in contacting Francis, who was entirely happy for me to have his phone number. I first contacted him in mid-December from a phone box – always these calls were made from phone boxes – about ten days before another trip I'd planned to Amsterdam. He was bubbly and friendly, and I warmed immediately to him over the phone. It was agreed that I would visit him on my return in January. In the meantime I'd also met a pleasant elderly gentleman in Brighton through Roy, and he had many stories of his adventures over a lifetime. He lent me some nice picture books, including one simply called *Twelve*.

I had two reasons for visiting Amsterdam in that Christmas holiday of 1986. One was to explore the sex shops and see if one could still buy some of the more interesting magazines I'd heard about. The second was to meet and stay with a woman clarinet player I'd met at Dartington the previous summer. She had a special music stand that I knew Barbara-Sue was looking for, as well as a clever device for standing a clarinet up, which one could only buy in Holland. She'd also spoken about her young sons, aged twelve and thirteen, and I was curious to meet them too.

I booked the flight and hotel through a local agent, and the very first evening was an eye-opener. I was on the top floor and the lift was spacious. One couldn't help noticing the smell of cannabis seeping out of the room across the hallway, but this was, unlike for many visitors to Holland, not one of the reasons I'd come. I'd smoked grass for the first time in Oliver's flat quite recently, and I'd found the effects pleasant but nothing earth-shattering.

As I was waiting for the lift down, prior to my first brief exploration of the city, a stark-naked girl of about seventeen emerged unsteadily from the room opposite, much to the objection of her boyfriend who tried to stop her. She became aggressive towards him, shouting and hitting out wildly, so he merely shrugged his shoulders and went back into his room. Rather embarrassingly, she held on to me for support as we waited for the lift to arrive. When we entered it, the girl was still clinging fast to me, and moaning softly though, to my surprise, nobody else seemed to take much notice.

When we arrived in the large lobby, I did manage to shake her off gently, and she sunk slowly to the floor, adopting the lotus position, with arms held out, palms of hands facing outwards, and appeared to be meditating. Again no one took any notice, and she was still there half an hour later when I returned with a Spartacus gay guide and a couple of new Coltsfoot Press books which I'd found on sale in a market close by. When I came down from my room after about forty-five minutes to find a restaurant, she had finally gone – back to her boyfriend, I hoped. Before my evening meal, I had an enjoyable hour drinking in a local bar, where an American told me what an unusual nation this was: "What other goddamn country has two names, Holland and The Netherlands, and another name for its goddamn language – Dutch?! Tell me that!"

When I returned to my room, I studied the Spartacus guide before going to bed. It was extremely helpful, indicating the shops where one could find the widest range of material. I thus sought out these places the following morning.

The third one appeared the most promising, and I gravitated over to a section of magazines which had the least hairy-looking nude males on the covers – I estimated their ages at around eighteen. Then a friendly voice behind me in a strong Dutch accent asked:

"Can I *help* you?"

I knew no better word and replied boldly, "Yes, I'm looking for the paedophile section."

"Ah, I knew it, as soon as you came in. I *knew* it!"

"Oh right!"

"I knew it, you know!"

"Mmm."

"I knew!" Slight chuckle.

I could not find any further response to make to this.

"But that is also illegal to sell in Holland now."

"Ah, I see!" I prepared to leave.

"But wait! I can help you if you follow me to another *special* room!"

"Oh, OK. Thank you – how kind."

I was shown into a small private area sealed off from the main shop by a single curtain and containing a large stock of magazines and films of various degrees of naughtiness, all of it rather expensive. I made my selection of three of the less hardcore-looking mags (though they still portrayed erections) and went to pay for them, anxious to leave. But the conversation was far from over.

"You can see some of the films beforehand if you'd like to buy them too!"

"Maybe later. This is fine for now, thanks."

"You know, boy-love is a very good thing. I had my first blow job from a man when I was twelve and enjoyed it very much."

"Oh, that's nice!"

"I also gave the man a blow job in return, as he was very attractive to me."

"How lovely!"

"You know, you are a very attractive man too. I can give you a free blow job if you like."

"Well, you are most kind. I'll bear it in mind …"

And then a sort of what-the-hell-what-have-I-got-to-lose? thought struck me. If this man fancied me, he might be useful.

"Erm, I just wondered," I added hesitantly as I handed over the money for the magazines, and he put them in a bag.

"Yeees?" (Smiling eagerly)

"Do you know where I might find the real thing … here in Amsterdam? Boys, I mean?"

"Well, as a matter of fact I do know this man. He lives in a large apartment and has many available boys visiting him. Some are as young as eleven and many are very beautiful."

What!? You're kidding me! Then as coolly as I could: "That sounds great, does he allow others to share them?"

"Yes, as long as the person comes well-recommended, and I can see you are a genuine, nice sort of person."

Inwardly I had a sort of aw-shucks reaction to this, but I didn't want to lose any of the amazing ground I seemed to have made in such a short time, so I remained silent and simply raised my head and eyebrows and smiled gently in quizzical anticipation. Surely this couldn't be happening? It all seemed a bit surreal.

He produced a piece of paper, wrote down a name and telephone number and handed it to me.

"Just say that you got this number from Stijn, and it'll be fine."

I offered Stijn my profound thanks, adding that I'd think about the films and would come back and let him know.

As I was leaving the shop, he suddenly shouted after me "Oh by the way!"

Oh Lord, what now? Was it all a hoax? Had I left something behind?

I turned round, half in and half out of the door, with other customers milling around close by.

"Yes?"

Loud and jovial: "Don't forget the free blow job!"

"Oh, no, right, thank you again. Goodbye for now then."

I dithered for some time, and finally plucked up the courage to ring the number from a call box. Perhaps it would be the local police station …

It was answered quickly: "Allo."

"Ah, hello, do you speak English?"

"Yah."

"My name's Stephen, am I speaking to Berend?"

"Yah."

"I was given your number by Stijn, is it alright to talk?"

"Maybe, it depends."

"He told me that you had available boys, and I was wondering what sort of age they were!"

Slightly narked: "Vould you ask such a question over ze telephone in your own country?"

"Of course not, I'm terribly sorry. Perhaps I shouldn't have called …"

"I said zat ze telephone iz not good for discussing zese matters, but if you want to come round and see me, you vill see how it is for yourself."

"Oh right, thank you. How about this evening?"

"Yah, that vould be OK."

Berend gave me his address and we agreed a time in the early evening. He stressed that every day was different, and maybe there would be several people there, or maybe none. His concluding remarks were, "You cannot tie zem down."

It sounded genuine enough, though I still couldn't quite believe it. Anyway, at around 7 p.m., I found myself in a posh suburb with large smart-looking flats and, after locating the correct one in the dark, rather nervously rang the bell. I was immediately buzzed in and soon found myself in quite a smart and spacious apartment on the third floor. Berend was small and dapper; the only other person in the flat was a blond boy of about fifteen who also looked extremely well-groomed. I was offered a drink, and we chatted idly for a while before coming down to exact terms.

The boys came and went as they pleased and, if they liked the look of you, they would go to the bedroom with you for about an hour; the price was quite high and non-negotiable. The blond who was there indicated that he was willing to go with me there and then but, as I was still feeling a little nervous and out of place, I knew that my "performance" would not be good, so I rather feebly made an excuse about needing to get the money, as I didn't carry that much on me. It was agreed that I would call back the following night, New Year's Eve, and see who, if anyone, was there.

On the way back to the hotel, I was cursing myself for my hesitancy. How often does a chance of sex with a Caucasian fifteen-year-old present itself so easily? I would certainly take the opportunity tomorrow if it hadn't already slipped through my fingers.

In the event, the same boy was there, and he hadn't changed his mind! He did make some apologies though, telling me he'd been to the naked swimming pool that afternoon (what naked swimming pool?) and had already come three times that day, but would do his best. For my part, it was not the best sex I've ever had, but it was fun and he was enthusiastic and did indeed manage a fourth orgasm. At twenty-nine, I was even then feeling rather ancient, only normally able to manage two, or maybe three "happenings" in exceptional circumstances in a 24-hour period – I subsequently met fourteen-year-olds who boasted of six or seven emissions in one day. Oh, how my teenage years were well and truly wasted!

I was to stay with the lady clarinet player, Hannah, and her sons the following day, and took a train to Schagen, where I was met. After three delightful days, I was driven back to Amsterdam with one of the boys in Hannah's car, and she was able to find me a cheaper and quieter hotel for the remainder of my time there. I got on well with her children, but remember little else except that Hannah told me they had liked me and that I was a very good ambassador for my country. Unlike the English of most of the young Dutch people in the big cities, theirs was poor, so direct communication had been a problem.

I first met Francis Canning on the Sunday before the start of the new term in 1987. He turned out to be every bit as approachable, intelligent and witty as my first impressions over the phone had led me to expect. Two of his young friends were there whom I shall call Bob and Jack, both by then eighteen and not attractive to me, which was probably just as well. We had a magnificent Sunday lunch with plenty of wine, and I became rather garrulous, and full of curiosity about how an active boy-lover lived and survived in England. Roy restricted his activities to overseas trips, and was only really interested in porn when in the UK. There were many funny anecdotes about him too and how he used to entertain the boys when they were younger with stories about his war exploits. One day Bob, then aged thirteen, had appeared out of nowhere, dressed in full army combat uniform complete with rifle when Roy was eating his lunch at the table, and pretended to attack Francis's guest. This hadn't gone down at all well with Roy, and Francis, though he had found the episode hilarious, had had to pretend to tell Bob off severely.

I was utterly taken with Francis, with his clever jokes and fruity deep voice, though I later learned that some considered it all rather an insincere act to conceal a deeply sensitive and insecure personality. His main passion was amateur dramatics, and he had considerable skill not only as an actor, but as a director and constructor of scenery too. He loved all sorts of word games and could polish off *The Times* crossword in a matter of minutes – *The Listener* would take him a little longer. He did have a genuine concern for others though, otherwise he would not have once worked as a Samaritan's volunteer, and I imagine a most effective one.

I soon became a regular visitor, mostly on Saturday nights, often sleeping over when the booze had been flowing particularly freely. Francis was a well-liked figure in his local pub too, even though they knew "all about" him. This might have had something to do with his legendary generosity – it was always difficult to pay for anything if Francis was present. There were about four regular young visitors in those days, three of whom were "retired" as far as bedroom activity went. I met Sam too, who was indeed still luscious, but I never tried anything on with him.

There were two main jokes about me in those early days. One was that I must be an undercover *News of the World* reporter as I was always so full of questions, and the second that I was Clark Kent. This came about because I always rang from telephone boxes, inside which I would clearly transform myself into Superman and wear swimming trunks outside my trousers. The nickname Clark Kent stuck and was playfully used for the next four years before Francis left to work abroad.

Through those Saturday evenings at Francis's, I came to meet many new people, including some I'd heard of during my reading at the British Library. This was most exciting, perhaps intensified by a sense of danger, but I made three or four firm friends with whom I am still in regular contact, as well as several pleasant acquaintances. Francis was full of optimism at this time, asserting that "our" time had arrived, and that boy-love would soon be as accepted as simply another form of homosexuality. This led to many an earnest discussion, in which I mainly listened – I certainly couldn't see any evidence for the truth of this, but what did I know? Francis had been involved in this area all his life and had not exactly had a trouble-free existence.

Meanwhile I was still visiting Roy on some Sundays, as well as attending the lessons at the Thai temple. I made the mistake of telling him about my encounter in Amsterdam, and of course he wanted the phone number. As I didn't think I'd be returning there soon – I was too focused on Thailand – I hadn't made a point of keeping it. I hadn't purposely thrown it away either; the scrap of paper had simply become lost. I learned from the man in Brighton that Roy thought I was deliberately keeping it from him and he was extremely put out by this, to the extent that he didn't want to maintain contact. I wasn't too upset about this; a friend who couldn't accept my word was not worth much in my view, but future events were soon to throw us back together again anyway, for a while.

I continued to see Miriam whenever I was in London and she told me she had an English contact in the Bangkok Symphony Orchestra. This could prove useful if I ever did decide to move permanently to Thailand.

I also received a couple of letters written in simple Thai from Lorn, enclosed in Adam's letters. My reading proficiency was not yet advanced enough to decipher the script, and I took them to the local Thai restaurant for translation. They were simply rather sweet and touching declarations of love, expressing the wish that he hoped to see me again soon. I asked Adam to assure him that the feeling was mutual.

My next Far Eastern trip was in the spring holiday of 1987, in some ways an even more eventful visit than the one of the previous summer. I was met again by Adam and Lorn, who recognised my suitcase before he noticed me. Adam had moved to a slightly more spacious house, still in walking distance from Silom Road and the heart of the city. It was wonderful being able to understand everything that was being said by Adam, and to be able to communicate directly with everyone I met. I'm sure my simple Thai was execrable, but all the boys understood and modified their language so that I could also follow everything they were saying.

Early on during the visit, I duly phoned Miriam's Bangkok Symphony Orchestra cellist friend and left a message on his answering machine along with Adam's number. When the cellist rang back, Lorn answered, and the cellist was clearly surprised that a boy should be living in the house where I was staying. Going by the old edict of "never explain, never apologise", I simply arranged to come to a rehearsal the following day and enjoyed meeting the musicians, particularly the bassoonists. They pressed me to show them alternative fingerings for the notoriously difficult top notes between top C♯ and F. I was beginning to feel very at home in Thailand, and had I not already got a job I adored back in the UK, would have seriously considered relocating, as many Englishmen I came to meet had already done, or would do so within a couple of years.

This second Thai trip was memorable for many reasons, but two occurrences remain firmly fixed in memory. I met an extraordinary new person, who soon became a firm friend and remained so until his death twenty years later. The second was a sexual marathon which went wrong on account of eating cheap food from a dodgy local eatery the night before.

The new friend, Peter C., had come for coffee one morning to Adam's house, and it was clear within five minutes that we were simpatico. He spoke freely of the hundreds of boys he had "known" throughout his life, and hinted at many adventures in different countries, continuing with his decision to relocate to Thailand from Australia. He had tried living in Portugal, but found the limited repertoire of the boys rather frustrating. He did though have a British contact there who might be willing to show me where to stay and how to find young companions, which more or less decided me on a visit to Lisbon as soon as I could. Peter was currently living with a boy whom he'd picked up in Pattaya nicknamed "Keem", as he adored being fucked and would frequently demand the favour by uttering "cream", meaning it was time to apply the KY which facilitated this activity. Peter was exactly thirty years older than me, and I received daily reports by telephone of his "soft quarter of an inch" languishing to the half inch, three quarters et cetera, as Keem's demands took their toll on Peter's virility; this was long before the days of Viagra.

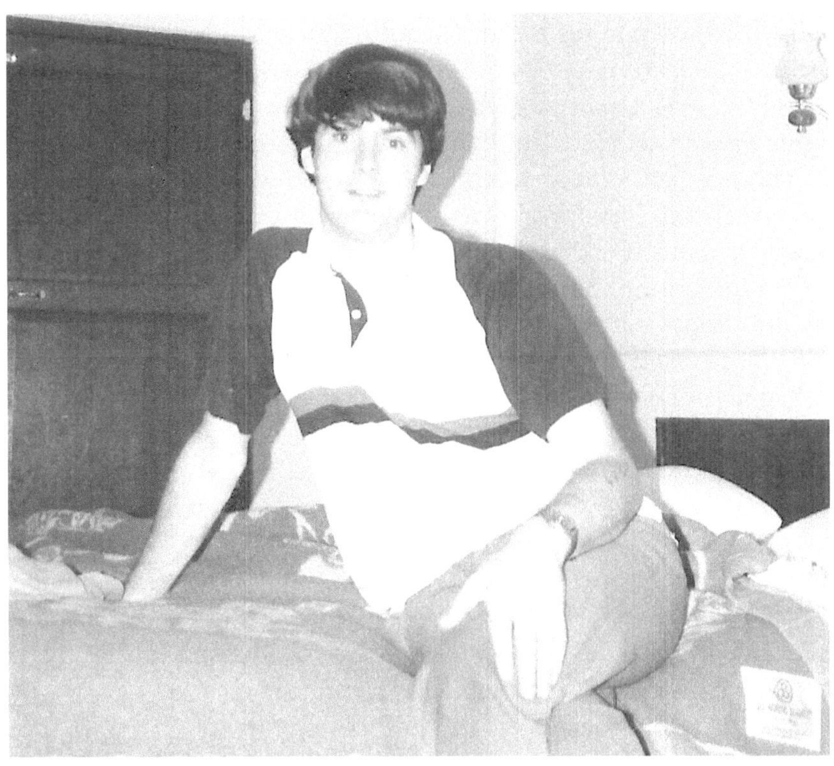

Had I known Peter better, I would have offered to oblige Keem myself, as finding a boy who enjoyed being fucked, in my experience, was something of a rarity. As it turned out, this would have been welcomed, but the knowledge came too late …

There is a footnote to the Keem episode, in that he stole a camera from Peter and was caught with it and arrested. For many reasons, Peter did not want to press charges, but was not given the option; he was highly nervous about giving testimony to the judge. As it was, his worries were misplaced: the judge clearly realised that Peter went to Pattaya "for the boys" and what his relationship with Keem had been, as if that were entirely normal and par for the course.

Regarding the marathon, I had decided to test out my newly acquired linguistic ability on my next trip to Pattaya, by initially avoiding boys who were obviously on the game. To that end, I had wandered round the town chatting up the prettiest numbers I could find, some of whom were clearly earning their living in a virtuous manner by selling various sugary items to tourists from a tray which they carried round everywhere.

I set up six "meetings" in my hotel room for the following morning, starting at 8 a.m. and finishing at 1 p.m. with little expectation: indeed, if only one turned up, the exercise would have been a success in my view. I had a frugal evening meal at a non-touristy backstreet café which Adam used to frequent to save money. I then found a boy for the night, who departed around 7.30 the following morning, somewhat to my relief, as during the night I had developed food poisoning and felt truly dreadful. I swore it would be the last time I would go to that café, but what I needed most of all was some extra sleep to shake off the pain and nausea I, most unusually, felt. I had all but forgotten about the assignations I had made the day before, not believing that any of them would materialise anyway.

How wrong I was. Almost on the dot of eight o' clock, there was a knock on the door and a smiling vision entered the room, lay his tray down carefully, and slipped out of his clothes and into my double bed. I manfully performed as best as I could under the circumstances, though I sensed some disappointment from the boy, who felt I did not love him enough! I gratefully bade farewell to him after fifty minutes and turned over for some much-needed restorative sleep, only to be thwarted by another tap on the door ten minutes later. The same thing happened four more times, and by two o' clock that afternoon, a drained Stephen was finally able to get his much-needed rest, swearing to himself that he'd had enough boys to last him a lifetime and that the rest of the holiday would be spent visiting temples.

Needless to say, this was not the case. On my first trip to the country, I'd returned to England with numerous pictures of normal touristy activities, but as I now knew I'd be visiting the Land of Smiles many, many times, that little deception was pointless. I told anyone who asked that I liked the culture and the people, which was entirely true, and left it at that.

True to his word, Peter did contact his friend IR in Lisbon, who said he would be happy to show me where to stay and the general lie of the land, should I choose to come there. In those days it was clearly not at all difficult to find what Peter would often refer to as "trade". So my next half term, always late in the summer, was now organised and I spent a memorable week there in mid June. As usual I spent a fair amount of time learning the basics of the language before going, so that I would at least be able to understand and communicate in simple Portuguese.

IR and I seemed to hit it off immediately, and I am still good friends with him today. We often reminisce about those days on the Iberian Peninsula, and also about a later Portuguese holiday during which I was lucky to escape incarceration. The *pensão* he recommended was cheap and cheerful, and run by a laid-back young man with long black curly hair and a permanent five o'clock shadow who didn't bat an eyelid at the guests one chose to entertain, except on the last day, when maybe the left eyelid showed just a hint of being batted …

The weather all week was superb and I loved sitting outside in cafés drinking half-litre *canecas*, smoking cheap cigarettes and eating *tremoços*, a type of salty bean whose taste I always associate with that holiday. As predicted, it wasn't difficult to find my first boy that evening, a very pleasant and obliging lad of fourteen whom I liked in every respect. I was rather disappointed when he said firmly that he did not wish to stay the night, but was pleased I had enough Portuguese to talk with him about his life and to negotiate further meetings. I told him that if he came the following morning, I would buy him new clothes, and offered him a generous incentive to introduce me to his friends making clear the type (blond preferably) and age-range I liked.

He proved a delightful and discreet companion throughout the week. He chose his new clothes with care, and looked stunning in them, though even more stunning out of them, and also provided me with many ravishing partners. It is sad that the photos, developed locally, since one would not dare take them to Boots on one's return, are now all lost, though the memory is still strong.

One incident I will never forget is when I decided to go hunting myself, and encountered a lively blond number hanging off the back of a bus. My basic Portuguese was enough to bring him willingly back to the *pensão* and action had just commenced when there was a loud knock on the door. Oh fuck, who could that be?! Quick. Clothes on! Another furious knock. Shit. Sit there. Here's a book, pretend to read – no, not upside down!

Fearing the worst, I opened the door. Imagine the relief to discover that it was none other than a surprise visit from IR, come to see how I was getting along ... He knew the boy in question and there was a lot of friendly banter. When, after IR's departure, I came to take some pictures, he stipulated that it was OK for IR to see them, but no one else ... I'd like to think I respected his wishes once I was back in the UK.

During the day, I met some colourful adult characters in the main local square, one of whom offered to find me boys at a price, but of course I had no need of this. I found out later that he was the notorious con man called Alan Perry whom Peter had been warned about when he was there the year before. He was charming company, however, and one could chat easily over a beer or two as long as one politely declined to listen to any of his proposals involving one parting with money. Peter joked that Alan said to him in a rather wounded manner, "Don't you trust me then?" and Peter had replied jovially, "Of course I don't trust you!"

On the last day of the trip, IR accompanied me and we explored further afield in a neighbourhood where a stunningly beautiful twelve-year-old lived. On the bus ride there, IR warned me that it was all a matter of luck, and maybe one would meet Jorge, but not to build my hopes too high. He was also the first to warn me that, just because someone shared one's sexual tastes, that was no guarantee that he would be someone one wanted to know. As someone then vastly more experienced in this area than me, he had come across a fair selection of shits in an area which could sometimes be fiercely competitive.

As luck would have it, we met Jorge quite quickly and he was with a slightly older darker friend, equally pretty in his way. They proved very happy to come back with me for a threesome. Our entering the *pensão* was, as mentioned, the first time the man behind the desk expressed any sort of surprise, but certainly not disapproval. Without going into detail, the threesome didn't really work, as the boys became too giggly in each other's presence. They were dealt with individually while the other waited in the bathroom. All in all, a memorable last day.

I continued to visit the Thai temple each Sunday for group lessons, and noticed in its English magazine one week that a Channel 4 film crew were due to visit Thailand, and that the authorities were rather unhappy about this. I asked the teacher about it, but he was not forthcoming about the reason for the filming, so it was clearly not going to be a conventional documentary about Thai culture. My worst fears were confirmed by Peter and others resident in the country that this was to be a big exposé of "sex tourism" focusing on the boy scene in Pattaya and it would be happening in the summer, just when I would be paying my third visit.

Partly on account of this, but also because he thought it would be a fun thing to do, Peter asked me to stay with him and then hire a car which he would pay for as long as I drove and we shared the petrol and any fines incurred. The plan was to go to Pattaya for a short visit and try out some of the boys, avoiding the notorious Siren Bar as far as possible, as the camera crew would surely be lurking there. We planned to find a suitable couple who would be willing to go on a two-to-three-week tour round the south with us, and very clear terms were laid down regarding a *per diem* allowance. It was important that the two boys would get on with each other as well as be willing partners for us and, after a day or two of testing, we both managed to find pleasant companions who were compatible and willing to travel with us. They first accompanied us back to Bangkok while we prepared for the holiday.

Before we departed, Peter was visited by a curious photographer called Raymond Varley, who was enormously attracted to my boy, Mong. With my permission, he disappeared upstairs with him to take some pictures – a process which one would have thought would take a mere ten minutes. After an hour, Peter went up to see what was going on and found a naked Mong precariously balanced on one leg in a provocative position, while Varley was occupied in activity in which the camera only played a small role. Rather sheepishly, he ended his session and rejoined us with a slightly bemused Mong following behind.

Later Peter recalled the name Varley as being someone who had caused the suicide of a good friend of his in England a while back. This man would also visit India and pretend to be a doctor doing research in penis size in relation to a boy's height, and would line up as many as thirty naked boys in order of tallness and photograph them earnestly. He clearly did more than this, as he had to leave India in a hurry and, even now, the authorities there are demanding his extradition, which the UK is refusing on the grounds that his health is too poor for the travel. A reversal of the usual situation and fortunate for him, as Indian prisons have little to recommend them.

The car trip went extremely well and Peter remembered it as one of the best holidays he'd ever had, even referring to it on his deathbed in hospital many years later. Mong and Da, Peter's boy, got on swimmingly and there was not a bad moment, though plenty of amusing ones. In one small town, after we'd found our hotel for the night, we went for a coffee in what we thought was a café, except that it seemed to be occupied by rather more young ladies in heavy makeup and revealing skirts than one would have expected. Moreover, they seemed to be looking at us with increasing hostility and the boys were becoming more and more uneasy. It transpired that we had blundered into the local brothel, and were thought to be pimps offering unfair competition. We managed to leave before things got nasty, as they might well have done had the girls' pimps arrived, and were able to laugh about it afterwards.

On Koh Samui, which in those days was almost free from tourists, one was able to rent a small bungalow for thirty baht a night and there was a good German restaurant which catered mostly for local *farang*. We passed a small café selling magic mushrooms, which neither of us had tried before, and decided to partake. They were liberally sprinkled over a pizza (needless to say, not the boys' one), and at first neither of us noticed any effect from them. However, after about two hours I was suddenly hit with an extraordinary light-headedness in which I saw beautiful colours, and all my heightened senses perceived everything with extreme intensity bordering on euphoria. When I ravished Mong in this condition he seemed delighted and responded eagerly. As trips go, it was exceedingly pleasant, with no corresponding depression afterwards, not that I've ever been strongly into mind-altering drugs.

I went next door to see if Peter had been similarly affected, but he was calmly lying on his bed reading a biography of Queen Victoria. According to him, I burst in crying "red, yellow, blue" and flapping around like a man possessed. It was clear that I would be in no state to drive to the restaurant, and this was one of the very few occasions when I experienced Peter's erratic driving. By this time, he too was clearly feeling some effects from the mushrooms, as he was singing Italian operatic arias at the top of his voice and careering madly from one side of the road to the other, whereas for me the effects were beginning to wear off. Mong's small solemn voice in the back kept making brief profound utterances such as *"Peter khap rot antaray* (Peter drives dangerously)" and, flatteringly, *"Stephen khap rot dee kwa* (Stephen drives better)". Miraculously, we reached the restaurant in one piece and, after a good meal, I was able to get us back to the bungalows.

Everywhere we went, we were greeted with warm smiles: be they fake or real, they would surely not have been forthcoming a few years later. Peter presciently pointed out that the days when one could roll into a town and cherry-pick two attractive boys to accompany one on holiday were definitely numbered. For the rest of my five-week stay in the country, we avoided the obvious pick-up places because of the presence of the camera crew, but I was still able to share my bed with someone each night.

The documentary was aired later that year, and I made a point of being out of the school when it was screened, as Karen, then living above me, would have known what I was watching. I did though videotape it, as well as view it in another person's house. It was as ghastly as could be expected with young boys, many of whom I recognised, being handsomely paid to recite a script about how horrible it was to have sex with men. Another teacher who lived locally, and whom I had recently befriended, was caught on camera in the aforementioned Siren Bar, surrounded by boys. He was fully expecting to be recognised and to receive a summons from his headmaster, but there was far less curiosity in those days about these matters and, fortunately, no one who might have known him had watched it.

Karen had of course seen it, and kept trying to bring the subject up. I simply had to blank her until she gave up referring to it.

I will conclude this chapter with a story which brought home to me what a dangerous world I now occupied as a friend and associate of known boy-lovers.

Francis Canning had been delighted to be once referred to by the gutter press as "the most evil man in Britain". As he was from a well-to-do family with influential connections, he considered himself fairly safe, especially as by now he was mostly going abroad for sex.

For Christmas in 1987, I went again to Thailand and stayed with Peter. He now had a large house on the Sukhumvit Road and an excellent maid, Ting, who shopped, cooked and looked after the house, including a large number of resident boys whom she would mother. Peter would get angry when visitors indulged in huge displays of physical affection in front of Ting. Although she was fully aware of what went on, he didn't feel it was right to rub her nose in it.

By this time I had acquired quite a large collection of "relevant" material, mostly printed word, but also some photographic albums from Germany (bought through a magazine called *Pan*) and two or three videocassettes of stronger material, which it was still legal to possess in those more enlightened days, though this was soon to change, with catastrophic results for many people. These precious items were kept in a large suitcase with a rather common and feeble lock and, as I was uncomfortable about leaving this in my school accommodation when I went away to the Far East, Francis cheerily said I could leave it in his house. He would himself be going away for three weeks at the start of the New Year.

Stupidly, I had forgotten that I had left inside this case a postcard (used as a bookmark) addressed to me from the then notorious boy-lovers' paradise, Pagsanjan. It had arrived at my Worthing home months before and been forwarded to the school where I was still working.

As usual, I arrived back in the UK a few days before the start of term to compose my next piece for the school orchestra, as had then become customary – always geared round the musical talent of the instrumentalists we happened to have at the time. Francis was still away "enjoying foreign parts", as his answerphone message wickedly put it, but, just after the start of term, I received a calamitous message sent from Peter via friends of his that I knew well in Surrey. Francis's home had been raided by police looking for porn.

In the normal course of events, the plod would not have been able to make forcible entry if the house had been unoccupied, but two of Francis's "exes" had decided to stay the night there and were able to tell me what had happened. The heavies had arrived with a search warrant at seven in the morning and woken up the two elderly teenagers, roughly demanding to know where the owner of the house was. On being informed that he was in Thailand, they proceeded with what was a rather desultory search, and soon found my suitcase under the bed in the spare bedroom.

They forced it open and were delighted that the obvious nature of the contents meant that they would not have to expend further time and energy going into the loft or confiscating other videos. It was clear enough that this was where Francis kept his stash, and one of the officers even remarked gleefully, "Bingo, this case is where 'e keeps the stuff 'e likes!" The fact that one of the books was a rare and expensive edition of Rolfe's *Venice Letters* and another was a long-out-of-print serious study of the Uranian movement by Timothy d'Arch Smith which had taken me months to track down (no Amazon or Abebooks in those days) meant little to them – it was all filth that these perverts get off on. But most worrying of all from my point of view was that wretched postcard.

At least Francis had had warning of what had occurred and was very careful about what he brought back through customs, as he was sure to be given the third degree, and indeed was, even being made to pay duty on a suit he'd had made. As he couldn't bear to throw away the photos he had taken, he posted them under his name to a respectable couple two doors down who eventually passed them on to him unopened. They were curious as to how the mistake in house numbers could have occurred, but asked no awkward questions.

Meanwhile I had to sweat it out back at school, wondering when, through the postcard, the police would twig that the suitcase was not Francis's, but the property of someone who worked in a boys' prep school close by. It was another difficult time. A few days after Francis's return in January, I went back home for my thirty-first birthday, as it fell on a Tuesday, my half day, and I was, most unusually, able to spend the night at home. My mother was out when I arrived, but she had prepared a huge welcome, with a large card on the stairs announcing that the champagne was in the fridge, when the thing I least felt like doing was celebrating. I was wondering if I might need legal advice and, before my mother returned, rang Edward Brongersma's Dutch number (given in *Pan* magazine), as he, generously as ever, offered free advice to brethren in trouble. He was kindness itself and gave me the number of a Dutch lawyer who might be able to advise me further should it prove necessary. I also phoned this man, who sensibly suggested hanging on and waiting to see what happened before going to the trouble and expense of consulting any lawyers in England he might be able to recommend. I also phoned Gabriel Strider, who was as supportive as ever, and pointed out that, postcard or no postcard, the material was in Francis's possession and he would have to answer for it. "I've no idea how that card got there, officer" would be my response if challenged with it.

I was thus able to enjoy my birthday meal a little more easily. Though my dear mother could always tell when there was something amiss, she now never asked questions. Even when the axe fell in a big way a few years later, she took the news remarkably calmly, but I'm jumping ahead. I now had many uncomfortable weeks of tense apprehension ahead, and faced the loss of much precious material diligently acquired with risk and determined hunting.

Karen was also able to tell that all was not well with me and, unlike my mother, kept dropping hints that she understood there might be trouble, adding that she could be trusted if I wanted to share it with her. In many ways I would have been pleased to do this, but I knew she simply would not understand the boy thing, as opposed to the concept of "gay", which she was determined to cure me of.

This might be a place to explain more about Karen, who at one level was a straightforward earthy woman who enjoyed a good gossip with the matrons and had a long-term plan to entwine her life with mine. In that year, 1988, for example, she proposed marriage to me on February 29th, after chapel on Monday morning, and was deadly serious about it.

She flew into tantrums if I left her alone after end-of-term concerts, and so that became a time when I would join her with a bottle of champagne to celebrate the successful result of our collaborative endeavours. We would usually watch a video in her room, as she had acquired a machine herself. I'm sure she hoped that these evenings together might lead to something more, or to personal revelations, but I always remained cautious with her. In fact, however much I have to drink, there are certain matters which remain safely unsaid, except to the "right" people – a ghastly way to live in some ways, as ordinary friendships always contain a strand of dishonesty, but as the alternative is unthinkable, one has to make do with the compromise.

Karen could also be kind and generous. I told her my friend Adam in Bangkok enjoyed snooker and could not watch the major tournaments over there. So she would record them all for me to take out on each visit – often as many as forty video cassettes! It was in fact Peter who was the snooker fan but, as Karen had only heard about Adam, it seemed simpler not to tell her about other people. Peter was a fine player of the game too, as I discovered the first time I played him in the coolness of the British Club. This was a calm oasis in the middle of a noisy city, with none of the gossipy snootiness which some of these places have – the one in Oporto for example. Peter and I would relax by the pool there, and there was always plenty of *farang* "talent" to admire.

Karen was also happy to lend me her VCR so that I could copy Thai films I picked up in Earl's Court. These I would watch during spare evenings, whilst imagining myself back in Thailand by drinking Singha beer and smoking Krong Thip – I always brought a good supply back with me from these holidays. Karen once said, as she lent me her machine, "Presumably it's to record your porn", as I'd felt a bit coy about telling her that I wanted to copy Thai films to improve my understanding of the language. She had at any rate guessed my reason for visiting the country, so I didn't want to keep reminding her of my South East Asian interest.

I could recount many stories which showed that in many ways the fate of Karen and me was curiously linked, and I hope the reader will forgive me if I relate one example of this while it is fresh in my mind, before reverting to the resolution of the suitcase saga.

We both had rooms in a beautiful house separate from the main school and were the only teachers there, the rest being domestic staff. One morning, I noticed a small package arrive at the house, which made my blood freeze, for it had a label announcing that it was from The Acolyte Press in Amsterdam. This was a successor of the Coltsfoot Press and also run by Frank Torey, who published and distributed books about, and I dislike using what has become an ugly and much *mis*used word, paedophilia – specifically related to men and boys. This was the sort of material that had been in my suitcase and which I was uncomfortable about having on school premises, let alone getting delivered there. What on earth was Karen *doing*, importing such explosive literature to a boys' prep school, when there had been stories in the press of headmasters getting arrested because customs had opened such packages and considered it unfit for those in charge of children?

She immediately realised when she saw me that I was freaked out by what I'd seen arriving through the door early that morning, and wrote me a note along the lines of, "What business was it of mine, and how did I know what the parcel contained anyway?" When we had a chance later that day, I had to have a long chat about it, with me explaining that I'd heard about The Acolyte Press (omitting to say how, but implying it was through the newspapers) and that the books were all about paedophilia – a word which, in her simplicity, she didn't know. She rang a woman friend of hers in the police force who confirmed that such books could lead to a lot of trouble if imported through the post.

She then tearfully told me the whole story. A colleague of hers at her previous school called John had asked her if she would take delivery of some books, making up some story about the mail service being unreliable where he was then living. Karen had innocently agreed, and had not of course been told about the nature of the books. She was furious with him and wrote to tell him that she would not be passing on these books and felt very betrayed by the deceit. There also remained the problem of the remaining books, five more to come, she told me between sobs, and thus five more chances of them either being opened by customs or, should they happen to be delivered to the main school instead of the staff house, spotted by someone else with sharp eyes such as the second master, whose knowledge of the world and savoir-faire were extensive.

Three or four uncomfortable weeks passed during which the individual packages gradually arrived safely. Karen of course felt she had to read them. They included such classics as *The Asbestos Diary* and *Vice Versa* by Casimir Dukahz. Her judgement of the books confirmed my instinctive belief that I should say as little about my own inclinations as possible, as she condemned the material as sad and sick – though I do wonder how much effort she made to understand it. When the final small parcel arrived, we were both relieved that we could continue as normal, without a sword of Damocles hanging over our heads. I include myself, as Karen would certainly have inadvertently let on about my knowledge of such material if heavily questioned, leading to much awkwardness.

Somehow I muddled through that term, feeling under a death sentence, and dreading the moment when I might be called out of a lesson to answer questions from DC Flatfoot of the Yard about my connection with Francis. Fingerprints would show that all material was mine, as Francis had never touched the contents of the suitcase, and the least I could expect would be instant dismissal from my job.

While I was still waiting for the outcome of this matter, it was announced that the law regarding "possession" would soon change, becoming a criminal offence in itself as opposed to merely being an indicator of guilt supporting an accusation of assault. Indeed, Adam had been to prison in the mid-seventies for sex with his pupils, members of a swimming club, the charges including attempted buggery. On his release, he was able to claim back all the property the police had seized from him, including a huge amount of hardcore porn. How much things had changed in the intervening decade – and yet, compared with the horrors to come, it was in hindsight still a relatively civilised time. At least the soon-to-be-introduced punishment for possession was only a fine, as happened to a clergyman with whom I later became acquainted, who was raided on the very first day the law came into force.

As to the search of Francis's house, clearly this raid on a former prominent PIE member had been undertaken to coincide with the imminent change in the law, and the orders for it may have come from people in high places, as Francis's brother was about to be appointed to an important post where national security was very much at stake and therefore needed to be thoroughly vetted before taking it up. Simultaneous vetting of his brother, a known "predatory paedophile", as Francis was later described to me by a member of Scotland Yard's obscene publications squad, was clearly part of the procedure.

Eventually Francis received a letter telling him to attend a certain local police station, which he did in the company of a lawyer supplied on legal aid. He was advised to give a "no comment" interview from which, in those days, nothing could or should be inferred. To the disgust of many a liberal-minded barrister, such as John Mortimer, who spoke fervently of the sacredness of the right to silence, the law on this was modified in the 1990s so that in certain circumstances silence could be regarded as self-incriminating.

The suitcase was in the interview room during the interrogation process, which, despite the refusal of Francis to answer a single question, lasted well over an hour. At the end of it all, he did his best to retrieve some of the books, but was told that "all this lot will soon be illegal". He didn't want to push the fact that the printed word was to be exempt from the new law, but did in the end manage to liberate the d'Arch Smith book and a video of my first Thai holiday in which Lorn could be seen frequently nibbling my ears as we, otherwise respectably, toured the ruins of Ayutthaya. This had also been of some concern to me and I was pleased to have it back. Needless to say, quantities of nude photos of Thai boys were not returned, nor a four-hour video of hard-core Golden Boy movies.

I guess I should have counted myself lucky that the case of the suitcase was wrapped up so easily, however much regret I might feel at the loss of so many rare books: "I did my best with *The Venice Letters*," Francis told me. One has to wonder what was achieved though, and what they learned from such a perfunctory raid. They hadn't taken much else from the house, address books, correspondence and such like, which would have been the norm, and it wouldn't have taken them long to work out that the material they had seized was probably not Francis's.

The witch-hunt mentality was not then as established as it was soon to become, as a similar investigation, even a year or two later, would surely not have ended there.

VIII. The Warm South versus the Frozen North

After the relief of the undramatic conclusion to yet another scare, life began to return to normal, or as normal as it could be. I knew that, even at this stage, my life could continue along one of two paths, one being relatively safe, the other fraught with danger but infinitely more rewarding.

So, like the art teacher in the school where I worked, I could even now choose to live a lie, pretending to be a red-blooded heterosexual and inventing distant girlfriends fooling no one, but keeping out of trouble. I would have to renounce the friendships I had formed which were potentially dangerous, sneak off to the Far East for holidays whilst claiming to go to Blackpool, and eschew any meaningful social life whilst in England.

The alternative was to live a richer, more fulfilled existence, meeting interesting new people, some of whom might become lifelong friends, and explore who I was, gaining greater understanding of myself and the convoluted sexual puzzle which Nature had bestowed on me, by comparing and contrasting my experiences with those of intelligent kindred spirits. I had been shocked when I first read Michael Davidson's autobiography that his friend and fellow journalist, James Cameron, should say in his introduction to the book that Davidson had been to prison for "being himself", but I had to accept that if I didn't choose to, in the words of the Beatles, "hide my love away", I risked public disgrace and incarceration.

There was no choice at all really. Having discovered, albeit fleetingly, the poignancy and richness of close relations with boys, the course of my life had changed irrevocably. There were no risks not worth taking for this very special intimacy, and most of my meaningful open adult friendships would need to be with people who either shared or, more rarely, accepted this important aspect of my emotional makeup.

Thus my network of friends gradually grew. Some of them I met through Francis, others while travelling or through friends already made. I encountered every type of person: predictably many teachers (including headmasters), a few doctors, but also the most ordinary type of working-class bloke whose sexual tastes could not be attributed to boarding-school education, lack of a father, or an overindulgent mother. One of these rode a huge motorbike and spoke with a heavy Essex accent, others drove lorries or worked on building sites. The motorcyclist had once had a boyfriend who'd told him, "I would never have taken you for a boy-lover, you seem far too ordinary!"

One of these friends was a schoolmaster like myself, and lived in Abingdon which was just conveniently close enough to drive to and spend a Saturday night. I shall call him Roger C. He was a softly-spoken and seemingly absent-minded Cambridge gradu-ate whose gentle manner concealed a razor-sharp mind, and an instinct for survival which bordered on paranoia. Not the slight-est reference, be it ever so obscure, that might give away what we were must be uttered within possible hearing distance of anyone at all who was not already a "member of the church". Forgetfulness of this unspoken rule could unleash a sudden frightening fury of which you would not have believed Roger to be capable.

I had resumed the habit of visiting swimming pools, and had extended my range much further to avoid visiting the same one twice for many weeks. I might sally forth for a good old session of ardent voyeurism about once a week. The excitement was in the unpredictability of it all: how many attractive boys were present, how they behaved in open changing rooms, the possibil-ity of the occasional naked shower or even some pleasant con-tact. Visiting a new pool always produced a frisson of excitement as one entered. What would the layout be? Were there good vantage points where one could see without being seen? If there were cubicles, how many people had been there before, drilling strategic holes in them? Much later on, I met a wonderfully wicked old soul in his eighties who always took his own "spy-ing" kit to swimming pools, which included various sizes of gimlets.

Roger, however, was in another class when it came to swim-ming-pool knowledge – an altogether truly international Olym-pian class, as he was extremely well-travelled. Whereas I might pootle out for a pleasant two hours of naughty fun in a single pool, Roger would plan a whole day or weekend round his trips, taking in several of them. This necessitated at least three towels, and a whole paraphernalia of "delaying" items and tactics such as foot powder, nail clippers, shaving kit, drawstring of swimming trunks getting stuck inside, or heavily knotted … it mattered not what, as long as he could justify the amount of time spent in the changing room.

At first I was in awe of such dedication, but was very happy to join in on Sundays. A typical day might start at Oxford's Temple Cowley pool, going on to Banbury and then further out to Bristol, and finishing at another Oxford pool. As we got to know each other well, we planned trips during holidays and half terms which took us round different parts of the country staying in B&Bs, and encountering all manner of odd landladies who still furnish us with huge amusement when we reminisce about those days over a glass or three of wine, or something stronger.

There were trips abroad too, to Germany, France, Spain and, of course, Portugal. In the last of these I had one of the scariest scrapes ever, perhaps rescued by the fact that it was a public holiday in August, the Assumption of Mary, and most senior *polícia* were taking the day off.

We had planned a three-week trip in my car, driving down through France and stopping at major naturist resorts – something new for me, though I had seen TV documentaries about them in the seventies. The bulk of the trip was to be in Portugal, where we were to taste "the real thing", renting apartments in Lisbon and Porto, and meeting up with mutual friends. Roger was clearly an old hand; in Porto we were able to drive to a district called Vila Nova de Gaia where flocks of eager boys were happy to be picked up by friendly foreigners, taken to the beach, fed and bathed. I must confess that I was a little more active than Roger, whose sexual requirements were very easily satisfied. Again, probably his wise caution.

When we first arrived in Lisbon, a vision looking every inch like a British prep schoolboy, twelve, blond, slim and cheeky-looking, approached me asking for a cigarette. We were outside the main station and the boy was alone; surely he was "on". My Portuguese was then lamentable, whereas Roger's was fluent.

Me: This one looks keen. Ask him if he'd like to come back to the flat.

Roger: No, he only wants a cigarette.

Me (mounting frustration that he might go away): Well, no harm in making the suggestion.

Roger: His clothes look too smart.

Me: Just try, please!

After a little more cajoling, Roger eventually did and was met with an enthusiastic response. There was a logistics problem in that we were meeting another Englishman, EV, who was going to go back to the apartment with us in my car, so Roger immediately hired a cab and whisked him away.

When EV and I arrived back, we were met with a very contented Roger and a very willing lad, who turned out to be rather mischievous. I took many photos of him, and he insisted on taking the camera and taking ones of me, something which I could hardly refuse.

Many and varied were our adventures in Lisbon, which in those days was teeming with boys. We nearly lost a series of pictures of another delectable blond when I was showing them to Roger and the boy grabbed them and refused to return them. A little gentle persuasion from EV however, in execrable Portuguese, soon restored the photos to me.

On this trip, I also met EV's adopted son Pedro, a boy he'd met in Lisbon a few years previously. EV had befriended the parents, who were fully aware of the nature of the relationship. They were delighted when EV offered to take Pedro back to England and put him through prep and public school, something which worked out extremely well. The boy is now in his forties, but still sees EV as a father figure, even though he frequently went home to visit his real family. Roger became enamoured of Pedro's younger brother and I can see the two of them now, hand in hand, in the water park, completely at ease with each other.

It was on the return journey that matters became rather more hairy. As well as the original group from Gaia, I had a go at picking up boys myself from near the river Douro, a surprisingly easy thing to do, even with my bad Portuguese. We were renting a spacious flat in Espinho and took the new group to the beach there, and then back to the flat for more fun and games – one rather naughty boy, Paulo, discovered that having his prick sucked was really rather nice, and kept demanding more.

At the end of each afternoon, I would drive them back to Porto and leave them where we first met. Part of the fun of this journey was that one of the other, extremely well-endowed boys would sit close to me at the front, and it's just so easy sometimes to mistake the gear stick for something else …

Usually we met them at the same place where we dropped them off each day, being where I'd first encountered them. On one occasion, however, they asked if the following day we could pick them up from near their homes, all close to each other, and explained to Roger where this was. Maybe this was to do with the religious holiday on August 15th, part of which they had to spend with their families.

Whatever, the next day's meeting was scheduled for one p.m. and, allowing time for getting lost, we arrived at the designated place more or less on time and waited for the boys to arrive. What happened next was as startling as it was frightening. Two large police cars suddenly appeared from nowhere, blocking me in by parking close to the front and back of my car. Roger was rudely ushered out of the front seat and told to sit in the front police car whilst a burly cop took his place in mine, and ordered me to follow the police car in front. The rear one, in which the three boys were seated, followed closely behind.

After this dramatic and well-organised coup, which the policemen managed to bring off with the discipline and precision of a well-oiled military unit, they seemed rather at a loss as to how to proceed, once we were back at their small, dirty, ill-equipped police station which ran to a telephone and a clock on the wall which didn't work. It seemed the trouble was all about Paulo, whose cock I had sucked, and who was, fortunately for me, well-known to the police as rather a troublemaker. Unnoticed by either Roger or myself, Paulo had pinched some Spanish coins from Roger's jacket pocket and his mother had found them and demanded to know where he'd got them from. If he'd possessed an ounce of intelligence, he'd have said that he found them in the street but, as it was, he told her all about the nice men who took him and his friends to the beach and then back to their flat in Espinho.

She'd then made him tell her about what went on in the flat and whether either of these nice men "touched" him. On learning that one of them had, she contacted the police, telling them about the next rendezvous which we had set up with the boys. Again fortunately for me, she was a loud-mouthed harridan of a fishwife who spent her entire time shrieking blue murder, and telling me how I was going to pay dearly for the terrible things I'd done, as Roger later told me. Somehow I managed to stay calm and look suitably bewildered at the accusation.

At first the cops were more interested in other matters – my car documents, insurance or anything which they could find legitimate fault with. When they discovered we were school-teachers, we were given old bits of paper on which to write our names and where we worked. I noticed that Roger wrote St Cake's School with a fictitious address, which I followed up with St Custard's.

Following this, I was asked about the boy's accusation, which I firmly denied, saying we simply felt sorry for the boys and wanted to give them a treat. Roger, who not only spoke the language well but had a deep insight into Portuguese culture, emphasised that as teachers we loved children, so why on earth should we want to hurt them? Questioned alone, Paulo tried to stick to his story but seemed unconvincing, wanting to know why he was here and not at the beach where he was hoping to go. His friends, with a bit more common sense, denied that I'd touched them in any way whatsoever, and also stressed that we were wasting time in this boring old police station when we could be at the beach having fun.

Things then took a more sinister turn as the cops became interested in the photos I might have taken, and it was at that point that my heart sank, for they proposed to take Roger back to the flat to perform a search. Surely it wouldn't take them long to uncover the stash of nude pictures I had taken and had developed in Lisbon, and which were unconcealed in my luggage bag.

Again, there was drama involved here. Roger was whisked off in a large Black Maria at top speed, with the siren wailing all the way back to Espinho, which was some distance away. Because of my lack of decent Portuguese, I could not be questioned any further and just had to wait until the car returned with two triumphant cops clutching my precious photos. All the while the woman was clucking on and on to everyone's evident irritation.

To my astonishment and relief, the search party returned empty-handed, and everyone now seemed anxious to bring the matter to some sort of conclusion. From nowhere, a more senior plain-clothes officer appeared and ushered us into his small office. I was to be questioned further and Roger was called in simply to act as interpreter, as no accusation had been made against him.

Again the question was raised of why we had taken the boys out on these trips, and the same answers were given. Then I was asked a direct question: "What happened with Paulo?" Having picked up why his mother had become suspicious, I spun a reasonably convincing yarn about catching the boy in the act of stealing coins and demanding that he return them, which he'd refused to do. I then grappled with him and managed, so I thought, to retrieve the money, though clearly Paulo had already hidden some of it in his pocket. I supposed it must be this assault that Paulo had told his mother about … I illustrated my story with a lot of physical movement to lend it verisimilitude and suspect that the officer knew it was a pack of lies.

But it was getting late, it was a holiday, they all wanted to get back to their families, Paulo was a pest who was always causing them trouble, and his unreliable word was the only evidence they had. I'm sure had one of these factors been different, or if one of the policemen had it in for *bichas*, what followed next would not have happened. We were led out of a side door and round the back of the police station to my car, but not before one of the other boys had asked me if we were now going to the beach at last. Once Paulo's mother realised I was being released, she created merry hell, and her screaming reached a new pitch, the noise from inside the building following us all the way back to the car. This no doubt was another factor contributing to my good fortune that day. Had she remained calm, the police might not have become so fed up with her, and would perhaps have been more inclined to be sympathetic to her complaint.

There was one chilling moment though as the police officer accompanying us back to the car issued a stern warning along the lines of "Tome muito cuidado com as crianças. Se alguém interferisse com meu filho, eu o mataria!" meaning, "Be very careful with children. If someone interfered with my son, I would kill him."

From his manner, and the way he spoke, there was no doubt that he meant it.

Roger wisely decided that we should not remain in the country a moment longer, just in case someone changed his mind or decided to take justice into his own hands. We hurriedly packed our bags, emptied the fridge and shelves which, as well as some food, contained plenty of wine and beer, and took the key back to the agency, which was about to close. We claimed that, because of an emergency, we had suddenly been forced to cut our holiday short, and not to worry about returning the money we had already paid for the remaining five days. Amazingly, the girl in the office insisted on reimbursing us, believing perhaps that some awful tragedy had befallen one of us.

I then drove nonstop to Spain, as darkness began to fall, drinking beer and wine and munching bread and cheese. Once we were safely across the border we managed to find a guest house which had spare rooms and was still serving an evening meal – thank heaven for the fact that the Spanish eat so late. Despite all the excitement, I slept remarkably well that night and gave especial thanks to my guardian angel.

There were other incidents on the return leg of that holiday, including my ramming a cyclist in France who landed on my bonnet and broke the windscreen, leading to another long, but much less worrying interview in a police station, during which I was breathalysed. Although the poor man's racing bike was a write-off, he was mercifully unhurt.

Roger insisted that by the time we arrived back in England, I should have somehow managed to dispose of the photographs which had so nearly caused a bundle of trouble. How those policemen had managed to miss them, he did not know – apparently they had looked everywhere except in the place in my bag where I'd carelessly left them: that guardian angel at work again.

I couldn't bear to throw the photos away, so phoned a friend in England who had a huge collection of pornography and was always keen to add to it. He was the one who rode a large motorbike, and worked as a professional driver, and I will call him Kevin. He seemed prepared to take the risk of me posting him the pictures, and, with some misgivings, I did so. This man was to be the cause of a huge amount of grief for many people, but that would be four years down the track.

One day when Roger and I were doing one of our silly swimming-pool runs, he told me about a businessman friend of his, CL, who had once worked in Copenhagen. CL told him how at every swimming pool it was obligatory to take a naked shower before entering the pool, and that this rule was rigorously enforced. Moreover, the attitude towards nudity was extremely relaxed and all boys would spend a large amount of time naked in the shower and sauna area. He also had an amusing story.

CL was just leaving a pool one day when he was stopped by an attendant:

Attendant: Excuse me, Sir.

CL: Yes?

Attendant: You were at the swimming hall yesterday, weren't you?

CL: Yes, I was.

Attendant: We know that when you were here you masturbated a small boy.

CL (spluttering): I've no idea what you're talking about.

Attendant: There is no point in denying it, we know.

CL: Well, em, well er …

Attendant: So, please, if you come here again, do not do this. Many people come here to look, but I'm afraid that's as far as it can go. Is that understood?

CL: Er, yes …

Attendant: So please remember: you can look, but don't touch!

"You can look but don't touch" became something of a catchphrase for us over the years.

But what about Denmark? I'd already heard all sorts of good things about this small country where everyone speaks English, including reports of extremely light sentences passed on those few men convicted of sex with underage boys. The age of consent was, I knew, an unconditional fifteen anyway and the attitude towards homosexuality was relaxed too. I had seen Lasse Nielsen's wonderful film *Du er ikke alene* with its catchy song at the end, and indeed, thanks to Francis Canning, had a video of it. I found many Scandinavian boys achingly beautiful, and the thought of seeing a whole load of them naked was too enticing for words.

How reliable was CL's knowledge? Was it already out of date? Did anyone know anyone who had been there recently?

There was only one thing for it. I'd have to jump on a plane and check it out for myself.

Before I describe this rewarding adventure, I hope you will bear with me while I make another diversion related to European travel.

In 1988 I started collecting Air Miles, much to the amusement of friends who thought I wouldn't have a chance of amassing enough for even a single short flight. One was though awarded them for all sorts of things, including petrol and money spent with the Nat West credit card, so I felt it was worth doing, if only for amusement. As usual when I put my mind to something, I followed it through with utter determination, using my Nat West card for all purchases, getting one air mile for every £10 spent, and always filling up with Shell petrol. Once when I went for lunch at Francis's, there was an envelope on the table saying "a present for Stephen"; inside were three individual air mile vouchers, and everyone round the table laughed.

To my delight, however, after a few months of collecting them, there soon began a great promotion, with petrol stations quadrupling the number of air miles on offer and, by Easter 1990, I had easily accumulated enough for a return flight to Copenhagen. Reclaiming them was rather a primitive business: one simply stuffed the required amount of vouchers into an envelope indicating which return BA flight one wanted to take, and back through the post came one of those large air tickets which are so rarely seen these days, in this case indicating a purchase price of £0.

What fun that holiday was. I got my usual smoking seat at the back of the plane, which in those days was not packed like a sardine can, as the regular price of a flight was considerably more than it would be today. I was served an excellent lunch and could drink as much booze as I wanted – all for nothing!

I found a good small hotel near the station for a reasonable price, which included a self-service breakfast, and nearby was a delightful underground pub which had excellent beer and large portions of tasty home-cooked food. Even if the pools turned out to be a disaster, my creature comforts would be more than provided for.

My initial impression was of a city where everything seemed to function like clockwork. People were friendly and helpful and it was easy to get maps and information about the various suburbs and the best way to travel.

On my first afternoon, I went to an inner-city pool which was a tad disappointing – I later learned that tourists who wish to swim usually get directed to this pool, probably because it was the closest to the centre of town. Surprisingly, the male changing area was segregated into adults and children, an instruction I chose to ignore being a silly foreigner who didn't know any better, and which no one challenged me about – not even the flunky whose enviable job was to sit in a small alcove and ensure that all the boys showered properly. There were even little diagrams on the wall indicating the five areas which had to be thoroughly washed with soap (provided by each shower) before entering the water: under both arms, groin area and feet. I do vividly recall the first boy I saw as I slowly undressed in the open changing room, trying to work out how the locker system worked. An unbelievably beautiful godlike silkily blond Adonis of about twelve summers parked himself next to me and immediately removed all his clothes, after which he did not know what to do and approached me to ask how the lockers worked. I was unable to enlighten him, so he, still stark-naked, had to get help from the man in the alcove.

Adonis then took a long shower which I was able to observe, unseen, from the toilets, and so began my Danish career of furtive voyeurism.

Each day I spent in Denmark simply got better and better. No other pool I went to had this odd segregation (I later heard of people being put off altogether after experiencing this as their first pool), and I proved my theory that the further out of the city you go, the better the pools are in terms of numbers, general friendliness and openness of behaviour. Naked boys would happily play with you and engage in horseplay under the showers, and there was no flunky on duty to spoil things. One of the highlights of that week began as a complete disaster. I arrived at a distant pool in Hillerød at about 2.20, only to find it almost empty, with the only customers being old men. I put up with this for a while, thinking surely there must be plenty of boys in this town, what on earth do they do on a dull Wednesday in Holy Week? Even the men were beginning to drift out after half an hour, and I was on the point of doing so myself when, at three on the dot, there came the heavenly noise of about thirty excited babbling voices into the changing area. From then on and for the next three hours or so, the room was heaving with naked boys of all ages, permanently filling the shower area and sauna, in which one might have two or three squeezed next to one with several standing right in front with everything displayed inches from one's face. Occasionally an attendant would wander through, and if he saw so much as a pair of swimming trunks hanging from a faucet in the shower room, would order the unfortunate lad to take them out and put them on one of the pegs provided by the benches.

The images from that extraordinary afternoon stayed in my head for days. That evening, I was due to take the night train to a small Swedish town called Gävle, where a divorced woman called Britt-Marie lived with her twelve-year-old son Ludvig. I had met Britt-Marie through Francis, when she had been staying with him a few months before. They became friends when Francis had taught in Sweden a few years back and she had been a pupil of his. She remembered him with affection as a great teacher and a warm, understanding human being. She knew all about his and my liking of boys and this did not bother her at all, and she had insisted that I should stay in her house if I was ever in Scandinavia.

After leaving Hillerød, I had some time on my hands before catching the late train to Stockholm, from where I would transfer to the line for Gävle, and so I decided to visit the only Thai restaurant in Copenhagen. I was greeted warmly by the proprietress, who became effusive when she found I could converse in basic Thai. Dispensing with the menu, I ordered my meal in this language, specifying that I wanted the red curry nice and spicy, and was told that, for me, she would make it twice as hot. I washed it all down with plenty of Singha beer. I cannot remember what else I ate, but the portions were generous, and I was pleasantly full by the time I was drinking the strong coffee and complementary chocs at the end, having paid a modest bill.

As I got up to go, the owner asked me eagerly, still in Thai, if I would like a nice girl to finish off the evening, and was fairly insistent. I replied politely that this was terribly kind of her, but I had a train to catch, and would not have time to enjoy such a treat properly. Maybe when I returned in five days' time after the Easter weekend …

The time with Britt-Marie passed agreeably, and she made a special effort to look after me well, as she'd remembered my generosity when I'd paid for a Thai meal at a restaurant in Kingston, in which there were eight other people in our party. I had of course used my credit card and earned plenty of air miles, but in truth I was glad to beat Francis to it, as he was always paying out huge amounts for everyone in restaurants.

Her son Ludvig turned out to be enormous fun, and we hit it off well. He introduced me to many of his friends and we would often wrestle together in the basement. There was one friend of whom Britt-Marie did not approve, as he was too streetwise, being allowed to wander around alone getting up to heaven knows what. "Just the sort of boy Francis likes," I remarked, receiving a rueful smile and nod in return.

There was a delightful pool where Britt-Marie took me and Ludvig, along with a couple of his friends. The boys were very protective of me and showed me the whole procedure for entering the pool, which in those days was very similar to Denmark. As well as having a lot of fun in the pool I was able to slink off alone to the showers and sauna and feast my eyes on the talent which was constantly coming and going.

I met Ludvig's father, who was a bassoonist, so we had much to talk about, including reed-making. Ludvig also played the bassoon, but somewhat reluctantly. However, when I was staying in his house, he was happy to play in front of me and I of course offered enormous encouragement, which pleased his mother.

In the many trips I subsequently made to Denmark before relocating there, I managed to stay with Britt-Marie and Ludvig at least three more times. Ludvig knew how keen I was on going swimming and, on the last occasion I visited, informed me regretfully that the pool had burned down. This was rather sad, but there was still plenty else to do.

Before returning to England after those few days in Sweden, I'd allowed myself some more time for exploring Copenhagen's watery paradises, of which there were many. Many more in fact than were listed in any tourist brochure or city map. I boldly went into the central library and asked if there were such a thing as a book which listed all the swimming pools in Denmark. Of course the librarian was not only happy to show me their copy of this seminal tome, but was able to tell me where I might find my own, at the Høje Taastrup Teknisk Forvaltning. He even gave me a phone number for this august institution, along with instructions on how to get there.

I phoned them immediately, claiming to be a postgraduate student studying the relative fitness of various nations in relation to the number of public sports facilities available. Yes, they had the book, and certainly, if I came within the next couple of hours, I could buy a copy.

As word of Denmark later spread among my friends, this book became known as The Bible, as it really was definitive, listing addresses, phone numbers, number and size of pools and so on. I felt like some sort of pioneer, as many followed in my footsteps, marvelling at the way the Danes were so laid-back about their bodies and sex generally.

Another massive change for me in 1990 was making the momentous and exciting decision to buy a flat near to the school. The prices in this part of Surrey were truly astronomical, and I could not have secured a mortgage if my aunt Ingrid had not agreed to pay half the cost of the flat as a loan, but one for which there would only be a Deed of Trust drawn up by the conveyancing lawyer. The idea was that if at any point I wanted to sell the property, she would have half the proceeds.

In the event, when I did eventually sell it twenty-five years later, she wanted nothing to do with the sale, claiming she might be liable for capital gains tax. It was clear to me though that the money had all along been a gift to help me onto the "property ladder". She had been my mother's eldest brother's fourth wife. My uncle Davy was the successful one, having amassed a fortune as Director of the World Bank, but he'd died very suddenly a year earlier. Ingrid, who was already phenomenally wealthy, had been his sole heir, and my mother had a theory that, not having expected to die so young, Davy had simply forgotten to include any other family members in his will. Ingrid's gift rectified this, though this was never spelled out.

One major advantage of living out of the school was that teachers were paid an additional £3000 per annum, the idea being to prevent valued teachers from moving on too quickly. I managed to find a ground-floor flat with a huge living room in a secluded and quiet area, but within walking distance of the school, though I did later buy a bicycle. The very first day I moved in was also eventful for quite unwelcome reasons.

I will need to retrace my steps to put this unsettling event into its full context. The previous year, Francis had left the UK to start a new job in North Africa, and had rented out his house. Until about a year before he left, I had been his closest friend, both regarding the distance I lived away from his house on the river, and also in terms of intimacy. However, when he eventually met Kevin, the motorbike man, Francis, to the astonishment of everyone who knew them both, reacted as if he'd experienced a road-to-Damascus-type revelation, and Kevin was suddenly regarded as, to coin a phrase, "the best thing since sliced bread". It was surprising in that, apart from a shared interest in boys, they seemed to have very little in common at all. Personally I didn't particularly mind, as Francis and I still remained close, but, whilst not disliking Kevin, it was very difficult for me to find common ground with him apart from our shared good sexual taste and then, at one point, video games which I tended to use to amuse boys when entertaining them. Through Kevin, I became rather good at them, and started collecting the expensive Sega Mega Drive cartridges: challenging him to the two-player games became a useful way of passing time with Kevin.

What *had* been annoying before Francis left the country was that Kevin was now nearly always with Francis, encroaching on special private times which we used to have together, such as our Monday-night snooker games at a local club, in which I could also unwind and share with Francis some of the issues I'd faced the previous week. This was impossible with Kevin present.

I also became subtly excluded from some of Francis's activities, such as the time he and Kevin went out in Francis's boat and picked up a group of lads at Sunbury with whom they started a friendship whereby the boys came round to Francis's house every Sunday. I stumbled upon this by accident when arriving early back from a trip to Abingdon. I decided to call in on Francis without warning, as there were matters I urgently wished to talk to him about. Sunday was a day I very rarely visited him now, except by prior arrangement. I was taken aback to find three or four young boys occupying the place as if they owned it, smoking, drinking alcohol and addressing both Francis and Kevin in a relaxed over-familiar manner. Francis was clearly embarrassed that he hadn't shared this discovery with me: "It was too early; I was going to," he said. For the first time, I felt a mild sense of disappointment that he should have kept an important secret from me. "The Sunbury Mob", as they became known, were later to feature in a heavy investigation into Francis's affairs and I felt that after all I had been lucky not be involved with them.

After Francis had left the country, he insisted that I should "keep an eye on Kevin" and include him as much as possible in whatever I was doing – he was adamant we should "stay together", which I found odd, but I made a point of keeping up with Kevin for the sake of my friendship with Francis. Much later on, this would prove impossible as I became torn between loyalty to Francis and Peter C., who had come to thoroughly despise Kevin.

Peter was still a very close friend at this time, and now became my closest. He was extremely perceptive, and although he and Francis had hit it off extremely well after I'd introduced them, Peter's character analysis of him, as well as of me on occasions, could be brutal in its honesty. He would say of Francis that apart from being a very poor judge of character himself, what he really craved were courtiers who would fawn upon and flatter him. This was not said behind Francis's back and Peter even repeated it to Francis's mother during the first period that Francis was unfortunate enough to spend a few months held at Her Majesty's pleasure: Francis had asked Peter to report to her after each time he visited him in jail, not wanting his mother to have the distress of seeing him there herself. But I am getting ahead of myself.

Though I loved Francis, I would never, I hope, flatter his ego in the way that Kevin now did, his reward being lavish hospitality – expensive meals out, free trips to Thailand and the like. Francis also played the grand host to Kevin's working-class parents, who were at first delighted until Francis's friendship with their son led to him facing "official" difficulties, and the really big trouble that Kevin later experienced resulted in many others having problems too. One acquaintance rather ruefully described him as "the big domino" – fine to know as long as things are going well, but liable to drag everyone down with him should he ever end up in a police station.

One result of Kevin holding number one place in Francis's affections was that he was asked to be an official manager of his house should any problems arise with the tenant. There may well have been a generous motive to this too as Francis would probably have paid him for doing this service, whereas he knew I wouldn't have accepted money for it.

This worked well for a few months until, in fact, the very day I moved into my flat. On my first evening there, surrounded by boxes and books and all manner of stuff to be sorted through,

Kevin arrived at about 8 p.m. in a jittery state of nerves. Apparently Francis's tenants had discovered material in his attic that he really should not have left there, and they phoned Scotland Yard to inform them that they seemed to be renting their house from a paedophile. Kevin, as manager, was rung at work and did his best to disclaim any knowledge of Francis's private life, but he was then faced with the enormous problem of clearing out his parents' house of all porn for fear of a raid – a massive task, which some used to claim jokingly would require three furniture vans.

So Kevin returned a few items I had lent him and stayed for half an hour or so to chat, before moving off to dispose of all the other risqué items which he had in his white van – the vehicle he drove when not on his motorbike.

My feeling was that Kevin had overreacted by immediately disposing of material, but being no stranger to that helpless feeling of mad panic which can distort all your finer judgment when faced with a threat that strikes to the very root of your being, I could well sympathise with his course of action. I and others reasoned that the Scotland Yard Vice Squad would be unlikely to respond with an immediate raid on Kevin's premises, but would bide their time, lulling him into a sense of security before choosing their time to strike – they have all the time in the world. This is in fact exactly what happened, with disastrous results, but it wouldn't be for another four years.

IX. Further Contacts and Adventures

Meanwhile I was entering one of the happiest, busiest and most productive periods of my life, whereby every aspect of it seemed to be falling into place. The flat was a huge success, modern but solidly built with pleasant neighbours who did not object to my music and with a cosy warmth about it which all who visited it remarked upon. I was now playing in three good local orchestras, still adoring my work and the boys, and able every holiday and half term to travel abroad: Europe when I only had a week off, and usually Thailand for the Christmas, Easter and summer breaks, though I did spend one Easter holiday in Sydney.

My circle of local friends and acquaintances was also increasing at a fast rate, and in my free time I would see people who lived as far apart as Surbiton, Islington, Sutton, Camden and Bracknell. I was also inundated with love letters from a pupil's mother, Mary, whose husband was a governor. These would arrive almost every day, and I eventually didn't bother opening them, though I still have a huge sack of them in my garage. She was a prominent member of the school choral society, and before her personal interest in me had become too obvious, she had invited me round to her house "for a drink and a chat". In my innocence, I hadn't realised that she planned a huge seduction and I was greeted by a rather scantily-clad middle-aged woman with expensive Champagne and assurances that her husband was away.

As ever, I played it cool and kept the conversation strictly on "shop" with many mentions of Karen who was supposed by many to be my sweetheart, as her attraction to me was evident to many in the school. This was perhaps one of the most difficult balancing acts I had to perform at this time – the parent and Karen were in a sense rivals, but contrived to be friends. I accepted many meals out from Mary, as Karen was always invited too, and, as well as the stream of letters she was always giving me, expensive presents and requests to set her verses to music, which she would then perform at choral society events. These were all love poems and aimed directly at me: one was called *When You Were There*, which I felt I set rather well. I found that, by a mixture of professionalism and airy friendliness, I could maintain good relations without her friendship turning into frustrated resentment, and I did actually like her, which helped. I even provided a name for her younger son's new puppy at her request.

At around this time I also, along with other members of staff, did a parachute jump for charity, and I recently discovered the video of a thin fit-looking young man rakishly clad in jumpsuit and backpack. He is someone I barely recognise today, but it gained me enormous kudos amongst the boys and some of the parents who sponsored me.

After a few months, when he had finally settled in, I went to visit Francis in Tunisia. The first time I stayed with him, he was living alone and still finding his feet, both in terms of the general culture as well as how to pick up boys. His first clumsy attempts had met with hostile reactions from elder brothers, and he'd had stones thrown at the windows of his little house situated on the edge of the beach. Now however, he had become accepted, and we were able to sit unmolested on the roof of his house in the warm spring sunshine, sipping our drinks, on the day I arrived.

There were many pleasant excursions and adventures on that trip, but I will relate the most amusing. One morning Francis drove to a crowded beach away from his home and with remarkable speed, managed to find two boys who immediately understood our interest. One was about fourteen, whom Francis said he would take, and the other was probably not more than eleven and definitely less assured than his friend. We found a reasonably secluded country spot with plenty of bushes and shrubbery, and parked the car there.

Because of some aversion therapy Francis had been more or less forced to undergo many years before, he was always notoriously quick to come when having sex, and he immediately vanished into a dense thicket with his boy, leaving me alone with mine. Being younger and greener, mine required many reassurances before he would remove any of his clothes, and when he was finally ready and happy to play with this strange English-man, Francis suddenly reappeared from nowhere: "Haven't you two finished yet? We've waited a long time, and thought you'd be done by now!"

They made themselves scarce again for as long as was needed, but the moment had been lost, and I had to start all over again before my nervous partner would feel confident enough to relax and enjoy himself. Eventually, though, we did achieve some sort of mutually satisfying result. This occasion was a first for me too, in that I'd never had congress *al fresco* before.

On this trip I also met for the first time a pair of English non-identical twin brothers aged twelve who were living with their mother, Babs. As well as being physically very different, the twins had utterly dissimilar personalities. Tommy was tall, outgoing and cheerful, with a large cock and oodles of confi-dence, whereas Bill was decidedly runty, puny and whinging, with a tiny cock and far less self-esteem. I first discovered this when we went swimming on a deserted beach, while Francis and their mother were at work. Very soon after getting in the water, Tommy removed his trunks and swung them above his head, challenging me to chase him though the water. Bill would cer-tainly not have removed his had we not both, in play, given him little option.

Later I was to learn that Babs had been something of a hippy, and had brought up the boys in Greece without clothes – there were many photos of them unselfconsciously parading around in the nude when younger. When they reached the edge of puberty and moved to a different society, their attitude towards nudity altered. Tommy was still sort of OK with it, but with Bill it was another matter and he did not like being seen naked.

Later on, after Babs had returned to England to live with her drunkard of a husband, the pair stayed with me for a week in my flat in Surrey. They were mostly delightful company, though they did have an annoying habit of locking themselves in the toilet to wank together. Inevitably Kevin had to be involved in this, at Francis's request, and I also became quite close to Tommy for a while afterwards.

Not long after I'd returned from this trip, Francis was joined in Tunisia by an old friend of his, Gavin M., who'd had to leave the country in a hurry a few months before Francis left England. I'd only met him once before, in Surrey, when he'd turned up at Francis's house laden with two-litre bottles of cheap red wine and three extremely presentable boys. It had been a fun afternoon, especially because they all enjoyed messing around in the Jacuzzi which Francis had had installed in his bathroom and which I'd never seen in use before.

Gavin had known these boys some time, and there had never been a problem with their parents. However, a few weeks after I met him, one of the brothers' aunts, a policewoman, came to stay with the family and was suspicious of his involvement. She questioned the boys closely and soon wheedled out of them the exact nature of his relationship with them. He was arrested and, amazingly, released on bail for a four-figure sum, which a close friend of his guaranteed before he fled the UK. He went first to Amsterdam and, after some months, joined up with Francis with whom he remained for another fifteen years, in various countries. It was always assumed they were a gay couple, which was a useful cover for them both.

The second time I visited Tunisia, things had definitely moved on. Gavin was a "hard operator" and, between them, he and Francis had acquired quite a network of young friends. One of the sunniest and most amusing was Hamdi, who would show up at any time of day demanding sex, and was more interested in that than any money that might be offered. One standing joke was that he would, for example, initially ask for twenty dinars, which was rapidly reduced to ten if he got no response, then down to five and then, with desperation, "no dinars" – at which point someone would oblige him. I managed to teach him a few tricks in the shower, which he thoroughly enjoyed, and after my departure, these had to be included in the repertoire of Francis and Gavin. Hamdi acquired a nickname from me – BIAT. This was based on the local bank, Banque (or Bonk) Internationale Arabe de Tunisie, as he would happily "bonk" with anyone who came along.

I also remember this holiday for the splendid picnics which

Gavin prepared, and for trips to Hammamet. Francis had befriended a family on the outskirts of this town, and the father was highly approving of the sexual education offered to his son, claiming that an important tradition was being upheld. The boy would often spend the night chez Francis and Gavin, and, during my trip, was happy to spend a night with me too. Francis regarded it as good hospitality to provide his guests with at least one boy in whatever country he was living in.

I will conclude this chapter by briefly describing a few more of my adventures during this golden period, before what became known as the "FOD" (Forces Of Darkness – or Scotland Yard detectives) began to interfere and shatter so many lives.

The fall of the Berlin Wall in November 1989 was to have a considerable influence on where people chose to spend their holiday, with the whole of the Eastern Bloc suddenly opening up for tourists.

After Christmas that year, Roger C. and I took a trip to Berlin, where the contrast between east and west was still very much in evidence. East Berlin was more innocent, as evidenced by a huge swimming pool we went to on New Year's Day. Many boys there were still happy to parade around naked in the changing rooms, had little sense of "stranger danger" and were happy to chat and interact with adults. This was in contrast to the Thermen am Europa-Center in West Berlin which was then, and still is, a place where everyone goes naked, but which is heavily staffed by flunkies who, even back then, were suspicious of single males.

1990 was of course well before the internet, which did so much to shrink the world and irrevocably change the lives of everyone in it, but even back then it could sometimes still seem a surprisingly small place. One evening we entered the Pinocchio Gay Bar, which was well-known then for having quite young teenagers. After we'd been there about ten minutes, I heard an adolescent voice call "Steewan" and, on looking round, saw a very well-dressed Thai boy whom I immediately recognised as Peter C.'s favourite when he'd been living in Sukhumvit Soi 101. He had been nicknamed BJ because he gave such excellent blow jobs, and was the only boy in the house off-limits to guests.

I gathered he'd now been adopted by a German and brought back to live in Berlin, where he seemed to be happy enough – happier at any rate than another boy I knew who'd come to live in England in a public schoolmaster's flat in Brighton, where he was cold and lonely. I also hoped that the German was luckier than the English housemaster, who was reported to his headmaster by an anonymous evil-wisher, claiming that he'd brought a young male prostitute back from Thailand. It couldn't, however, be proven that there had been a sexual motive for the boy's presence, and everything was in order with his paperwork, so fortunately the man escaped with a warning to be careful.

In Berlin at this time, there were a good many shops specialising in boy "material". The most famous was Galerie Janssen in Pariser Straße, but there were others which sold quite hard porn, including extremely risqué photo sets. As Francis was unable to obtain such items in Tunisia, I agreed to post him some magazines and pictures, which unfortunately never arrived. I also bought some for myself, intending to take them back to England.

I'd arranged to spend several days longer out of England than Roger, and it seemed a good idea to take an overnight trip to another European city, as the train fares were remarkably cheap – just a few pounds to go to Copenhagen or Warsaw, for example. Never having been to Eastern Europe, I decided on a whim to visit the latter, much to my regret as it transpired.

The train departed early in the evening and I'd brought plenty of booze and food to consume before attempting to sleep by stretching out on the seat. On entering Poland at about 22:00, the border official had warned me to "watch my bags", which advice I should have taken more seriously. The only other person in the carriage was a pleasant young Polish girl. She spoke excellent English and had just completed a long university thesis which she was taking home with her. She didn't seem to think there was much risk of robbery on the train either, but I hadn't appreciated that this train stopped at almost every station, so it would be an easy matter for someone to slip into our carriage, quickly half-inch anything not secured and then leave the train before it set off again. To my horror, I saw that both my bags had been taken along with the Polish girl's during the couple of hours or so we'd been asleep – inside mine were all my money, credit cards, clothes and books, along with the rather naughty material aforementioned.

For the first and only time in my life, I pulled the communication cord which brought the train to a grinding halt. However, no one came to investigate and, after a few moments, it simply started moving again. Luckily, I still had my passport, which I'd kept on me after showing it, but the poor Polish girl had lost everything, including the only copy of her precious thesis.

Via the British Embassy, I was given emergency spending money. They also found me somewhere to stay in Warsaw, and purchased an air ticket to England on British Airways for me, with money wired to them from England by my mother: a sad end to what had been a fun trip. The only bit of good I was able to do in Warsaw was to pass on the return section of my rail ticket to a penniless student anxious to go to Berlin. His genuine gratitude was at least heart-warming, as there was no other opportunity to meet and get to know the locals.

Eighteen months later, this ghastly experience had a surprisingly pleasant outcome, as a Polish mother, ashamed of how someone travelling in her country had been treated, invited me to stay in her Warsaw flat along with her son, with whom I got along very well at school. He had been a playful lad, who enjoyed physical contact and often initiated mock fights which ended up with him wriggling in my grasp, giggling gleefully. As this behaviour was very open, I'd thought nothing of it, though I did learn later, via Karen, that one of the spinsterish matrons had considered allowing this sort of behaviour "inappropriate", as I was far too physical with the lad.

Unfortunately, by the time I stayed with him in Warsaw, he had hit puberty and was far less fun – a pity, as I was left alone with him all day while his mother worked. We still had a pleasant time though, and it was perhaps just as well that the physicality we had both enjoyed didn't go any further.

Getting too fond of the boys I taught was always a danger, but there was only one with whom I fell head over heels in love and felt my feelings returned. In other circumstances we could have had a fun and mutually beneficial relationship, but in the gold-fish bowl of that environment I had to behave as correctly as possible and demonstrate my affection for him without unacceptably crossing any boundaries. Even then, this inspired the furious jealousy of Karen, who did everything she could to discourage me from having more than strictly professional dealings with him, and slagged him off to matrons during staff supper in front of me – intending no doubt to provoke a reaction.

I was now using all the short breaks from school to visit Denmark and other European countries on Air Miles, which had really turned up trumps. I ended up doing around ten trips using them, saving on average around £180 each time, and then I was able to sell the remainder to a collector when I left England for good in 1994 – no one was laughing at me now. I was still also going to Thailand at least twice a year, even though from about 1990 onwards the situation there gradually became more and more sour.

Police were now routinely arresting *farang* in popular tourist areas, hoping for a large bribe instead of throwing them in jail and allowing the legal system to take its frustratingly slow course. A few residents actually kept the required large sum ready in cash and would enter into agreements with others to pay their release "fee" quickly, which could be as much as 500,000 baht – well worth it to escape the privations of a Thai prison.

Thanks to local knowledge from friends who lived there, one learned where the safe places were. There were still boy-friendly hotels which could be used, usually ones with separate villas and no central lobby. Yet, more and more, it became a question of meeting a boy in a well-known pick-up area and taking him back to Peter C.'s house in Bangkok.

One memorable morning, I took an excited phone call from Peter at my hotel because two extremely well-dressed twelve-year-olds had turned up on their bicycles at the Crystal Gardens in Pattaya, and were clearly curious about what this sex-with-men thing was about. The Crystal Gardens, where Peter was staying, was one of those hotel compounds consisting of separate anonymous villas, and I had only just been with him a short while before, when we'd had breakfast at a nearby café. Peter's amusing words over the phone were: "A week might be a long time in politics, but half an hour is a long time in pederasty. Come straight here now!"

Fortunately I was in time, and the lads hadn't ridden off or been discovered by someone else. What fun that was – Peter had his regular boy with him and I was able to enjoy a threesome with the newcomers in the adjoining room. I remember now the glorious sight of their unsullied nudity, and the implied question of "now what?" After realising that this sex-with-men-thing was in fact rather jolly, as well as lucrative, they were both happy to accompany us back to the capital in our hired car. They just had to take their bicycles back home, wherever that was, and explain that they were going away for a few days. Unlike the next boy I will be describing, we had no idea who they lived with or what would be thought of them suddenly heading off to Bangkok for a week, but they assured us that all was fine and they were trusted and given freedom, so we didn't enquire too deeply.

One was a stunning blue-eyed blond, appropriately nick-named Lang, who mostly became my companion for the next few days. There were many mixed-blood boys around at that time, and they were always in demand! The first I'd had, three years earlier, was one of the crop fathered by American G.I.s during the Vietnam War.

Besides Lang's beauty, he was a thoroughly pleasant character, with an equable temperament – laid-back, amusing and lan-guidly sensual in bed. The other was pure Thai, handsome and equally engaging. They could easily have been two pupils from my school.

There was only one hairy moment: when we were taking them back to Pattaya after a wonderful week in Bangkok, the car was stopped by the police as a matter of routine. Had they realised the nature of the relationship between the boys and ourselves, matters might have become extremely sticky and, at the very least, we would have been detained for questioning. As it was, as soon as we saw ourselves being flagged down, Peter immedi-ately urged the boys on the back seat not to utter a word and to pretend they didn't understand if asked anything. Fortunately this worked like a dream. Peter and I were very polite, and when there was no response to a question sharply fired at one of the boys, they asked us if we were "embassy". Yes, indeed we were, and so with a low respectful *wai* we were quickly ushered on our way.

The earlier mixed-blood boy referred to above was an instance of where my basic knowledge of Thai proved extremely useful. Having entered the well-known pick-up bar on my first night in Pattaya, I encountered a sandy-haired vision whom I was easily able to engage in conversation. I proposed taking him back to my hotel for the night and then perhaps to Bangkok the day after; he told me that he didn't want to go with me right now, but would meet me at a certain beach tomorrow and spend some time with me, after which he would take me to meet his mother. If he felt he wanted to, and she agreed, he would then come back to Bangkok with me. Fair enough.

He then left the bar and I was immediately accosted by a loud-mouthed, slightly tipsy Australian who greeted me with:

"Yeooh BAStard!"

"Erm, sorry …"

"Yeooh utter BASTARD! YEOOH UTTER UTTER *BAS-TARD!!*"

"Oh, right."

"I've been comin' in 'ere every night for a week and haven't been able to get anywhere at all with that kid, and you swan in and pinch 'im from right under me bloody nose. StrOOth!"

"I wasn't aware he belonged to anybody."

At which point, having said his piece, he stormed off, somewhat unsteadily.

The next day I was met as promised and, after playing on the beach and having some lunch, we duly went to meet his mother in their tiny little shanty-town-like house. I accepted a glass of tea and chatted as well as I could with the lady, who adapted her speech so that I could understand her. Occasionally she would fire off fast remarks at her son which I could not follow, but all in all everything seemed amiable enough.

After half an hour or so a decision seemed to have been reached, and a small bag was produced in which he packed his essential belongings. I offered the woman some money, which was refused: her abiding concern was for the welfare of her son, and she'd had to be clear that he was happy to be going away with me. Her final remark, in English, was rather poignant, and I will never forget it or the simple undramatic way in which it was articulated: "Look after my baby."

It was clear that evening that he had never been with anyone before, and his trembling excitement was highly infectious. From the start, he was lost in some sort of ecstatic pleasurable world of his own. Without wishing to sound like some third-rate hack pornographer, it would not be exaggerating to say that his rock-hard organ was literally throbbing, and dripping oodles of precum – the like of which I'd never seen before. When his first explosion came, it was almost dry by comparison, but it was accompanied by bodily writhings and moans of pleasure. Almost as soon as it was over he wanted to go for the next one, and the next …

I was with him for ten days, and each night his passion became a little less ardent, though he continued to be an inventive and responsive lover, and it was a huge wrench to say goodbye. One does wonder if one might have corrupted him, as I learned later that he'd become, for a while, an accomplished professional little tart, donning his Noel Coward-style dressing gown and, though I suspect this was exaggerated invention, smoking expensive cigarettes via a cigarette holder, selecting his clients with care and charging high prices. But if it hadn't been me first, it would certainly have been some other extremely fortunate person.

There were many happy encounters in Thailand, and I could probably fill a single book with reminiscences of the numerous boys I was privileged to befriend there. I will leave South East Asia with a brief account of a second car trip, this time to the อีสาน (north-eastern) region and in the company of another resident, MB, who had recently moved to the country from the UK to escape potential problems arising from a heavy scene in Birmingham.

After the idyllic holiday I had spent with Peter in the company of two very compatible companions, the trip to the north-east was far more fraught. To begin with, MB was even more highly sexed than me and expected to find a suitable boy companion in every town we visited. A new phrase was coined on this trip: when Peter suggested going to see some famous ruins at one of the cities we stopped at, Mike retorted, "Fuck the ruins, where are the boys?" Fuck The Ruins, or FTR, became synonymous with not bothering with the cultural heritage of a place one visited and concentrating on personal pleasures.

Later on, I went to visit Francis when he was living in Athens, and he emphasised in his letter to me before I arrived how much there was to see there, and there would definitely be *no question* of FTR.

There was an amusing incident in one of the first hotels we stayed at in the north-east, when MB was smitten by a particularly good looking room-boy aged about twelve. I fussed over him a bit, took a couple of photographs of him smiling proudly in his pristine uniform, and thought no more of it: he was clearly a working boy with no thought in his head that guests might have any designs upon him.

After an exploration of the town and a pleasant meal out, I retired to bed at about 11.30. Much to my surprise there was a knock on my door just after midnight and, to my great astonishment, there was this same room-boy in the company of a rather dubious-looking man I hadn't seen before.

"You like this boy – yes?"

"Er, well, mmm, yes I do."

"Do you want him for a short time – 400 baht?"

"Oh gosh, well … yes, thank you!" I didn't start to argue that I could find willing boys for 200 baht where I'd come from. This boy anyway was in a different class.

So he was ushered in, and was clearly bemused, perhaps expecting a small grope or even a quick wank. I'd have been happy with this had he removed his clothes, but he was reluctant to take off so much as his jacket.

I opened the door to the man outside.

"Sorry, the deal's off. He won't take his clothes off."

After wishing them both goodnight, I got back into bed and switched off the light. About a minute later, there was another knock on the door.

"It's OK now, he'll remove his clothes!"

To the boy: "Are you sure?"

From the boy by way of answer, a nervous nod.

From the man: "But the price is now 600 baht."

I pretended to demur at this, but finally agreed and the boy once again came into the room and this time coyly removed his jacket and shirt.

"No more?"

"No more."

I opened the door and once again ushered the boy out, explaining to the man that I expected the boy to be fully naked, that it was fine by me if he didn't want to undress properly, but in that case I wasn't interested.

I went back into the room, and this time kept the light on – just in case!

Sure enough, two minutes later there was yet another knock. Heavens knows what agreement had been struck out there, but I was assured I would this time have the boy cooperate fully …

"But the price is now 700 baht."

"OK, fine!" I said with a sigh.

True to his word the boy stripped in front of me, rather slowly and nervously which, I must confess, I found unbelievably erotic. We soon settled into a pleasant session in which the boy became much more relaxed when he realised that nothing terrible was going to happen to him.

After forty minutes I delivered him, fully dressed and pristine again, along with seven 100 baht notes, to the man outside, went back to bed and fell asleep quickly.

I was awakened about an hour later by the bedside phone ringing.

Sleepily: "Hello."

"Hello. I want to know please, do you have one of our room-boys in your bedroom."

"What? I don't know what you are talking about."

"I said, is there a room-boy with you?"

"Of course not! I think you must have a wrong number – good night!"

On which firm note I hung up, half wondering if the phone would ring again, but it didn't.

During breakfast later that morning, I recounted the incident to Peter and MB, who was mad with envy, and didn't mind showing it. Peter took a different view and suggested we check out immediately and get on our way, in case there were any awkward questions.

It was with some relief that we were on the road thirty minutes later. However, we were stopped after only fifteen minutes by a police car. Whether he spoke in jest or not, I don't know, but I didn't for a moment take Peter seriously when he said: "I expect they've just been told how you mauled that room-boy last night."

MB was driving and, as usual, driving too fast. It was simply another 200 baht on-the-spot fine, which went straight into the policeman's pocket and into a small logbook of ours where all traffic fines were noted down along with who paid them, as all expenses connected with the car, such as petrol, would be divided evenly between the three of us at the end of the trip.

Our next stop, Udon Thani, was bigger than the previous town and MB had high hopes of scoring here. We decided that the best way was to hire a *samlor* driver and tell him what we wanted. The *samlor* is a rather bizarre contraption, essentially like a tricycle with one wheel at the front and two at the back where there is also a seat just large enough to fit two large Englishmen.

The young man riding the machine had clearly developed strong thigh muscles and took the pedalling in his stride.

We offered him a considerable tip if he could find us a boy each. I spelled out very clearly the sex and ages we were interested in, and he seemed confident that he could fulfil our rather unusual request. After fifteen minutes of strenuous pedalling, we arrived at a rather nondescript building, and he showed us in. We were met with the rather degrading site of about twelve young scantily-dressed women behind a glass screen – comparison with a goldfish bowl would be particularly apt here. One was presumably meant to choose a girl who appealed and then be taken along to a separate chamber with her – hardly anyone's idea of romance. I discovered later that this was a very common arrangement for a brothel in Thailand and still exists today.

We quickly retreated outside and I again had to articulate very s l o w l y exactly what we were looking for, and added that, if he couldn't oblige, that was fine, and we'd pay him off there and then. But no, he understood now and off he pedalled again. However, we ended up at a similar establishment with young Thai girls, although this time there were also ladyboys on offer. Whilst intrigued by the *kathoey* as a social phenomenon, and having been fooled by one when I had my hair cut on my first visit to the country, I could not pretend to be sexually interested in transvestite young men, and again we hurriedly left the establishment.

MB was becoming impatient by this time, but the driver insisted that he knew somewhere private where we would find someone to suit us both. We were now well out of the centre of the city, and had I been alone, I might have started to get uneasy. After another fifteen minutes we arrived at what looked like a private house, and the door was answered by a young woman clearly in an advanced stage of pregnancy, who would be happy to service us in turns.

MB, now really rather angry, declared that he was going to take a taxi back to the hotel and advised me to join him. But, still high on the eventual success with the room-boy and his unlikely pimp, I stupidly decided to persist. Surely this man must understand that I wanted a boy: such a preference can't have been unknown, even in a provincial city, in a country where sex was still regarded as just as natural as going to the loo, and where questions of taste were no more significant than whether one liked sugar in one's tea or preferred savoury dishes to sweet.

Off he pedalled again, now with a solitary passenger in the back. At least it's not such hard work for him now, I thought. But by now I *was* becoming a little alarmed, as we seemed to be moving further and further away from civilisation on quiet uninhabited streets. Then it became dark rather suddenly, as it is wont to do in this part of the world.

When we reached a secluded spot, he suddenly stopped, leaped out of his saddle and indicated to me to follow him. I was feeling very uneasy, and stopped walking after a short while. He then turned to face me, made a "come hither" gesture with both arms outstretched, indicating that he was offering himself to have sex with me there and then, and started removing his shirt. I declined as politely as I could, fished some hundred baht notes out of my pocket, threw them on the ground and legged it away as fast as I could, before he had a chance to follow. It took a good forty-five minutes to find my way back into town, and a little longer to locate the hotel. The evening had not been a success, but was maybe quite instructive.

We stayed in the town for two nights and we had more luck the following evening. Having just about given up on finding boys, MB and I went into a café, purely with the intention of having a coffee, and noticed that it was run by a fairly large family which included mother and father and various boys and girls. I tried out my simple Thai on the mother and immediately everyone was charmed by the daft *farang*'s efforts to speak their language, crowding round the table and asking endless questions.

At one point someone asked us about our wives and was answered with a firm "no have". As there was nothing to lose, I then told them we preferred males, preferably young. This was met with a few giggles; how different would the reaction have been in England! I then started telling the mother how good-looking their sons were and asked how old they were. In reply, she made the three boys tell us their ages: eleven, twelve and fifteen – all with genuine beaming smiles. MB had taken a shine to the fifteen-year-old, whereas I was more attracted to the two younger brothers.

The question then came up of their sexual experience and whether any of them had ever had any. The older brother proudly declared that he had, but that his brothers hadn't, with the implication that it was high time they did. Everything was going rather nicely, and bit by bit it was agreed that MB could take the older boy for the night and I would take the younger ones, with the proviso that there would be nothing too heavy.

There may have been some money involved in this, but, if there was, it certainly wasn't a major consideration, and I'm sure the parents would have been shocked at any notion that they were offering their children as prostitutes. Had there been any hint of unwillingness, they would not have let the boys come with us. As it was, they seemed curious about us and seemed to find the idea of spending the night with these two funny foreigners rather a jolly adventure.

It all worked out very well and, in my case, the sex was light, beginning with nude massages which became gradually more intimate. I won't pretend it was a night of hot passion, as with the other virgin described above; rather it was simply a pleasant romp for the three of us. In fact Peter, who dropped into my room the following morning and had a session with the twelve-year-old, had greater success in stirring the lad into ardent action, declaring that he was perhaps more experienced than he'd let on.

X. Further Acquaintances in England and Adventures Abroad

This chapter will aim to portray how my already-busy life was becoming ever more pleasantly frantic and fulfilled from every point of view – creativity, friendships and professional success, along with intellectual as well as musical growth.

I was playing in three local orchestras and improving my bassoon technique by seeking out the best teachers and practising regularly every day. Through one of these orchestras, I met a wonderful pianist with whom I practised regularly, and met many of her other friends, with whom I played chamber music and still do to this day. She had an extraordinarily talented friend whose professional name was Marvin Hanglider. His real name was Mike Hatchard, and he now has a significant presence on YouTube, but is still virtually unknown. He could improvise songs at the piano in any style and on any subject matter thrown at him, rather like Richard Stilgoe, but sharper and more amusing. I remember an extraordinary one-man show he gave at the Royal Festival Hall in which he managed to sing *My Way* and accompany himself at the piano, but in a different key and a beat behind, to amazing effect.

He took part in a concert we gave at my school on behalf of a cancer research charity founded by bassoonist Laurence Perkins (whose wife Susan had died of the disease), and brought the house down. Although the school hall was only a small venue, we managed to collect over £200 for the Susan Scott Musical Fund for Cancer Research, and Laurence was delighted.

Marvin also agreed to write a musical for the school to perform, but it was so smutty that the headmaster had to veto it. Pity, as it was based on boarding-school life with unflattering portraits of masters and dubious juvenile heroes, which would have gone down very well with the boys if the production had been allowed.

It is hard to say which of my lives was the more real – the respectable one where I mixed in good society and enjoyed performing and meeting talented people as well as famous musicians, or the trips abroad where I could allow the more primitive part of my makeup freer expression. Perhaps a comparison could be made between the artistic and animalistic sides of my nature as Apollo versus Dionysus, or Schumann's stormy impulsive Florestan as opposed to the dreamy Eusebius. I dreamed of a world where these two conflicting parts of my nature could happily co-inhabit, but apart from the rationed visits to English swimming pools, most of my sexual adventures had to be abroad if I were to survive.

I did however make plenty of like-minded friends outside the school – possibly too many. There were the odd couple, Bruce and Ted, who lived in Surbiton and whom I met through Peter C. Both were over sixty and had spent much time in Australia, having originally fled the UK many years before. Ted was definitely the more skilled when it came to making friendships with boys leading to consensual sex, and it had worked so well in the antipodes that Bruce had invited Ted to live with him rent-free in Surbiton, in the hope that he would continue to provide him with young talent the way he had in Sydney. Neither had quite realised what a different society Britain in the late eighties was from the one they had left in the sixties and, after a couple of fairly barren years, Bruce was rather brutally to throw Ted out.

Living next door to Bruce and Ted was a divorced mother with two sons aged fourteen and twelve, who spent much of their free time in Bruce and Ted's house. The mother was intelligent, friendly and grateful to get the boys off her hands for a while. She frequently invited Bruce and Ted round for supper and I was often included. She was also delighted that I would quite often take the younger boy, Christopher, out for the day.

Ted, who had designs on both of them, was less delighted, but he needn't have worried, as I had no intention of trying to seduce Christopher, even though he was a classic fair-haired blond beauty. With fun to be had abroad, I had resolved to keep my hands as clean as possible in England, so I simply enjoyed his company, having lunch together, playing snooker or going bowling. My friendship with Christopher started shortly before Francis left the country, and he suggested I should bring him back to his empty house while he was at work, to see if I couldn't "go a bit further" with him. Francis had plenty to entertain boys in the way of computer games and videos, so I agreed that I would take Christopher there on our next outing and see what transpired.

Francis had made a huge effort that day and the house was spotless; also ready were the computer games console and a large selection of games for Christopher to play.

It was obvious from the start that Christopher was rather nervous about this deviation from our usual plan and, although he was happy to play on the computer, he did keep asking me, rather anxiously, why I had brought him to this strange house on the river.

He'd probably picked up a little of my nervousness too, as Francis was notorious in the neighbourhood and everyone, including the local police, knew about his "proclivities". Because of his exuberant personality, he was tolerated but, as evidenced by the suitcase incident already described, he was certainly under some sort of casual surveillance, and I had probably already been officially clocked as an associate of his.

I resolved to give it another few minutes and then take Christopher away to somewhere that felt safer. The living room faced directly onto the river and there were large windows affording a wonderful view. Christopher suddenly looked up and his expression altered.

"Hey, Stephen, look, there's a policeman outside!"

Sure enough, when I turned round, I beheld the alarming spectacle at the window of a large burly copper in uniform, complete with helmet, indicating for me to open the door. Oh no, what was this about?

It turned out to be the friendly local bobby who'd known Francis for years and clearly didn't regard him as a monster. All he wanted to find out was if Francis had renewed his gun licence, and I was unable to enlighten the good cop.

At one point the constable turned to look at Christopher and then back to me with a grin and a knowing wink. There were to be no awkward questions about who this boy was, who I was and what the nature of my relationship with him was, for which

I was grateful. It might, however, have been a different story had Christopher been discovered déshabillé in the bedroom.

The PC left a note for Francis to contact the police station and, when I next met him, he roared with laughter at the extraordinary coincidence of the bobby arriving at just that moment. To me it emphasised just how important it was to keep one's hands clean in GB. Another piece of advice from Francis, which I ignored, was to hug the pupil at school whom I so adored. One might have got away with such displays of affection in the sixties and seventies, but in buttoned-up Thatcher's Britain with its Section 28 amendment outlawing any so-called promotion of homosexuality in schools, it would have been suicidal madness.

One day I turned up at Bruce and Ted's house in Surbiton to be greeted by both the next-door boys and a dashing young Australian man called Howard. The boys were clearly impressed by this fit young man who had recently been in the Aussie equivalent of the Territorial Army, as well as a PE teacher in New South Wales, telling me I'd better "watch out" now that they had special protection!

Later I discovered he was a fugitive who had boarded the first plane out of Sydney to avoid his trouble escalating. He had known many of the same people in Oz as had Peter, as well as Bruce and Ted, and they offered him a bed in their house until he could find his own feet.

We got along extremely well. He was amusing and charismatic and full of stories about characters in Australia, some of whom I would later meet. He quickly got a job as a security guard in a department store, and was given a posh smart uniform which also impressed everyone.

Howard was soon introduced to Francis, who made a huge and immediate impact upon him, as he had upon me and so many others on first acquaintance. A mutual friend once unkindly observed that Francis would have made a brilliant second-hand car salesman, such was his possibly-superficial charm and magnetism. He also, through me, met Adam's friend Oliver, who had been instrumental in paving the way for my first trip to Thailand, and the two got on famously. It transpired that Howard was what I have heard described as an "anything in trousers" person. Not only did he seduce Francis's ex, Sean, who was then nineteen, but he also had sex with Francis himself and with Oliver on at least one occasion. Rather flatteringly, he expressed an interest in "doing it" with me and I had to politely refuse, at which he was rather miffed.

He was primarily interested in boys though, and became rather good at "cottaging" – something which held little appeal for me. Bruce was also an ardent cottager, and it struck me as extraordinary that someone could get his kicks in a filthy smelly public toilet who was so fastidious about cleanliness in his own home. He frequently berated Ted for his sloppy cleaning and would do half the bathroom again after Ted had supposedly cleaned it, just to show just how sparkling it could be. But then we all have multiple sides to our natures.

From Howard, I heard the story of the boy in the New Addington cottage. I had heard about this public convenience from Bruce and others, but had never followed it up. There was quite a risk involved, as the cottages were known to the local plod, which to dedicated cottagers forms part of the dangerous allure.

Howard went there one Saturday afternoon and spent a fair amount of time simply standing at a urinal. After a while, he was joined in the building by a presentable lad of fourteen or so, who seemed furtive and nervous, and not at all interested in relieving himself – well, of urine anyway. Howard smiled at him and received a nervy acknowledgement followed by a quick head movement towards one of the cubicles. The message was unambiguous.

As soon as they were together and the door locked, he indicated that Howard should lower his trousers and pants, and his face became transformed into one of blissful reverence. "Oh that's so beautiful," he sighed, "so *so* beautiful." Gazing was soon followed by touching and caressing and sucking, and the boy was quite happy to reciprocate, allowing himself to be similarly fondled.

Arousing as Howard's description was, I still decided that I should stick to my policy of abstinence while in the UK. I had so much to lose.

There were riotous evenings at Oliver's flat in London, where we would sit and drink and smoke until the small hours. Once, when the cigarettes ran out, Oliver phoned a taxi company to bring him more from a 24-hour garage – a fairly ordinary event apparently. Quite often there would be cannabis passed around, and this was my first experience of smoking it. The effects were pleasant, but did little to raise my level of well-being, which was generally pretty good anyway during this period of my life.

Mad times. At about 3.30 in the morning, I would get into my car, full of booze, and drive back to Surrey, leaving Howard to spend the night at Oliver's place. I would have to be up at 7.30 later that morning for an 8.00 choir practice, and somehow managed to function normally the next day. Oh, to be young again.

Howard confirmed many of the Australian stories about the various characters in Sydney, which I had heard from Peter and the Surbiton pair. In particular, there was a diehard Aussie nicknamed John the Hoon, the meaning of which I had no idea. He ran a stable of extremely beautiful boys who would perform any sexual act with anyone, and they were very carefully selected, using a checklist in which every box had to be ticked for any new boy to be considered safe and suitable to join the group. For example, John the Hoon would see a ravishing angel playing on his own in an amusement arcade and send one of his lads in to test him out.

John's lad: "Whatcha, mate! What's yer highest score on this thing?"

Angel: 7320.

John's lad: "Jeez, is that all, I managed to top 10,000 the other day."

Angel: "No kidding!"

John himself: "Tell you what, let's play doubles. I'll pay."

Angel: "Yer on mate."

John would then deliberately play below his best, encouraging the angel and at the same time making more small talk. This was where the real process of whittling down began: as soon as there was a "wrong" answer, John would take his leave with a "Jeez, is that the time?! Guess you are better than me after all!"

Examples of important questions might be: "Do you have brothers and sisters? What do your folks do? Do they mind you wandering about on your own? Do they ask difficult questions? Are they happy for you to spend the night away fairly often?"

If stage one was passed, stage two would move carefully on to more intimate questions about sexual habits, and what experience the boy had had, and such like. There were not many who passed this high level of scrutiny, but it was a guaranteed formula and, amazingly, John the Hoon never suffered any trouble with the law. He would say to Bruce: "This is a high-risk industry mate, and yer just can't be too careful."

There were also many less happy stories about police corruption, which led to a huge enquiry in which Peter later had to give evidence via video link from London. One of the most colourful characters was Robert "Dolly" Dunn who was, of all the alcoholics I ever met, one of the most hardened. At one point he was gaining immunity for his own activities by "dobbing in" other peds and helping the New South Wales vice squad collect huge bribes for their release. It only came out later that he and one other had been "helping" the corrupt coppers, and there was a huge NSW commission into the whole affair which can be found online.

After hearing all the stories, of which there were many many more, I decided that rather than visit Thailand one Easter holiday, I would go to Sydney for three weeks. It would make a pleasant change, and perhaps still a few wagging tongues at work. "Mr. N. is off to Bangkok yet again. I wonder what he gets up to there."

Before describing this rather odd trip, I need to say a few words about one of Bruce's favourite boys called Stephen.

Before leaving Australia in something of a hurry, Bruce had taken some candid video of some of his young friends there, nearly all performing with each other or alone. However, the exception to this was the video he most prized; it was of a pleasant fresh-faced twelve-year-old who visited his home every weekend. Shortly before leaving Oz, Bruce filmed the final "performance", showing the boy arriving, slowly stripping off and playing with himself to a commentary that went something like: "This is my mate Bruce's house and I come here every Saturday afternoon for some fun …"

After about five minutes of the boy arousing himself, the shot cut to a naked Bruce bending over his bed, and Stephen in something of a frenzy mounting him. Bruce had been very careful, so he thought, to keep his face out of shot, and all one really sees is Stephen's pert little bum going up and down as he gives Bruce a good rogering, shouting out "I love you, Bruce" in between ecstatic moans and groans, culminating in a quivering orgasm that certainly could not have been faked.

This video was predictably to land Bruce in a fair bit of trouble, but that was still some time off. On learning that I was to visit Oz, Bruce gave me a huge wad of Australian dollars with which he wanted me to pay off his credit card bill. He hadn't been going to bother, but they had somehow found out his English address, and were sending him nasty letters and he was worried about the thing escalating. He also, for whatever reason, wanted me to give money to Robert "Dolly" Dunn and to Stephen, with the idea that I might have a little fun with him myself along the way.

Peter C. was still in Bangkok when the arrangements were being made for my stay in Oz, and he later on castigated both Bruce and Howard's choice of host for my brief stay. I could apparently have been introduced to John the Hoon and another gentleman who was known as "fat Lloyd", both of whom would have been guaranteed to supply me with willing boys.

As it was, arrangements were made for me to stay first with a gay friend of Howard, Vince, who worked for customs, and then another person called Brian, whom Peter later described as "the most boring person in Australia", before I spent the remaining two weeks with Dunn.

I flew fairly cheaply on what was then known as a courier flight. One's hold allowance on the outward journey was used by a company transporting goods, and one had no idea of what was being carried, which was perhaps just was well. The outward journey on Qantas was broken in Singapore, where one was given a hotel for the night. Much of the next day could be agreeably passed wandering round the city, which was amazingly clean to the point of being sanitised, and easy to get around. One day there was probably enough, however, as everything looked rather boringly the same.

I thus landed at Sydney relatively refreshed and free of jet lag, and was met by Robert Dunn, who eagerly took the litre of duty-free whisky I had on me and which I never saw again. Great mistake: I should have saved it for Dunn's gay friend, Vince. It might have made my arrival a tad more welcome, seeing as I was to spend the first few days at his house and then Brian's, before staying with Dunn for the rest of the trip. Vince hadn't been told that my interest was solely in boys and, within ten minutes of my arrival, he attempted to make love to me, which was rather embarrassing as I then had to explain my position.

From then on I was merely tolerated. Fortunately he was at work all day, allowing me to organise my first meeting with Stephen, who was sent by Dunn to the house to be my guide in Sydney until he was free to entertain me himself. On my first meeting with Stephen, he came into Vince's house and chatted away happily as I told him of my plans, including hiring a car from "Rent a Wreck" which leased out old cheap, battered vehicles. In spite of their appearance, these were in fact reasonably reliable and roadworthy. I gave Stephen Bruce's money, which was substantial, before we both left the house so that I could explore the centre of Sydney with a good willing guide by my side. He was quite surprised by the large sum and said to me, looking up somewhat forlornly, "Gee, thanks, Steve, I guess you want something back for this, eh?"

I assured him that the money was not intended to buy his favours and that if he didn't want to do anything, that was fine by me. In retrospect, I could have been a little more forceful, as he may have simply wanted me to make the first move. It just didn't feel right though. Later that day, Dunn told me that Stephen was addicted to heroin and that the money from Bruce was a bad idea as it would simply go to feed his habit. I realised too late that this was probably one of many lies that Dunn told me: in his normally befuddled state, he was full of all sorts of stories, told in a chirpy, credible and emotional way. He had an engaging personality and plenty of charm, but seldom allowed the truth to spoil a good narrative.

I saw Stephen most days before moving out of Vince's house. He went with me to hire the "wreck" and loved being driven about in it – all the way to the Blue Mountains on one afternoon. Unfortunately, I had chosen a very bad time weather-wise to visit New South Wales, as it rained most days, so that the Mountains were completely obscured in a mass of cloud.

Stephen was always delightful company and I never once tried anything with him, believing it would be wrong to take advantage of a drug addict. Perhaps that was Dunn's intention.

The few days with Brian were as dire as could be expected. He spoke in a constant monotonous droning drawl on uninteresting topics, and seemed to lack any sort of sparkle whatsoever. He was frequently visited by rather superannuated youths who seemed to treat him with utter contempt and demand money off him in a rather menacing way – the blackmail unspoken, but always there in the background.

One of the more delightful aspects of the trip was remeeting Robert Scoble, the fluent Thai-speaking diplomat whom I'd first encountered in Bangkok. We spent many a pleasant hour together, eating out and discussing books and mutual acquaintances, but he seemed ignorant of those who might have been able to set me up with some live action.

Despite his drunkenness, the most enjoyable part of the trip was spent chez Robert Dunn. We ate out every day at excellent restaurants and he ferried me everywhere, no doubt putting our, and many others', lives at peril because of his almost permanent state of inebriation. He showed me the places on Bondi Beach where he'd had the most luck picking up boys, and drove me round to the houses of friends of his, some of whom were extremely amusing and with whom I maintained contact. It was in Sydney that I met a man close to death from AIDS – a first for me.

Dunn had a phenomenal collection of porn which he kept in a large lock-up, much of it featuring himself fucking young boys, which he was proud to show anyone who'd watch. Each video had a story behind it, such as meeting the boy on the beach and petting him in the water until it was clear what he was after. The remarkable thing in those days was that they all seemed happy to come back to his place for sex, although Dunn was sly where the video camera was concerned, telling the boys that it wasn't switched on if they expressed concern about it.

On a similar theme, he had plenty of footage of a local nudist beach where he'd set up his camera hidden in a bag. Part of this I was allowed to take back with me and Howard was delighted to see that a teenage boy he'd long fancied had been captured for posterity. He'd been told that this footage existed, but hadn't believed it until he saw it.

As well as meeting some of the more notorious Sydney peds, I did some normal sightseeing and had a respectable tea one afternoon with an old schoolfriend of my mother, who was keen to be updated on how things were back in England.

The only visual memento of that trip I was able to bring back was a four-hour tape of commercial soft porn, including a few of Dunn's hidden-camera items, which I admit to finding rather stimulating in a kinky, different sort of way.

I told Bruce the whole story of Stephen and the drugs and he was suitably horrified but, as I say, it may have been pure invention. Peter C. was extremely irritated to learn that I'd had anything to do with Robert "Dolly" Dunn, who later, once he lost the protection of the bent coppers, was hounded out of Australia and lived some time as a fugitive in Indonesia, before finally being caught and brought to "justice".

The Australian footage I have seen of how he was eventually apprehended fills me with sadness. He argues well the case for pederasty when interviewed for TV, and it became clear that all the boys in Lombok, where he had spent much time hiding out, had enjoyed their time with him. Many of the locals too seem frankly bemused about Dunn being arrested for such a harmless reason, so despite the heavy slant the Australian film-makers gave their documentary to prove how evil Dunn was, he doesn't come across as any sort of a monster at all – more a rather pathetic creature doing his best to pursue personal happiness.

Having had my first experience of nude beaches with Roger C., I was persuaded to try the famous resort near Montpellier, Cap d'Agde. Originally this came about through a psychiatrist friend of mine, Charles Douglas, who was friends with a naturist film-maker who then called himself Rebelo and focused on filming boys – he is still producing films in the Ukraine but, for reasons of safety, now concentrates mainly on girls and women.

They were planning to stay in Agde with a group of Portuguese boys whom Rebelo had already filmed extensively, the plan being that these boys would befriend other young holiday-makers and thus supply many more subjects for Rebelo to film. Charles invited me to join the party, conditional on the approval of an ex-Harrow teacher, JDT, whom I'd not yet met.

In the event, JDT did not think I should join what was already a rather large group of disparate individuals, but this didn't stop me from later making my own way there and meeting some fascinating new people. Not having booked anything in advance, I discovered that there was no accommodation to be had, and ended up paying a beach bum a large sum to stay in his hut for two nights until a flat became available, as he was perfectly happy to sleep on the beach. He'd gone on to me about all the dubious characters now coming to the resort, clearly meaning people like me. However, his high moral standards hadn't prevented him from drilling discreetly placed peep holes in his hut, from which one could spy on most of what was happening on the beach.

Later on, when I did eventually meet JDT, we became firm friends and there were no hard feelings at all about the initial snub. I also heard much background about the filming which was eventually achieved by Rebelo and then released commercially. It seems to have been rather a fraught holiday, and Charles, in his usual generous way, ended up spending a fortune hiring boats et cetera. JDT, on the other hand, managed to quarrel with Charles and also with Rebelo, after striking one of the latter's favourite boys, who had become spoiled and obnoxious. Ironically this holiday marked the end of what had been a rather close friendship between JDT and Charles, but there may have been more to it.

One of the famous Agde characters was an Australian called Scott, who in the early 1990s worked in an international school in Frankfurt and was remarkably successful with boys. He dominated an area on the rocks, carving out his own special niche and focusing mainly on fishing. This attracted quite a crowd of boys, especially as he had a large collection of state-of-the-art equipment, including baseball caps which he handed out liberally. After we became friends, he once remarked to me that I wasn't trying hard enough to befriend the boys, and with a rueful shake of the head observed in his broad Aussie accent: "There's no point in going on safari without all the right gear y'know!"

I saw him quite a few times in England when he would fly over from Germany with video tapes full of clips from the many TV shows which featured boy nudity at that time, including a rather charming advert for soap powder. At the other end of the scale, he had also been involved in filming many beautiful boys at Agde who seemed very happy to perform sex acts for him to capture – a willingness no doubt aided by a small monetary consideration, but also largely on account of his charismatic personality and charm.

I recall one incident in Epsom. Scott had needed to use a phone box and some mischievous schoolboy had left a note inside, along with the other usual sort of cards advertising the services of prostitutes, informing everyone that Jason in his class was gay and giving a phone number for "anyone interested in sex with Jason". I thought it might be a police sting, but Scott just had to find out and dialled the number, which was answered by a man.

"Hello," said Scott in his most unctuous voice, "is Jason there please?"

"Yes, who shall I say is calling?"

"Tell him it's Scott, a friend from school!"

A few seconds later an unbroken voice uttered a somewhat hesitant "Hello …"

"Hello, Jason, it's Scott here!"

"Sorry?"

"Y'know, Scott! I heard you like to have a bit of fun."

"Do I know you?"

And with a final "Yeah, c'mon it's Scott, S-C-O-T-T," he lost his bottle and hung up.

Well, we'd established that the number was genuine, but not the tantalising question of whether Jason was up for it or not – probably just as well.

On another visit Scott went through my entire porn collection, berating me for not having a better filing system to indicate what the nature of the material was (hard, soft et cetera), and transferred what he considered the best parts onto a single video tape. He then unscrewed the cassette container and removed the small reel of videotape inside, such being the way he always transported tapes through customs. He bought a box of chocolates and very carefully removed some of the cellophane covering it, and then three of the chocolates, putting the small reel of tape in their place before sealing up the box so that it was really impossible to tell that it had been opened. He wrapped it in colourful birthday-greetings paper and signed a card "to Auntie Jenny", before wrapping the whole lot securely in brown paper and addressing it to a friend in Australia, a PO box number, under the name of Mrs. Jennifer Bowen.

This was the first time I had witnessed such incredible caution. I later learned that the chocolates had not in fact arrived, but at least there had been no trouble for anyone, largely thanks to these elaborate precautions, I imagine.

On one visit to Agde I found myself sharing an apartment with Scott, an arrangement which suited us both in terms of spreading the cost and enjoying mutually compatible company. On one occasion, I was preparing to go to the main swimming pool when Scott said: "I've got a video camera here which I can conceal in a bag. Why don't you take it with you and see if you can preserve some of these wonderful sights."

I recoiled from this idea, certain that I would be caught. Scott tried to assure me that it was easy and he knew this guy in England with a huge amount of material captured in English swimming pools, leisure centres and camping places, including boys masturbating in public toilets. He'd even installed one-way mirrors in his flat so that he could film boys naked in his bathroom and wanking on his toilet.

Naturally I was intrigued, and Scott offered to introduce me to this person next time he was in England. Appropriately enough, his surname was Daff, as he turned out to be one of the most unusual people I'd ever encountered. He deserves a few paragraphs of description if I am to do this complex and troubled soul any justice at all. He was to play a major role in my life at this time and later on as well.

I had been warned by Scott that Daff was something of a "loony", but that did not prepare me for the complex, multi-layered personality I slowly began to apprehend as I got to know him – very definitely what at that time would have been described as manic-depressive, with huge mood swings which were uncomfortable to witness at either extreme. His highs were characterised by a loud, unrelenting, rabbiting monologue into which one could hardly get a word in edgeways, as he delightedly reeled off corny jokes, tales of his conquests and the mad behaviour of others. These ups were, on balance, preferable to his lows and sadly rarer. During the lows, he would bleat constantly about how badly the world treated him, his lack of money, his hatred of his family, particularly his mother whom he walked out on when still a teenager, how people took advantage of him and only liked him for his camera skills and so on. At times, he would simply clam up after a particularly lengthy recitation of his woes and sit hugging his legs closely to himself, whilst swaying backwards and forwards in a semi-catatonic state.

He had an extraordinary instinct for survival, and had decided from early on that other people owed him a living. His view of friendship was that someone was only worth knowing in direct proportion to how much you could get out of them, and he would maintain a useful grasping relationship by promising all sorts of goodies in return, which seldom materialised.

From the start, his choice of "career" had been cunning and calculating. He was a reasonable musician, and might just have made a decent living as a piano teacher. He claimed to have an Associate of the Royal College of Organists diploma, but his level of keyboard performance skill made this seem unlikely. He hated sport, except for one aspect of it: the showers which would always follow training and matches in those days. For this reason alone, he became a football coach, running teams in Bracknell leisure centre and insisting that they all shower after each session. When I first met him, he also had a job in a small day prep school, and ruled over the showers there with a rod of iron, making himself unpopular by taking over this duty exclusively, and making an enemy of one dear old long-serving music teacher by depriving him of his weekly thrill. Daff never budged from his position here, claiming that, as *the* sports teacher, it should be he, Daff, and no other who should perform this arduous supervisory task.

There was a strong streak of ruthlessness in his make-up too. If, when in a swimming pool changing room for example, he realised someone else was lingering and cramping his style, particularly when it came to filming, he would confront them and threaten to report them if they didn't leave immediately. This threat was by no means idle, and he did indeed manage to get other men thrown out by means of his self-righteous indignation: he was so truly disgusted and affronted by the obvious perverse behaviour of others that it would have been unthinkable to accuse him of the same – he would have simply thrown a wobbly of huge proportions and threatened a defamation-of-character lawsuit and heaven knows what.

During those times when he was not at either extreme of his mental range, Daff could be amusing and fun company. His mood would also suddenly change for the better if he encountered a boy whom he fancied, magically switching on a Pied Piper charm which was seldom detectable in his dealings with adults, beguiling and enchanting potential young friends with a range of quirky tricks which included pretending to shake hands and snatching his away at the last moment. He would also reel off inconsequential jokes which would have the lads helpless with laughter.

I first met him in his council flat in Bracknell, where I was taken by Ross. He agreed to lend me one of his "glimpses" tapes, provided that I had something "fresh" for him to look at in return – all dealings with him were on a quid pro quo basis. "Fresh" became a key word when it came to porn, as he tired easily of even the highest-quality material.

I had recently acquired a tape of the aforementioned Agde holiday, and there were a fair number of naked beauties on it, so the deal was struck. I heard later from Scott that Daff had whinged that this was a very bad exchange because, although they were both four-hour tapes, his had a much higher concentration of naked boys than mine did. This was another Daff trait which was to persist all through the time I knew him – he would be fine to your face, but slag you off remorselessly to mutual acquaintances. He did this so consistently that it almost became meaningless. He was always picking arguments directly with others too: employers, friends, strangers, anyone against whom he felt he had a legitimate grievance.

However, one thing that all who knew him were agreed upon was that he was superb when it came to hidden camerawork, and indeed he called it "work" as he had to get everything so precisely right. Roger C. and I nicknamed him The Master, as the results were really quite stunning. When on an "up", he would lecture you for hours about the best way to operate, how to place the camera in the bag, how it was important to distance yourself from it once the camera was running. He would spend hours adapting ordinary-looking sponge/wash bags into containers for his precious video camera. He discovered that the sort of transparencies used on overhead projectors were the best for filming through, and would carefully sew a label holder round the hole through which the camera was filming and put the plastic transparency inside, so that the lens could barely be seen unless one looked very closely.

I would meet Daff every Monday evening at his flat and we would exchange stories as well as porn. I assume his initial disappointment with my first video offering was soon forgiven, as he never mentioned it to me, and he often expressed great delight at my offerings. I soon had copies of all his precious material, though it was a work in progress as, sometimes when I arrived, he'd proudly tell me about a group he'd just filmed, managing to get a brilliant shot of such and such a boy who'd eluded him before.

Sometimes he would manage to delete the sound from his videos, but quite often his loud, high-pitched, raucous voice was to be heard ordering the boys where to stand, or to form a line, or to move away from the shower area and "not stand there gawping" at the others. The ages of his football teams ranged from eight to sixteen, and he proudly told me he had every single boy naked on video. There was a particularly mischievous imp of about ten who invariably got an erection after about ninety seconds in the showers. When this was pointed out by his friends, he would proudly twang his penis so that it slapped against his belly.

Even more extraordinary were the hours of filming he'd done in public pools at a time when British boys had no qualms whatsoever about nudity. It was rare to see a naked shower, but he managed to capture all sorts of naked shenanigans in the open changing rooms, towel fights, wrestling, or simply prolonged almost-unconscious posing once the trunks had been removed. Apart from their erotic value, such candid videos should be preserved simply to illustrate what a completely different animal the British boy was in the 1980s. Then there were the holiday camps such as Butlin's, where Daff would follow a boy who was dressed only in tight Speedos around for a while, and often into a toilet where he would film him over the top of the cubicle as the boy masturbated. He'd also devised an elaborate system of mirrors so that he could capture the image from the adjoining cubicle by strategically placing a mirror between them at the back, or sometimes putting it on the floor and filming the inverted image.

All these secret filming methods are relatively well-known today, and video has of course become omnipresent. In those more innocent days, it never occurred to most people that someone might be secretly capturing them.

It was of course his great obsession, and he would go to any lengths to add to his already-large collection. He once spent hours in a cramped lumber room situated above the showers in the place where he worked and, by drilling holes in the ceiling, was able to film the boys taking part in a huge annual swimming gala.

He had great ambitions to live in Holland and had befriended a rather simple-minded Christian member of the fraternity, Nico, with whom he used to stay. Nico eventually tolerated his presence for five years so that Daff, claiming to be Nico's gay partner, could apply for a Dutch passport, but that was a few years ahead.

I mentioned the Danish pools to Daff, and his first reaction was negative. Oh no, he'd been to Copenhagen, and the first pool he'd been to had segregated adults and children. I laughingly told him that this was the first place I'd been sent to as well, and that it was probably the only pool in the entire country where they did this. He became extremely excited about some of my descriptions of Danish behaviour and resolved to return there as soon as possible – with his precious camera.

This he did at the next half-term in the summer, and returned deliriously happy. Not only had he managed some extraordinary footage in the regular pools, but he'd also marched into sports halls and filmed squash players, or basketball teams, or any participants in after-school activity that he could find. He stayed in a large youth hostel and was delighted to find many school groups staying there from all over Scandinavia – all of whom used the communal washing facilities in the mornings, creating another superb cinematic opportunity. Normally Daff would be exceedingly reluctant to give out copies of his "work" without something equivalent in exchange but, as I'd given him much information about Copenhagen, he was happy for me to have a copy of his first Danish trip – on this occasion.

Slowly Denmark was becoming my country of choice to visit, and perhaps relocate to, instead of Thailand. To begin with, it was much nearer England should I need to return in a hurry because of a problem with my mother, for example. From their friendliness and open behaviour there was a definite sense that boys were available, and the age of consent was fifteen, with no strings attached as was so often the case in other countries. Daily boy nudity was at that time guaranteed and, as a society in general, Denmark seemed relaxed and liberal – pleasingly free of interfering busybodies such as you commonly found in the UK.

Meanwhile, my Air Miles were accumulating fast and I was able to do a few more trips to Copenhagen on them as well as to Prague, Bucharest and Amsterdam again.

Prague I visited almost on a whim, doing very little preparation for the visit. It was known that after the Berlin wall came down and the imaginary Iron Curtain was lifted, many of the former Eastern Bloc countries were released suddenly from a repressive Soviet dictatorship. Before effective local governments could be established, there was a feeling of mild lawlessness about these countries, and seeking out men having sex with boys was given low priority until it became evident from the number of "sex tourists" visiting former Soviet territories that some action would have to be taken. Later on I heard many stories about Moldova, and regretted not visiting the place when I had the chance.

I arrived in Prague early one Saturday evening in June of 1992, refreshed from all the free food and booze provided on the free British Airways flight, and prepared to pay over the odds for decent accommodation. I found a promising information desk and explained that I was looking for a furnished apartment for one week and, if it was too late to find one that evening, I would stay in a recommended hotel and look the following day. To my astonishment, I was presented with a key and the address of a large central apartment, along with instructions on how to get there by tram. The cost worked out at less than £8 a night, payable there and then at the desk; when I left the following weekend, I simply had to leave the key in the flat and pull the door shut. They also provided me with detailed city maps and tickets for what turned out to be very efficient public transport, so that I didn't even need to take a taxi to get there.

On reflection, this accommodation would have been ideal had I known where to find boys willing to come back for the night, or even for a short time. Such boys would certainly have existed at this time and I did my best to find them by going to a well-known gay bar and making my interests known. I was introduced to a young gay Englishman who had no problem with my tastes, except they were not his and thus he could not help much. I can see him now, a true liberal whose motto was "C'est interdit d'interdire", which he repeated a few times over the course of the evening. I also wasted a couple of evenings checking out addresses of Czech peds in the suburbs, none of whom proved to be at home – though the information was probably out of date too.

The pools, however, were another matter, with an even more relaxed attitude than in Denmark. For example, Danish boys would get embarrassed about erections and often seek to cover them. Not so here, where even fourteen-year-olds scarcely seemed to notice them.

So, all in all, it was a pleasant week of good cheap food and conversation with my "c'est interdit" friend most nights. He was keen to know how I'd got on, and seemed rather disappointed at my lack of progress.

The lack of hands-on sex was more than compensated for by a trip to Bucharest a few months later, but, before getting on to that, there were some disturbing developments in the UK which I at first dismissed as being something which had no connection with me. It started with the raid of my friend DB in Beckenham in 1991, which seemed to happen out of the blue – he wasn't someone I was that close to and, as far as I knew, he didn't have my contact details.

Apart from some hard-core porn, what the plod seemed most delighted to find was a hand-written letter from Francis Canning in Alexandria, which concluded with a paean of recommendation for the city: "Alexandria is a city of boys, 99% of whom are available." I had thought that with Francis out of the country he would represent a small risk as far as my own chances of being turned over were concerned. However, from the way DB was questioned, it was clear that Francis was more than ever a person of interest in Britain, and may well have been the reason that DB was targeted. Early the following year, I met Francis when he was over for a brief visit, and he was equally mystified at the sudden interest. No one knew then that a sociologist friend of his, Peter Righton, had recently been in trouble, initially for importing soft porn through the post from Amsterdam. He'd kept many diaries detailing his liaisons with partners of many ages, but mostly mature mid-teens, including a couple of Francis's boys who used to go to his house in Evesham for weekends – much to Francis's annoyance at the time.

I'd vaguely heard of Peter Righton, but could never guess that, because of his "position of trust", his case was to become a major investigation into all single men working with boys in boarding schools and other such institutions. There had recently been a huge scandal at a school called Crookham Court, which had even led to social workers coming into my place of work and lecturing staff on "signs of abuse to look for in vulnerable children" and other such nonsense – the earnest ladies received short sharp shrift from me! So, I suppose it was only a matter of time before the Scotland Yard vice squad had the fun of their lives opening as many cans of worms as they could, as their computers randomised contacts between known and unknown sexual offenders. In the course of the next three years, these arbitrary raids became more frequent, though a vague pattern became discernable. By late 1993, it was clear that sooner or later they would get round to me and the need for one's house to be squeaky-clean became more and more urgent. Until you actually experience these thugs desecrating your home, you can have no idea of their degree of malice and prejudice, their desire to inflict hurt and their single-minded hatred of anyone whom they suspect may possess good taste.

The last significant Eastern European jaunt I made before leaving the UK altogether was the aforementioned one to Bucharest. I had met a few people who had been to Romania and heard of many more, including a lorry driver who used to enjoy the company of several young companions while travelling through the country. Unlike Prague, this was a trip which would need some careful planning to find the right form of accommodation, as well as the best places to go "cruising" and items to take with you. Video games such as *Tetris* on the Game Boy Tetris, along with a Rubik's Cube, could be relied upon to keep a boy entertained for some time, but more fundamental than this was the need for decent clothes.

Thanks to Nicolae Ceaușescu's rigid stance on abortion and contraception, there were many young people choosing to live rough on the streets, some actually finding this preferable to staying in orphanages. This meant that many of the boys possessed only the filthy rags they wore from day to day, though this was by no means always the case, especially as they became more established in their trade. Some boys, normally introduced by others who had decided that you were a "safe" foreigner and worth knowing, had become extremely sophisticated with their diaries and Filofaxes with which they would make appointments for weeks ahead.

I find it hard, in retrospect, to comprehend just how much we managed to pack into those eight October days of my final half-term holiday of 1993. I was travelling with JDT, already mentioned in connection with Charles Douglas and Agde, and we were well-prepared with special treats and suitcases full of clothes and blankets, mostly donated by my local Romanian charity shop, a chain which became Link to Hope.

I felt this trip would be different and interesting even before we boarded the Tarom flight (one of the few short-haul journeys I didn't make with Air Miles). Passengers were talking to each other at the boarding gate, and someone asked JDT in a friendly way why he was going to Bucharest, which was considered unusual as a holiday destination. He replied that he was studying the language and was, fortunately, not then required to compare linguistic competence with his interlocutor. I also noticed quite a large school group and hoped they wouldn't be sitting too far away.

Fortunately, this group was only three rows up from us, and I was immediately drawn to a stunning-looking boy of about thirteen who was imitating the stewardesses as they were giving the safety instructions in Romanian, and generally seemed to be a charismatic and delightful character. I noticed that the seat next to him was empty, and, bold as I was in those days, found myself sitting next to him almost as soon as the seat belt signs had been switched off.

Far from being suspicious, as an English boy might have been, he was delighted that I should choose to sit with him and chat: his English was excellent and he was very open and friendly. His name was Bogdan, he'd been staying in an English prep school as part of some sort of exchange scheme, he loved England and was sorry to be returning so soon to his own country and, yes, he'd love to meet me in the city and show me round. After a good thirty minutes of stimulating chit-chat, I decided to return to my seat to give him some space to be with his friends, and he gave me his address and phone number.

Our first night in the city was spent in a hotel, but on the second day we made a determined effort to find a flat where the owner did not live too close-by. We'd been given the name of an agency who'd found something suitable for a mutual acquaintance of ours and, after viewing some clearly unsuitable places, we were taken to a large spacious apartment where a family were living – grandmother, mother, father and two girls aged twelve and thirteen, whom JDT, who swung both ways, took an immediate shine to.

The idea was that we would pay the family for a week, in cash, and they would move out, leaving the place exactly as we found it. After some friendly chat, in which JDT helped the girls with their English homework, they decamped, presumably to a relative's house, and I went out to explore local shops and was astonished to be able to buy pleasant bread, cheese, salami and good wine at ridiculously cheap prices.

Later that day I went exploring, and from a known pick-up point outside one of the larger luxury hotels an attractive boy immediately responded to my appreciative glance, eagerly joining me in a taxi back to the flat. As with the first lad I met in Lisbon, he turned out to be a regular for the week, and a most useful fixer. However, no sooner had he departed with plenty of money, new clothes and promises to bring back other boys to the flat than the doorbell rang. It turned out to be the girls that JDT had taken a shine to; they must have formed the impression that he wanted to see them again. It was a narrow escape, and after he'd spent twenty minutes or so "teaching" them English, they had to be shown the door with clear instructions from JDT that they shouldn't come back: the message was received and understood and luckily that was the last we saw of them. Although I suspect JDT had a minor regret or two, this was more than made up for by the fun we had that week.

Several delightful boys were brought to visit us, and some I encountered on the street. It was the latter who were usually happy to stay the night, although most seemed to have achieved a level of independence to the extent they did not pretend a huge affection which they did not feel. On one occasion our mischievous fixer arrived with rather a beautiful companion whom JDT immediately took into his room. Master Fixer was smirking away, and told me that my friend was in for a big shock as it was "not a boy". In the event, JDT was delighted at the discovery, and Master Fixer's joke fell rather flat.

There was one rather sophisticated, freckled lad. He had tolerable English, was dressed like an English prep school boy and had a sort of self-assurance to match. He told us he'd been "at it" for some time; he knew many men in the city and produced an appointments diary for his next visit to us. As there were only a couple of days left and we were uncertain of our movements, we said we'd let him know through Master Fixer.

Somehow, JDT and I found time to explore the city together, checking for example whether the swimming pools were of any interest – they weren't. We trolled the main station too, which proved disappointing as a pick-up place, though JDT thought he'd hit it lucky when he gestured to a pretty boy of about thirteen to follow him, which he did. It then became apparent to me, as a spectator, that the boy was not alone, and that the man with him was probably his father, as he called out his name, along with a sharp question in Romanian: "Vlad, what are you doing?" I quickly apprised JDT of this situation and we both beat a hasty retreat.

I spent an interesting few hours one afternoon visiting Ceaușescu's huge palace and hearing stories and opinions from local people. It is hard to imagine a national leader more universally reviled by his own people.

Meanwhile, Bogdan had not been forgotten and we arranged to meet twice in different parts of the city. In a sense it was pleasant to meet an ordinary boy and be able to chat about his life in Bucharest. It could be argued that the more unfortunate lads who found themselves living rough weren't any less ordinary, but communication with most of them was far less easy, and of course sexual contact with most of them was assumed.

One or two clearly didn't have a clue about the sex and it wouldn't have seemed right, but they were very responsive to affection in the form of hugs and kisses.

I felt certain that Bogdan was aware of my attraction towards him, and that he was curious about it. He certainly didn't find it strange or off-putting, and of course I did nothing to intimidate him. For our third, and probably last, meeting he was keen that I should visit him in his home. He assured me that his father would be out, and that we would have some time alone together.

When I arrived, dad had clearly changed his plans, understandably keen to know who this curious British man who was interested in his son was. Bogdan stood behind his father as I entered their apartment and gave me a somewhat exasperated, apologetic glance. The next hour was not at all awkward however, and I felt I'd passed some sort of test, especially as his son seemed so relaxed and happy in my company. Had I been staying longer in the city, I'm sure there would have been no problem seeing Bogdan alone.

When the time came to go, we exchanged full addresses and telephone numbers, and there was a brief correspondence as well as an exchange of Christmas cards. This was rudely cut short by events in March 1994, and I still bemoan the sudden ending of a promising friendship. Just before leaving him, I decided to give him ten dollars – a paltry sum for me, but a fortune in Romania at that time. Bogdan's father did not want his son to accept the money at first, but it didn't take too much persuasion for him to change his mind.

JDT and I agreed that things were becoming out of hand in the apartment, and we had no way of knowing how much of our activity had been clocked by the neighbours, or if we might suddenly get a knock on the door from a disgruntled older brother – or worse. So we left a day early and stayed the final night in a good hotel, before catching the mid-morning flight back to Heathrow. It had been a remarkably successful few days, and a trip we would have been able to repeat, as it took some time before the country would be spoiled by the do-gooders and sensational documentary-makers.

So I returned to my busy routine in the UK, with my usual pre-Christmas trip to Copenhagen which was great fun, as usual. Various factors had convinced me that I wanted to live in Denmark for at least a year and I started exploring employment possibilities. Some sort of job would be desirable, though I would go there willy-nilly, even if it meant washing up and playing honky-tonk piano in some lowlife nightclub. As far as Denmark was concerned, there were many positive reasons I wanted to relocate, and the negative reasons for wanting to leave England were mainly concerned with my job and a new, diminutive Welsh headmaster who didn't have a clue how to run a school. It was obvious that, within two years, all that had been built up by his predecessor would disappear, and the place would become mediocre at best. The first indication of this was the decision to take girls, not for ideological reasons, but because pupil numbers were falling and this would be a quick temporary solution.

Funnily enough, I hadn't appreciated just how dangerous Britain was becoming for people of good taste and their friends and associates. I still thought that if you hadn't done anything in the country or been arrested in the past, you were pretty safe from police raids. My swimming pool incident of 1986 was long buried. I had discovered that the file containing the papers relating to the case would have been destroyed after three years, and there were of course no digital records. And there had been nothing else. Nevertheless, it rapidly became apparent towards the end of 1993 and the beginning of the following year that something strange and deeply sinister was going on and I no longer felt safe in my flat.

Early in 1992 Bruce had given Ted an ultimatum: either he pay rent for his share in the Surbiton house or he find somewhere else to live. Such was Bruce's disappointment with Ted's role as provider. Ted went to live in a large tower block in Camden Town, where he was joined some months later and fifteen storeys higher by Peter C., after his hurried retreat from Bangkok. Peter had returned to the UK for a couple of reasons, the first because he'd been told he could apply for free housing and was running out of money. Secondly, and more significantly, he'd heard that the New South Wales police were looking for him in Bangkok over some rather dubious business dealings.

From the exterior the building looked run-down and grotty, but the flats were pleasant enough and well-sound-proofed and, amazingly for their location in a colourful part of London, the apartments in this block were rent-free. I was a frequent visitor, either driving, there being plenty of free overnight parking in those days, or catching a number 24 from Victoria station.

The first shock was Ted getting raided towards the end of 1993 for no apparent reason. He would *later* ingratiate himself with a large Bangladesh community, and have all sorts of fun and games with a number of young friends. Though the police found out about this too, their investigation would come to nothing as no one would talk to them. However, at the time of his raid he was squeaky-clean. There was even cause for amusement, because Peter had given Ted a large number of snooker tapes for safe-keeping in his garage, Peter's flat not having one – about half the number which I'd given to Peter in Bangkok, representing many, many hours of snooker action. Given that Scotland Yard had to go through every inch of videotape which they seized, they would have wasted a lot of time looking for hidden naughty bits in these tapes: snigger!

Bruce was also raided twice. The first time, in the summer of 1993, it was more of a routine visit without a determined, thorough search of the premises. Bruce had hidden important material in the garden, including my copy of Bradbury Robinson's *Young Thomas*, which I had recently acquired but had not got round to reading. Much to my annoyance, he, in a panic, then destroyed this photocopy, which I had painstakingly made in Worthing library. I was unable to make another, as the person I had copied it from had returned it to its owner, a distinguished organist in a London cathedral. It would be twenty-six years before I was able to read this book in its original form.

In January 1994 Bruce was raided again: a more determined search which included the garden. He didn't know the reason for either of these visits, but concluded that it had something to do with events in Australia. Fortunately, Bruce had rid himself not only of the Bradbury Robinson book but of anything remotely incriminating. He still had a dramatically-acquired passport in a false name, but with his photo, for "emergencies", but that was safely lodged in his bank. Mildly worrying was that they had taken his address book, and I knew he had my details in it.

Things were hotting up as the spate of raids increased and I was hearing more and more stories of friends of friends getting raided. The wonderful free democracy in which I thought I had been living appeared more like an ugly dystopia in which dissidents could disappear in the night for "thought crimes". Indeed, Bruce had planned to greet raiding officers, should they ever come, with the words "Ah, it's the thought police," but of course, in the heat of the moment, never did. One evening I received a chilling international phone call from Francis informing me that motorbike man Kevin, AKA the big domino, had had an early morning call from six detectives, and I knew that it wouldn't be long before they got round to me.

From being a pretty heavy sleeper who found it difficult to get up in the mornings, I was now always showered and dressed around 6.30 each morning, ready for the dreaded ring of my doorbell at 7. I put important things in my pockets: small address book, passport and such like, as I learned that they didn't search you – the warrant being for the household only. It was always a relief when seven o' clock came and went, and one knew one was safe for another day.

I had a fair collection of priceless material, which I was loath to lose. At this stage everyone knew that I intended relocation to Denmark, and I had already handed in my notice, so, deviously, I asked Joy, my lovely cleaning lady, if I could store some precious things in her attic so that "they didn't get mixed up with stuff that I would be throwing away". Though she was happy about this, I felt bad about leaving a large caseful of illegal material in her house, but I could honestly think of no other solution, as banks and lockups required much paperwork which I wouldn't want police to find.

I also discovered some possible employment opportunities in Denmark, including the Tvind boarding schools, which were controversial and paid very badly. Nevertheless, I was rather put out when Thomas Daff of the hidden camera, who was also keen to move to Denmark, went and got himself a job in one of them, after I'd told him I was interested in exploring them. He stayed several months, enjoying the huge affection of the unusual kids there and filming in swimming pools most days. Daff, as will be remembered, found it impossible to have a job or friendship and not argue fiercely about something. He objected to some of the jobs he was given to do in this egalitarian community, such as sweeping the floors, so it was agreed that he'd be better off returning to England. With my skills, however, there was a possibility of a serious music job in one of them, so I retained the Tvind schools in my shortlist of chances of a decent job.

From extensive research, I narrowed my options down to three possibilities:

1) Just one Tvind school that was situated some way out of Copenhagen, but that took music very seriously and already had an Englishman coaching their wind band who was paid a decent hourly rate. After my initial approach, I had quite a few telephone conversations with the head, who, uniquely amongst the people I contacted, was very curious as to why I was eager to move to Denmark. I had the most plausible story ready, namely that I had a Danish girlfriend, but, under the head's questioning when I finally visited the school, I was to make it somewhat implausible.

2) A variety of *aftenskoler*, or adult evening classes, where I would be able to do instrumental teaching on a variety of instruments, either in groups or individually, paid on an hourly basis. These schools were dotted about the capital in various *kommuner*, and, I learned, pupils might enjoy the kudos of being taught in English.

3) The regular state schools were not feasible until I'd learned Danish to a pretty high level, but there were two excellent international schools which I had nothing to lose by exploring.

In the meantime I was endeavouring to teach myself Danish via the Linguaphone course, which I completed, and expensive private lessons every Tuesday afternoon, my half day, in London. As part of this, the teacher lent me videos of a long classic Danish TV soap opera, *Matador*, with Danish subtitles which I was able to copy bit by bit. I also rewatched Lasse Nielsen's *Du er ikke alene* and found that I was able to pick up more and more of the dialogue.

The spring term ended quite early that year but Karen had entered the choir for a national competition, which meant I had to be back for the second week of the holidays to play for it. So, no sooner had term ended than I was off to Copenhagen for my usual fun on March 19th. Only this time I had managed to arrange three interviews in the different institutions outlined above, so I had to pack a suit!

The most promising had seemed to be the Tvind school, where they were keen to have me but not to pay me too much. I met the charismatic English wind coach, who was quite enthusiastic about the school, and met a lot of the students who were different in a pleasant way. I was staying, as usual, in the youth hostel, which was surprisingly comfortable as well as being affordable, with excellent cooking facilities. The astute Tvind head was clearly curious about why I was not staying with my girlfriend, as he'd asked for a phone number in case he wished to contact me. On the spur of the moment, I made up some story about her being in a wheelchair, which at least stopped the head asking questions, but hardly satisfied his curiosity.

The *aftenskole* I visited seemed well-organised, if not very stimulating and was the option I least favoured, except for getting a foot in the Danish door.

Surprisingly, I had managed to secure an interview with one of Denmark's best international schools, Copenhagen International School, which went tolerably well. I was able to show the American principal some of my compositions for children's orchestra and choir, about which she made intelligent and perceptive comments. I discovered that she was leaving, along with the present music teacher, because of the curious tax situation in Denmark for Americans. The first two years they enjoyed complete tax-free status, but then they were suddenly taxable at the full rate – effectively halving their salary. Consequently, the turnover for US citizens at the school was very high.

On the last day of this trip, Thursday 24th March, I was not going to go straight back home, but had planned to call in on Bruce in Surbiton because he had an unusual dinner guest. Kevin had been invited round because Bruce, having heard of his raid, desperately wanted to know whether the fuzz had seized the videotape which he let Kevin partially copy of him enjoying a bit of weekend fun with Stephen. Some months beforehand, Bruce had implored Kevin to get rid of it with all the raids happening but, despite Kevin's assurances that he had, Bruce had had his doubts. The purpose of the dinner was to make clear to Kevin that Bruce didn't mind whether he had disposed of it or not, but just needed to know, as it would affect his plans.

After a smooth early evening flight, I turned up towards the end of the dinner, and witnessed Kevin affirm that the cops had *not* got the incriminating tape. Bruce was insistent and followed up with, "Are you absolutely sure, Kevin? I do not blame you if you'd kept it, but I just need to know." Needless to say, Kevin *had* kept the video and the lie was to have catastrophic consequences for Bruce six months later.

After an hour or so it was time to go, and Kevin offered me a lift back to my flat. It was the first time I had seen him since his raid and we had a lot to catch up on.

We talked until about 3.30 in the morning, and I had details of his whole ordeal, including amusing banter the mindless filth had exchanged, such as, "'Ere, Serge, there's a drawer 'ere without any porn in it …" How ironic that this day, Friday 25th March, was to be the day when I would receive the early-morning seven o'clock wake-up call, after going to bed at 4 a.m. and not having even unpacked my bag, not to mention got ready for the possible invasion.

It is impossible to describe the sinking feeling of foreboding, which has remained with me whenever I think of that moment when the front door bell went.

At first there were only two of them, Constable Flanagan and Sergeant Passingham, who were to feature in many subsequent raids in what was code-named Operation Clarence. Apparently, they had tried to ring me the previous evening, but evidently before I arrived back with Kevin. Constable Flanagan used my phone to ring for reinforcements, and pretended the police had been tapping my phone with the comment "I had better get us off it!" Passingham considerately handed me my large address book which lived by the phone, so I could make a note of important telephone numbers and addresses before they seized it. What they did not know was that all my important numbers were recorded in a much smaller book which would normally have been safely in my trouser pocket by 7 a.m., when I would also have been fully dressed.

I had been strongly advised by Peter C. to avoid any sort of conversation with the pigs, but this proved easier said than done, as they clearly had all sorts of techniques for loosening the tongue. When I was asked how long I'd lived in the flat and I remained silent, Flanagan regarded me with something like irritation: "It's easy for us to find out, you know!" During the course of the raid, they deliberately asked leading questions such as, "How long have you been abusing boys in Denmark then?" the denial provoking me into saying far more to them than I needed to. When the two reinforcements arrived, they uttered not a word, so it was Flanagan and Passingham who took centre stage, for example taking it in turns to play good cop/bad cop.

I did not now have in the flat any examples of what they were looking for, and was able to answer confidently their first question: "We are looking for indecent images of anyone under the age of eighteen, or *apparently* under this age. Do you have any such material?" But as the search progressed, their attitude became steadily more hostile: "You were expecting us, weren't you?" and "You have moved your stuff, haven't you?!"

My bassoon was standing in the corner of the living room near the doorway and Flanagan joked that it would be a simple matter to smash it up, but for the fact they weren't allowed to do such things anymore and the Metropolitan Police would have a large bill to pay. As with Kevin, they kept picking up objects and asking, "What's that worth then?" They also found letters addressed to my mother's flat and wanted to know if I had two addresses. Passingham even demanded a cup of coffee when I made one for myself, but then didn't drink any of it.

Around 9 a.m., the post came, and they could see that one of my letters was a phone bill. It was from a new company, Mercury, that claimed to be the best value on the market and itemised every call. They immediately seized that, as it listed, amongst the many UK calls, all the calls I had made to Denmark as I phoned prospective employees. One of the "silent" cops drew Flanagan's attention to a brochure from Agde because, along with the many naked pictures of adults, there was the odd one of a child, which I had thought nothing of. The other silent one pointed out the number of Thai visas in my passport, which I would also have had on my person, if I had been properly prepared for the invasion. But at least they did not take the passport away as they did, completely illegally, on subsequent raids of church members. I'd even bought a copy of *Mayfair*, so when Flanagan asked me if I had pornography in the place, I was able to point it out, with the comment "I don't suppose that is illegal, is it?" He gave me a quizzical look: "No, it isn't."

It did not take them long to find my small address book where all my important names were listed, including Bogdan in Bucharest. I had long ago listed my cleaning lady's phone number in it, and had deemed it wise to tear the page out, without considering that there was no surer way of drawing attention to it. They immediately focused on this: "Why have you torn this page out?" And for the first time in ninety minutes, they managed to frighten me, as they would not let the subject drop: "You might as well tell us because a forensic test back at the Yard will soon reveal all the data you've tried to hide from us."

By now they were convinced I was hiding something somewhere, and they were determined to find it. After two and half hours of searching in the flat and car, and filling umpteen plastic bags with videos, photos, correspondence and various miscellaneous items, including my childhood diaries and an intimate diary from university which they never returned, they told me they wanted to search my office in the school. This involved signing a piece of paper "to save time" as otherwise there would be a delay while they got a magistrate to authorise it, and naturally you want to get rid of them as soon as possible.

They were delighted when they found in my school cupboard my camera, containing undeveloped photos of my Romanian holiday, more letters, including some from Scott in a German prison, and various Danish videos which I was using to help me understand the language better. Amongst these was my teacher's copy of *Matador*, and the seventies classic *Du er ikke alene* which got them very excited – I subsequently discovered that this was top of a list of films which "paedophiles" were likely to own. Flanagan, much happier now, asked me if there was anything in the movie likely to be incriminating, and I replied: "Well, there's a shower scene."

"What? We're not interested in shower scenes! Look at the famous one in *Kes*, do you think we'd prosecute people who owned that?!" At which I shrugged my shoulders.

Believing me to be well stitched up, they then became more affable and personal. Flanagan, his voice full of concern, asked me if I had ever been abused as a child. Passingham told me that they weren't really interested in me but, if I could give them information about my associates, they would leave me alone – to which he received a blank look. Referring back to the Agde brochure, Flanagan virtuously asserted he went to France for the good weather and the food, and then questioned me about my trips to Thailand: "Do you go by yourself or with another man?" and then, "Do you realise how wrong it is to exploit poverty?"

He also wanted to know why I had not expressed more surprise at their visit. "It's because you knew we were coming," he reiterated. "How did you know?"

He referred again to the address book, which he was keeping in his jacket, as top priority, saying that the Yard would deal with it first. "Come on, who is the person that you don't want us to know about?" I finally made up a plausible name which seemed to satisfy him.

When they at last dropped me off at my flat, the first thing I did, although I was utterly drained, was to go round to Joy's house to retrieve the suitcase. This was muddled thinking, inspired by worry that, as they said they could, they would find out that day who the names were in the torn section by studying the imprints on the two other pages around it. If they'd been cleverer, they might have waited and followed me; as it was, I was informed by a neighbour that Joy and her husband were away on holiday and would not be back until the following Tuesday – agonising!

Later on that day I was to discover all the small malicious bits of damage that the pigs had done, just to let me know what they thought of scum like me. These included cutting the cords in my car so that the hatchback wouldn't open, and ripping the pockets of three of my jackets.

I sank to floor in despair. I had a meeting about the choir competition with Karen at lunch time, the reason I had returned from Denmark early and, as there would be a parent there, I must be as professional as possible. Not easy in the circumstances.

Later on there would be much to sort out, and with so many uncertainties, I felt completely overwhelmed.

*   *   *   *   *

The only thing that Stephen wrote for this memoir after this episode was the titles of the remaining chapters and the description of Edmund and Tancred Marlowe given in Chapter XIV, besides documents written long before which he intended to include in Chapter XII. The editor has tried to fill in some of the rest of Stephen's story from their correspondence. He quotes from Stephen where possible and tries to recount events from Stephen's point of view, but he is unwilling to invent speech by Stephen, so the rest of the story has had to be told in the third person.

In his correspondence, Stephen concluded the story of "one of the worst days of my life" as follows:

A couple of hours after the filth had finally left me to clear up their mess, the phone rang asking me to confirm a request for full information about the recipients of all the telephone calls I'd made. They'd taken my latest itemised bill and wasted no time!

Magistrates issued search warrants at the drop of a hat in those days (perhaps they still do). All the police needed to say was they had firm grounds for believing such and such was a serious danger to children because of his associates, and that was enough.

They voiced suspicions that I might have moved my "hoard" to my mother's place, and, I learned later, were annoyed I left the country three months later, having at least been able to keep my passport. That might explain why they were even harsher in subsequent raids, confiscating passports et cetera, as happened to a friend of mine a year later who claimed that they broke every one of their own guidelines. My friend had to sign a permission slip for them to raid his parent's place too, or, again, wait a further few hours while they obtained another warrant.

Meanwhile, Feltonfleet learned that Stephen had been raided and the reason for it. He agreed to leave the school immediately, though he was paid for a while afterwards. He never had further contact with Karen.

Once the police had examined all the booty they had seized from Stephen, they must have discovered none of it was illegal, so no charges were brought against him and he was able to depart for what would prove to be twenty-two years in gentler lands.

XI. Denmark

Fortunately, no word of Stephen's ordeal spread to the schools in Denmark where he had applied to teach and he was given the job he wanted most, at the Copenhagen International School. He found teaching there stimulating and ended up staying in Denmark for five years, some of the happiest of his life.

Mostly, of course, this happiness was occasioned by the ease with which Stephen could meet naked boys in swimming-pools and find ones enthusiastic for sex: fifteen-year-olds, legally unproblematic but near the upper limit of what strongly attracted him, as well as younger ones. To this time belongs the incident to which Stephen alluded in the "Interlude", when he went to a boy's house to "greet his parents as the man their son has just picked up in the pool."

To give an idea of the effect such encounters had on him, here is what he said about one with a boy called Hendrik:

> If I tried to rewrite that extraordinary Danish encounter I'd have to relax completely into myself and recapture the unique ecstatic frame of mind which remained with me for days and days afterwards.

Staggeringly liberal as Denmark was compared with Britain, he did, however, run into trouble. The first was after he had been there about three years. He had a lesbian colleague whom he found so sympathetic a friend that he foolishly (as he later saw it) confided in her about his essential nature. This woman told everything to the school administration. After negotiations, he left the school with some months' salary in lieu of notice, and then claimed the generous Danish welfare benefits for his remaining two years in the country. By this time he was living in a tiny flat he had bought near the main Copenhagen railway station and later sold.

After this, Stephen twice had trouble with the law. Both these "rows", as he called them, following Michael Davidson, arose from his swimming-pool voyeurism. Influenced by Daff's success, this had become more over-the-top and included filming.

Members of the public alerted pool staff to his suspicious behaviour. He was lucky to be fined only, especially when he repeated his offence. No detailed account of these rows is preserved, so it is worth reporting two observations Stephen made near the end of his life.

The first is that of the multitude of active boy-lovers he knew during the quarter of a century during which he was active himself (if voyeurism is counted as activity here), "not a single one avoided *some* sort of trouble, although of course the degree of trouble varied enormously." Such had become the unprecedented danger facing these men.

The second is that of all these men who got into trouble over dalliance with a boy, he did not know of a single case where the trouble started with a complaint from a boy. Always it was the result of investigation by police or journalists, or reports by informers, whether these were unknown observers or friends who were mistakenly trusted.

Today, when most people are as sure that it is right to inflict punishment (sometimes worse than that for murder) on men sexually involved with willing boys as the mediaeval inquisition was sure it was doing the right thing burning heretics, it is worth pondering for a moment what distant posterity will make of all this.

As regards voyeurism, might not our descendants think it a strange sort of serious crime when the "victim" doesn't know it is happening and doesn't suffer from it in any way?

Stephen's story, together with the few others that anyone has dared to publish in recent times, should make it clear that everywhere there was an abundance of pubescent boys eager to try out sex with men until society indoctrinated them into believing it was disgusting and severely threatening. What will people of a future age make of a society in which essentially the only boys to complain themselves about sex they had willingly engaged in are ones who come forward, usually long afterwards, after being cajoled into doing so by suspicious third parties, being offered strong financial inducements to present themselves as victims or having it hammered into their heads over long years by the media and everything else they hear that they "must" have been severely harmed, however willing, happy and excited they had felt at the time?

Here follows Stephen's account of how he came to know the distinguished sexologist Preben Hertoft. Hertoft was the leading Danish expert on sexual relationships between adults and minors, having edited (and written a sympathetic introductory chapter to) a book translated into English as *Crime Without Victims*, consisting mostly of his interviews of boys and men who had been involved in such affairs.

To put it briefly, it was my second row in Copenhagen and there was a good chance of my being sent to prison. To pre-empt this, I went to see my local doctor, who arranged "counselling" with Preben Hertoft. When the court case came up, it was deemed, as I'd hoped, that I was taking responsibility for my misdeeds and I escaped with probation – on condition that I continued, at the taxpayer's expense, to see Hertoft, as well as a female social worker who turned out to be a gas. One of the most understanding and accepting people I dealt with by far, she was fascinated by boy-love, which far fewer people then imagined they knew anything about, and kept begging me to tell her more.

From my excellent weekly sessions with Hertoft in 1998, I would say that he was a man of great integrity. We had many a lively discussion about why he chose to work in this area, where he spent as much time counselling married couples as he did exploring other relationships, which he regarded as of equal interest – "right or wrong" was never an issue.

He was also greatly respected by the Danish establishment, including medics, press and the police.

Much of the advice from Hertoft concerned the best ways to pick up fifteen-year-olds, "who can often look much younger" he said, in such places as shopping malls and swimming pools. "At fifteen, they are considered adults and can geeve you no trahble. No matter how loud their parents scream, it can't make the slightest difference!"

One amazing thing Hertoft tried to do for me was get some seized video tapes returned, as the police owed him a few favours. Unfortunately he was just too late, as they'd been destroyed.

Stephen's rows thus hardly had any unpleasant repercussions. He later observed that if he had had such serious trouble in Britain then, "It would have been all over the gutter press, but it didn't merit a mention in mid-nineties Denmark. It took a further seven years for all this to change there."

He also travelled in nearby countries before leaving Denmark:

Then there was the delightful boy seemingly waiting for me ten years later at the Tallinn ferry port, when I once made a day trip there from Helsinki. We spent the whole time together, and if I'd known even three words of Estonian I might just have been a teensy-weensy bit bolder.

XII. Turkey

In September 1999, Stephen took up a post teaching English in a boarding school in Istanbul. He was charmed by some of the cultural differences he had not encountered before: "It was sweet in Turkey to see boys walk around arm in arm, and happily kiss each other and their teachers."

Much later, he was to say of the boys he had known everywhere:

> In my experience over the years I have found it has been one *or* the other: lots of slap and tickle without commitment, or deep love which sex would somehow trivialise or even spoil. The latter cases are also the ones where I've tended to maintain the contact.

The most outstanding of these latter cases, the boy he loved most in his life and with whom he did indeed maintain contact until his death, was one of his new pupils in Turkey, a boy of twelve and a half named Isa Can. Writing much later,

> I can picture him at the school I taught in, his arm unselfconsciously wrapped around another boy, whose arm would be around his, deep in some discussion as they amble along comfortably sharing each other's warmth. Such human intimacy is natural and healthy – all those boys would have been astonished at the idea there was anything remotely "gay" in open displays of normal affection.

> Isa told me that when he first laid eyes on me, with all the new staff, he knew we would be friends, and we have of course remained so. At the outset it was very intense and satisfying and brought out all my best characteristics, but the sexual dimension was not strong.

Here follows Stephen's much fuller account of the rocky first fourteen months of their friendship, of which he said: "I broke my own rules about never putting anything in writing."

*   *   *   *   *

AN EXTRAORDINARY STUDENT

When I first came to Okul I thought I had made a big mistake: the atmosphere was stifling, the buildings unfriendly and ugly and the administration inflexible and uncaring. There was *nothing* in my flat for many days – in short, it was the poorest welcome I had ever received. Three weeks of no school did not improve matters.

I was prepared to leave at the first opportunity when something happened to change my view. I had a skills lesson with class 7H and after it amongst the many students who came to talk – "What is my name?" et cetera – was a boy with short fair hair, quite dark eyes, a confident smile and a clear if somewhat nasal voice. He had written on his name card, "The best wishes from Isa, do not forget me until you are dead." He supported this with many – I thought at the time – typical student flattering comments about my appearance and manner. I replied, "I bet you say that to all the teachers," and was met with a flat denial: "No, I would not tell any other teacher he was sweet."

Over the next few days, Isa seemed to follow me everywhere – usually with a couple of his friends, and bombarded me with questions and kisses. These were not the normal sort of schoolboy questions about football teams or whatever, but deeper, thoughtful enquiries about myself: "I want to know all about your life," he said.

Whether or not he was being genuine, his attentions soon produced a strong feeling of love in me such as I have seldom felt for anybody. His intelligence, humour and liveliness combined with a sensitive, even rather fragile vulnerability awakened feelings in me I had long since forgotten about. In looks he was striking, reminding me of two students I had met at another school called Teoman and Bahri – mix them together and you would get Isa. So the obvious nickname for him became "Teori", or Theory in its English version. He seemed to approve of this.

For whatever reasons, the Okul administration does not seem to approve of friendliness between staff and students. I have heard numerous stories about teachers being asked to go because they got on *too* well with their pupils – no suggestion of any professional misconduct either. The feeling among the staff in that first year was, "Your job is to teach them English and nothing else" – and education is *so* much more than what happens in a classroom: an unnatural situation at the best of times.

Thus, the only chances I had to speak to Theory were in the classroom or the concrete "garden". No privacy at all – other students nearly always joining in – thus the conversation was normally fairly trivial. I had understood very quickly what an unusual boy Theory was: way ahead of his peers in terms of perception, general awareness and intelligence. I also sensed a huge sensitivity and empathy: the ability to tune into the feelings, moods and even thoughts of others. One morning I was walking along the corridor past his classroom – I was not feeling well in myself that day – a bit sad and detached – he immediately sensed this mood and said, "You're strange today." I thought I was smiling as usual, and had hardly uttered a word.

Anyway, I felt I wanted to know Theory better: find out what makes him tick – what his real opinions are, what makes him sad or happy, where his hopes and dreams are. He seemed happy in my company, and always when we talked together I felt a positive energy that was too important and urgent to be ignored. It was not something I wanted, or even particularly welcomed. It was rather disturbing, an added complication in my life, which was already pretty full of unwanted drama.

It seemed the natural thing to suggest we try and meet outside the school – away from the oppressive atmosphere, triviality of the other students and soul-destroying monotony of the Okul routine. Theory seemed keen to do this, and even said he might have time (if I did!) at the Cumhuriyet Bayramı: disappointingly, he phoned to say that family commitments prevented him from leaving the house.

This didn't prevent him from spending time with me at school whenever possible. He would always be waiting in the classroom at the end of the lesson: often with quite challenging questions to ask me such as, "If you could live in any period of history, which would you choose and why?" or, "Is there anything in your life you have not done that you would *like* to do?" Talking with him was a joy in a job I was finding increasingly tedious, frustrating and unrewarding. Kissing the teacher, too, seemed also a far more significant act for him than with most of the students. He almost made a ritual of it: "I won't kiss you now – I'll see you after the ceremony," or I would be leaving him and he'd say, "Haven't you forgotten something, Sir?" I never managed to get him to use my first name as children would in Denmark, but I suppose it would not have been right within the walls of Okul.

Then one, in itself unimportant, incident occurred within the classroom that appeared to change everything. I suppose it had been obvious to other students that I loved Theory more than any other – but he also happened to be by far the best student in the class. He always turned in excellent work, listened hard in lessons and contributed pearls of wisdom to class discussions. His essays were models of neatness and good organisation and the content was always interesting and thought-provoking.

The head of department had suggested a sticker system for rewarding good work, which I happily used. Competition for these stickers was fierce in 7H, and needless to say Theory *earned* the most, all the time. It would have been far easier if he didn't! Anyway, it was near Christmas and I was going back to England to celebrate the holiday. Normally I would've taken in the books and stuck the stickers in at home, but there wasn't time before leaving. So in the final lesson that day I went round the class giving out the stickers that students had earned, not really seeing how important it was for them.

Theory had amassed many stickers and after a certain number, I had decided to change to a slightly larger one for students with at least thirty. Seeing Theory receive these seemed to infuriate the class: the whole atmosphere instantly changed. What had been a responsive, fun group of pupils suddenly became hostile, restless, completely uninterested in the lesson and very hard to control. In the middle of this warlike atmosphere, I could see Theory looking wretched, disdainful (either of me or his peers – or both!) and hurt. Seeing this hurt me too – after the class he vanished quickly, while I fielded off a crowd of angry students accusing me of favouritism. That day was the end of what had been an excellent relationship with a class and its best student. I met Theory shortly after by the steps – he looked sad, but not cross with me: he said he had explained that *any* student who got thirty stickers moved on to bigger ones. "Kiss me," he said. That was also the last time he ever asked me to do that. Words cannot describe the misery I felt over something I had felt was just a routine class matter: the giving of stickers. How could it be seen as so important?!

After this in itself small and trivial incident, things were never quite the same, either with the class or with Theory. Even though I tried to explain to them (perhaps mistakenly) that in the class situation people get rewards by working well, not because I happen to like them, the students were for a time less responsive. Theory's work too noticeably deteriorated – as if he was sending a message to others: "Look! I don't crawl to Mr. N. See! I haven't done my essay this week – he's just a pathetic man anyway." He would still often wait behind after the lesson, but more in the background, part of the group – often just to say, "I have training now," or something equally boring. I sensed he wanted to talk, but was worried about his image and what other students would say to him if he were thought to be too friendly to Mr. N.

He also at this time began to develop a slightly unnatural arrogance, or "swagger" as I described it to him: maybe a defence mechanism against being hurt. The only time he really opened up again was towards the end of that year, when he asked me to send an email to one of his old teachers. He could easily have gone to a computer and done it himself – but the content of that letter revealed far more about himself than anything he had said to me since the sticker incident. I almost felt he was saying, "Look, my feelings haven't changed, but this place doesn't let me show them, so I am telling you like this." At the bottom of a "make-up" essay about jealousy, he also wrote, "Stephen – I <u>do</u> love you", something I would have ignored in most pupils – but felt Theory had written after thinking quite carefully.

When you love someone, you must also know when to leave them alone. This I tried to do with Theory. I couldn't control the way I looked at him, or how my eyes were, but along with my love was an enormous respect for *his* feelings, his personality, his way of dealing with life. In a way, this detachment made life easier – I could easily leave the school now without feeling I was deserting him.

But, so far, I'm still here and I do find time to talk to him. In some ways it is easier not being his teacher but just a friend, as he remarked in his essay about me. I do not know how much longer I will be at Okul, but I have a strong sense that in some way I will always be in touch with Theory. I think he has a marvellous career and future ahead of him, and I feel privileged to have known and taught such a remarkable human being. As he goes through the difficult, disturbing years of puberty, he will probably experience all the passions and traumas of being a teenager – that overwhelming intense sexual love for another that is often not returned, but will never be so important in his life again.

It will be interesting to see how he looks back on me. I suspect that as a young man he will forget me – or laugh with his friends about that crazy foreigner who said he loved him. As he reaches my age, his view may change again. My view of him will never change: he *is* an extraordinary student who will achieve greatness in whatever he decides to do with his life.

12ᵗʰ November 2000
  [Can it be essay of the year, Theory?]

*　　*　　*　　*　　*

A side story to the preceding concerns the old teacher whom Stephen emailed on Isa's behalf, Henry Stamp. Isa adored him and kept a photo of them together. As a result of Isa insisting Stephen contact him:

We had a lively email exchange and I slowly came to realise that he had been involved in the Crookham Court scandal alluded to earlier, and had been to prison before coming to Turkey.

There was clearly much hanky-panky occurring in this small Berkshire boarding school where, by amazing coincidence, I had been offered a job in the early eighties – how different my life might have been if I'd accepted. It was all exposed by that unbelievably evil scandal-mongerer-in-chief Esther Rancid (as *Private Eye* had her), causing her to set up her wretched "Childline" and changing the ethos of boys' boarding schools forever.

At the height of our correspondence, *The News of the World* started a massive naming and shaming campaign with photos, life histories et cetera; even the police disapproved of it. Stamp was comprehensively outed on the last Sunday of the campaign, at the end of my first year at Okul, and I never heard from him again.

Stamp was one reason the staff were so against closeness between pupils and teachers at Okul. The administration there was ghastly. Stamp also made comments in his letters to Stephen about the rigidity of the system, including its teaching methods. However, as Stephen was to recall:

The pupils were on the whole delightful. By the time I wrote this essay to Theory, I had rented a flat in Kadıköy where I was able to escape for weekends, and several of my favourite students came to visit me there. As the second year progressed things became more positive thanks to this element of freedom and I ended up being rather sorry to leave the school and often went back to visit. I offered to do part-time work there, but this was rejected.

The distancing between Stephen and Isa described by the former in his essay was soon overcome. Not long afterwards, "Isa spent hours and hours rattling off all sorts of nonsense, whilst I sat with both my arms firmly clasped round him feeling his emotions as if they were my own". Then a year and a day after writing the foregoing account, Stephen added to it with the following one:

TO:
SOMEONE SO SO SO SPECIAL

Is this important for "me"

It is true, I love the world more because you exist in it. But this is not about "me"; it is about objective appreciation and apprehension of the wonderful aspects of Life and Nature. It is numinous; it is outside of "me". It is an independent reality.

260

Because of you, beautiful music, art and sex have deeper resonance: the spirit that moves creative souls to produce magnificent and lasting works is more easily sensed, more closely perceived.

Seeing you, feeling your energy, I forget "me". With a new awareness of wonder, hope and "aliveness", I know that there is indestructible meaning amidst the temporal chaos.

For your life, I thank the benevolent force and source of all existence. You have been, and are. You cannot die. That is what is important.

16:55 Thursday 13th November 2001, Kadıköy.

The following anecdote evidently belongs to around this time:

When he was fourteen Isa was extremely serious about running away from his boarding school and coming to live with me, where *no* one would think of looking of course. One of the many snags to this plan was that he wanted to bring along his very naughty friend Halid, whom I nicknamed Fiddle – a joke based on his surname. Fiddle later invited me to his summer-house in Antalya where we shared a bedroom – but that's another story.

Isa was of course much better-looking than his friend, and I remember thinking at the time that this was a case of "the dish running away with the fiddle" (hey diddle diddle).

Isa later recalled that when he was fifteen:
"I was feeling particularly suicidal, and Stephen was the only person in the world whom I could relate to with an open heart. I hesitate to say my juvenile contemplation of suicide was rather of a philosophical nature but I remember how I was thoroughly swamped with emotional turmoil just at the unreasonable prospects of being alive. I would often tell Stephen in fits of melancholy how I was quite seriously pondering on ending my life because of all the complications of growing up in a time which seemed to me totally 'out of joint', to quote Hamlet, and the letter which follows was his kind and loving

reply to me just to keep my spirits high and remind me that the show must go on."

Stephen wrote:

<u>NOT</u> until:
1) You can speak at least ten major languages fluently, and have read the major literary works in those languages.
2) You have explored, understood and absorbed the ideas of the most important thinkers since the beginnings of Philosophy in Ancient Greece and India.
3) You have studied, perceived and felt the inspiration behind all the world's main religions, and can articulate why you think they are invalid.
4) You have made love to at least three hundred people who suit your ideals.
5) You have travelled extensively in the world, and experienced and empathised with many different cultures.
6) You have listened to and apprehended the world's greatest music, and felt its impact and message.
7) You have tasted the world's finest wines and most exquisite-tasting food.
P.S. and not before I'm dead!

Stephen showed both the "essay" of November 2000 and the "declaration of love" of November 2001 to Isa when he was about fifteen. When he left Turkey three years later, Isa wanted copies, but Stephen thought the risk of being incriminated as a result was too great.

Here is how the adult Isa was to regard their friendship in 2017:

Tele-jokes and video-smiles aside, you know what you mean to me as a guide in this "lost highway" of a galaxy … Indeed, you have always been a real northern star to this vagabond sailor for so many years.

I have been through times of incredible mental strain, stifling spiritual quest, and sometimes plain, ordinary adolescent confusion, and you were always there for me with a senior's patient wisdom for mindful orientation and amicable rehabilitation through music, literature, philosophy and your genuine humanity.

When I call you Captain, I do mean it with all the authentic trust of ancient mariners in each other against the vast darkness of the world's seven seas. In this fashion, you have indeed been a very reverend "First (and Last) Teacher" of mine. Wholeheartedly, I thank you for just being around. As a friend, as a true "meister"!

Though the most important thing in his life in Turkey, Stephen's essentially chaste love affair with Isa did not prevent him from having light-hearted erotic fun with boys who, as always for him, had nothing to do with the school he was teaching in:

The closest I came to a "scene" was in Istanbul when taking footage at a famous bathing place, and hitting gold. A rather plain boy of about fourteen kept insisting that I go off with him ("I have lovely cock" et cetera), but I was too interested in the lovely natural scene. I was also never short of obliging boys there anyway….

For amusement, a friend and I took a couple of his students (from a school for exceptionally gifted students – my God, some stories there) on holiday to İzmir once.

We all shared the same very large bed in the hotel, and it didn't take them long to work out what Mr. N. was about. One of them turned to me and said, with a wicked grin, "You're a boyeur, aren't you?!"

Nor were Stephen's amorous adventures during these years limited to Turkey. He could not travel to exotic lands nearly as much as before, as salaries were low in Istanbul, so much so that he was fairly hard up and dependent on the rent he received from the flat he still had in England. Nevertheless, he continued to travel a little more to the Far East:

> One of my happiest holidays was in Sumatra, the least spoiled part of Indonesia at that time (2001).
> My experiences there bear out what the locals said about not being suspicious of strangers and happily allowing their children to mix with anyone. Neither was sex any big deal; it was simply a source of fun. All boys up to about fourteen were starkers on the beaches. I must tell you one day about the things they loved doing in front of my video camera … Two fully-dressed women appeared at one point wanting to be filmed and were rudely pushed out of the way, much to their disgust.

He had gone to Sumatra to meet up with a man who had somehow got himself there following imprisonment in Britain over boys. This man had set up some sort of youth club for which he was forever pleading for funds and was last heard of in China where he had got into some terrible scrape and needed – surprise! – money.

On a quite different note, here is what Stephen had to say about "Anna, the beautiful blonde Swedish astrologer whom I worked with in Istanbul":

> She claimed in our early days of hanging out together to be "very clairvoyant" so I thought: that's alright then, I don't have to tell her anything. How wrong I was! She was convinced we'd shared at least one past life together and described in detail our simple shared existence in a log cabin. She also told me of techniques for recovering memories of former lives, which I never felt brave/stupid enough to try.

Presumably belonging to near the end of his time in Istanbul is the following anecdote, which he recounted in the context of mention of the future Prime Minister Boris Johnson's article in *The Telegraph* in 2006 expressing outrage over an incident on a

British Airways flight: a stewardess saw him sitting next to children and, not realising they were his own, ordered him to move elsewhere in keeping with the airline's policy of not allowing men to sit next to unaccompanied children.

Stephen dated his contrarily "lovely experience on Azerbaijan Airlines" to well afterwards, but said it was "on a flight back from Gatwick to Istanbul", which suggests otherwise.

Such a lovely fun boy, and a sensible mother who said "I don't believe in this not-talking-to-strangers nonsense. How's he ever going to meet anybody?" The mother was Georgian (perfect English) and the father was a Brit (not on the flight), and the boy was a jewel – full of mischief and fun. It started with me offering the boy my window seat and then sitting in the middle between mother and son; he'd been on the aisle seat originally. I normally hate this position, but on this occasion it made the flight go with a definite swing! I even got told off by the Azerbaijani stewardess – and that takes some doing. On another flight there was a bunch of young oafish Brits dancing in the aisle as the plane landed, and the staff made very little attempt to stop this.

XIII. France and Portugal

By the middle of 2006, Isa was nineteen, and Stephen moved on to teach English in the Pas-de-Calais department in northern France, in order to be nearer his ageing mother living on the south coast of England. He was there for two years, but nothing seems to have happened that stirred good or bad enough memories for him to think them worth recounting later to Edmund.

Then, in 2008, he accepted the offer of a teaching post at the British School in Oporto. Portugal was a country he called a "paradise" in the 1980s and 1990s, when he had been there. Not only had willing boys been easy to meet, as already related, but the attitudes of the "authorities", whether parents or police, had sometimes been astonishingly tolerant. The latter point is not clear from what he related of his own experience of those days, except in his story of EV. Two other stories from the same era that his friend Charles Douglas told him are therefore worth recounting, so that the depth of his disappointment with the Portugal to which he returned may be understood.

On one occasion, Charles and a friend were engaged with two twelve-year-olds in the back of a camper van in naughty, naked activities. To their horror, they were interrupted by a knock on the door. Hurriedly redressed, they found themselves faced by two policemen, apparently alerted by the shaking of the van. The latter, however, briefly peered in, laughed when they took in a rough idea of what had probably been going on, and explained that they could not park their van where it was and must move it on.

Another anecdote Charles told Stephen was of attending a party at the home of another boy of twelve he was enamoured of. He was puzzled by the hostility with which the father greeted him until, later in the evening, the man came up to him in a much friendlier mood and explained apologetically that he had earlier misunderstood that it was his wife rather than his son whom he had thought Charles was interested in.

The Portugal Stephen settled in half a generation later was sadly different. Worst of all was the school, where he encountered a conformity and fear of cultural diversity in lamentable contrast with his previous experience of teaching at the international school in Copenhagen. He did of course realise that, being British-run, it would have taken on board putrid British attitudes, as he had already experienced this when applying for the job:

I had to submit *four* references, and as I was on good terms with the referees, of whom Anna was one, I knew exactly what was asked: many questions about possible "proclivities" that only just fell short of:

"Have you any reason to suspect this man might fancy young boys or girls?"

"Has he ever seemed too friendly to children?"

"Have you ever witnessed him masturbating over naughty pictures of anyone under, or *apparently* under, the age of eighteen?"

"What sort of people (or animals) does he like to fuck?"

Oh, and by the way, "Do you think he's a good teacher?"

He was astonished, however, "to hear loud-mouthed pupils uttering 'paedophile' as a general insult, in the way that 'gay' used to be a general term of abuse a few years earlier. The disgusting behaviour to be observed there was, I'm sure, partly the result of resentment caused by forcing Portuguese children to abide by British codes of conduct, dress, et cetera."

Unfortunately, however, he found that Portuguese society as a whole had been contaminated to a ruinous degree. Portuguese boys were simply no longer open to sexual adventure with men, and he attributed it to their now being indoctrinated in the way British children long had been to be fearful and suspicious of strange men.

An incident that brought this home to him in his first year living in Portugal occurred on a train where he saw a beautiful boy of about thirteen standing alone. As had been his way since he became an active lover of boys, he gave the boy a friendly smile. Twenty years earlier, experience had already fully honed his senses to what was possible with a particular boy. He could tell from if and how a boy smiled back whether a conversation would be welcomed and if it was, as frequently used to happen, he soon just "knew" whether or not the boy was "on" for sexual adventure with him. In the present case, the boy reacted as he had never experienced anywhere before, with a look of such immediate and obvious hostility that Stephen was shaken to the core and beat a hasty retreat.

On reflection, this event ended his life as a potentially active boy-lover. He realised that not just Portugal, but the world as a whole had become hopelessly poisoned against men with his longings. Never again did he travel to distant countries with erotic hope in mind. Not only had boys been generally frightened off, but the means society had at last nearly everywhere adopted for spotting in its infancy and pre-empting any man/boy relationship that might nevertheless arise were so effective that mutual attraction could no longer practically be acted on without insane danger.

Though he could never escape hard feelings towards society for its injustice and inhumanity, he resigned himself philosophically to the new reality and sought other outlets for the harmony of his soul.

Stephen disliked the British School at Oporto so much that he gave it up after a year, but this time he did not seek another teaching post nor did he move country or even accommodation. He still considered Portugal a fine country to live in, albeit no kind of paradise. He did not mind living frugally, without heating in the winter and with only the cheapest boxes of wine, and for this his rental income from his flat in England sufficed without employment. He thus retired at fifty-two and led a peaceful existence interrupted by only one scare.

Stephen knew his old friend Francis Canning, whom he had not seen for many years, had become not only inactive with boys long before himself, but uninterested in them even as a subject. Nonetheless, due to a vindictive journalist, in 2013 Francis ran into new and severe trouble over his activities as a young man more than forty years earlier. Stephen was sufficiently frightened that their known former association might somehow lead to investigation of his own affairs, that when the time came for him to pay his annual summer visit to his mother in Worthing, he dared not leave his magnificent photographic collection unattended in Portugal and destroyed it all. This included a large amount of rare boy erotica and, most heart-breaking of all, the photos he had taken himself of the boys he loved and which had been bringing him such happy memories in his new, duller life.

Stephen's two greatest pleasures for the rest of his life were to be meetings with his several close and very long-standing, like-minded friends, with whom he reminisced about happier times, and literature. Most of what he read was fiction and biography at least vaguely connected to the topic of boy-love, and of this he was a great collector of rare books.

One of the authors he had always most admired was Michael Davidson, concerning which interest two things soon happened which were to have long-term consequences. First, he introduced himself to the writer and artist Colin Spencer, whom he knew from his introduction to Davidson's *The World, The Flesh and Myself* to have, as a young man, been one of Davidson's greatest friends. Spencer proved friendly; he was eager to talk about Davidson and to show Stephen his collection of Davidson's photos and unpublished writings. Stephen accepted his invitation to visit him and found him fascinating. As he later recounted, "Colin, despite being rather a sexual polymath, is entirely sympathetic; he also told me he'd had an affair with a boy of fifteen."

Next, Stephen was delighted finally to locate and buy a copy of the extremely rare and unexpurgated, American edition of Davidson's *Some Boys*, much sought by collectors. This brought him into online correspondence with Mark, an interesting young man who had been seeking the same book avidly but in vain. One day, they had an exchange on which writers on the subject of boy-love were friendly enough to exchange ideas with their readers. Mark mentioned an Edmund Marlowe who had written a novel he liked set at Eton and whom he'd found a friendly correspondent, "even though he's a toff."

At first, Stephen did not take seriously Mark's recommendation to read Marlowe's novel, *Alexander's Choice*, "as I have found few contemporary writers who are able to tackle this subject well: either it is an unrealistic Mills & Boon type fantasy or a condemnation. Generally too, the narrative is presented from at most two points of view." Soon, however, "I ordered it out of idle curiosity." Contrary to his expectation, he was immediately enthralled by it and promptly wrote to the author to say so. A lively correspondence about both the thinking behind the novel and wider literature on the subject ensued.

By this time, early in 2016, Stephen was already wondering whether he should move back to England, principally because his ninety-year-old mother was becoming incapable of looking after herself and needed his care. Then the plummeting of the pound in June following the disastrous outcome of the British referendum on leaving the European Union made living in Portugal much less attractive for him.

To cap it all, over the summer, he experienced terrible pains in his legs. As a man of robust health who had barely been near a doctor for decades, he was reluctant to take it as seriously as he should have and did not have himself tested until the autumn, by when cancer was suspected. With the upcoming results hanging depressingly over him, he spent November packing all his possessions up and left Portugal.

XIV. Nunc Dimittis

Stephen moved into his mother's house in Worthing, where she had lived for thirty-five years. It was also the area where he had been born and spent most of his youth, boarding school aside.

He was told the results of his tests for cancer the following week and they were devastating. He had left it too late to see a doctor and he had aggressive prostate cancer, which had already spread to his pelvis and lymph nodes, hence the leg pains. The best he could hope for was up to five years' remission. For the time being it was controlled through nasty hormone treatment, which amongst other things caused him to put on a lot of weight (so that he lost the fine figure he had hitherto enjoyed) as well as extinguishing his libido: "chemical castration", as he put it. Between February and June, he underwent chemotherapy.

The initial shock of knowing he had so little time to live was obviously profound and led to him to withdraw from most of his usual activities while he came to terms with it. But this, with his gentle philosophical nature, he was well-equipped to do.

Two months after the bad news, he was back in his stride, corresponding with his friends about literature and cinema, mostly still boy-related. He and Edmund now talked much more seriously about meeting in person, both eager to open their hearts to one another and talk without fear of the surveillance state. They finally met when Edmund came to London in June, just after Stephen had finished moving himself and his mother into more suitable accommodation in a bungalow outside Worthing.

Their brief evening together transformed them from lively correspondents to real friends, though neither of them anticipated quite how close a friendship it was to become when Stephen went to stay in Edmund's home in France in August. Edmund was certainty not, however, his only friend there. He joined in the life of the Marlowe family, became fond of Edmund's wife too and, in due course, all their children, though the elder ones were not there on his first visit. Unsurprisingly, the child he was most drawn to was Tancred, a good-looking, lively and sweet-natured boy of thirteen, and the only one young enough to be at home throughout the holidays. He did, however, say of Edmund's daughter, when he met her, that, "I can honestly say that if I'd ever considered marrying, gentle, intelligent and perhaps slightly vulnerable Penelope would have been my ideal soulmate."

"I realise now I had imagined I had reached a stage in life when I wouldn't make new friends of truly serious importance to me. How spectacularly wrong I was! I already miss you," wrote Edmund in his first email to him after he returned home.

"There are no words to express how much I value your friendship, coming so suddenly and unexpectedly as it has at this challenging time of my life," wrote Stephen.

From this time until just before his death, Stephen and Edmund corresponded nearly every day, and it is largely thanks to this that Edmund is able to fill in some of Stephen's life after 1994, though Stephen preserved his exciting stories for their personal reunions. Meanwhile, Tancred became, the next month, a new boy at a public school fortuitously not very far from Stephen's home, so Stephen was able to take him out for the day on several Sundays.

Stephen's ninety-two-year-old mother had been in severe physical and mental decline for two years and had to go into hospital in January. As a good and loving son, he visited her every day and cheered her up by playing the clarinet to her in her room. He knew the end could not be far away, but was nevertheless devastated to go into the hospital to visit her one morning and find her bed empty. No one had bothered to inform him that she'd died.

In his misery, he reread Edmund's account in *Alexander's Choice* of the main protagonist's mother's death when he was a boy at Eton, as he had found those passages especially moving. Stephen knew Edmund had based his account closely on his own mother's death when he was a boy and, for some reason, he looked up on the internet the date it had happened. He sat for ages, dumbfounded and yet finally not surprised, after finding their two mothers had died on the same day of February.

So fast did his friendship with the Marlowe family deepen that it seemed a matter of course that he joined them on their next family holiday, which was to Sicily the following March.

They began their wandering around the island with a stay in the pretty town of Taormina. A fishing-village until late in the nineteenth century, it had then become internationally fashionable for more than a generation through being the adopted home of the famous German photographer, Wilhelm von Gloeden, who spent many decades there loving and photographing the local boys. In one of those enigmatic examples of the tolerance and understanding often shown in gentler times to pederastic activity that was obvious and barely hidden, von Gloeden's sensual photos of nude boys posing in tasteful classical settings had become so widely admired that his visitors came to include, not just the men of the age best known for sharing the photographer's taste for boys, but international royalty.

Obviously aware that, well before he was born, the days had ended when the mayor's wife had acted as a match-maker, setting up visiting foreigners with suitable village boys for the duration of their stays, Stephen was nevertheless intrigued to investigate whether all memory of von Gloeden's days had been effaced in the new age of unmitigated social hatred of boy-love.

He and the Marlowes wandered through the sunny streets, enquiring amongst the great-grandchildren of von Gloeden's young friends as to the location of the great man's house, and finally discovered it had been turned into the police station! Heavy symbolism there, they would have thought, had not the occupants of the building already turned out to be quite different to their expectations. The charming policeman they ran into when they went in with their still-unanswered question had no idea they were all standing in the very place, so he helpfully telephoned his mother to ask where in the town it was, and it was she who revealed the truth to his evident delight. He enthusiastically promised to mention to the mayor of Taormina Stephen's suggestion of putting a plaque up to von Gloeden's memory. He also telephoned around to find out where they should go for souvenirs of von Gloeden, which turned out to be none other than the town toy shop, one room of which was a sort of von Gloeden museum shop, with prints of pubescent beauties strewn all over the walls. The proprietress was very happy to show them all she had, though unfortunately their poor Italian limited their search for knowledge.

From Taormina, they went to Catania in pursuit of other ghosts of the past. Michael Davidson had devoted one of the chapters of his evocative *Some Boys* to a vivid description of what he witnessed on the rocks beside Catania's beach of the "marathon of masturbation", whereby throughout the warms days of the year, dozens of naked boys could be seen openly wanking without the slightest sign of shame. There were no signs of the discothèques and other commercial venues that Davidson speculated might eventually be built over the rocks, but Stephen was sad to see that the rocks were likewise and more predictably barren of boys.

The other places they went to in Sicily were of more conventional interest, but it was during this time that Edmund convinced Stephen that he should write the book you are now reading.

True, as always, to his word, he began writing only a few days after his return home. The very first thing he wrote was a description of Edmund and Tancred. The editor has only reluctantly included the description of the former, since it is an embarrassingly over-sympathetic portrait of himself. He has done so simply because he has been following without exception the wishes of Stephen, who remained adamant that it should be in his last chapter, so here it is:

> He is gentle, considerate and though liberal-minded, a man of firm principles; of rare decency, honourable and trustworthy, ready to see the good in others whilst not being blind to their faults. Knowing that to be human is to be imperfect, you will rarely hear him criticise the weaknesses of others, though he will frequently chastise himself for lapses which even those closest to him would be hard-pressed to spot, let alone condemn.

He is intolerant of anything second-rate, especially where questions of logic are concerned. Be prepared to justify fully any remarks or judgements you are foolish enough to proffer without due consideration, as he will be quick to point out, in the most kindly way imaginable, any unsubstantiated opinions you may happen to let slip.

So whilst woolly thinking is never tolerated, he is less stringent with regard to smaller matters and adheres to a clear and consistent code of values. Issues of little importance, such as a person's dress sense or hairstyle, excite little or no comment. He is quick to forgive unintentional mistakes in others (though less inclined to condone his own) and, as a man of rare perception, is able to recognise the validity of points of view he does not share and can readily empathise with those whose circumstances differ markedly from his own.

His warmth and obvious integrity inspire total loyalty. He is someone upon whom you feel you can rely completely, and you would be demeaning yourself if you did not return his unconditional trust in the same free and open way it is conferred upon those fortunate enough to earn his friendship.

Do not be fooled by his gentleness: it conceals passionately-held convictions and a volatile artistic temperament which can erupt into a sudden, but generally short-lived burst of temper when affronted. His vilification of behaviour, beliefs or acts which arouse his sense of righteous anger can be frighteningly savage in its intensity, but always remains rational and rooted in his sense of what is right, just and fitting.

Above all, he is man of discrimination and fine taste. His thirst for knowledge along with a deep appreciation of beauty in both art and nature reflect the essential goodness of his soul. Modest about his extensive learning and achievements, he will only reveal the extent of his expertise when exploring any given topic to discover its worth and uncover its essential truth.

A devoted husband and father, he is happiest when at home surrounded by his loved ones, treasured books and artworks. He might not be the first person you would think of asking for help should you want to erect a set of shelves, mend a faulty tap or cook a gourmet meal, but I feel sure he would observe your bungling efforts from a safe distance and offer comforting words of encouragement and reassurance.

This is how Stephen described Tancred, who had then just reached fourteen:

Fun-loving and playfully mischievous, he is a person who brightens up your life merely by being in the same room. Although capable of deep thought and thoughtfulness, he will never allow himself to waste too much of his abundant energy pondering unfathomable mysteries. To him, life is a gift to be explored, savoured and experienced in the moment.

He is also a gift to life: one beyond price to his parents, siblings and those blessed enough to know him as a friend.

Of lively intelligence, he will seldom allow himself to be defeated by any task thrown at him and accepts challenges in a healthily competitive manner. When inspired by something, he will commit fully to it and is frequently harshly self-critical of his own achievements, knowing instinctively that though perfection is unattainable, its pursuit is always worthwhile.

Insatiably curious and unafraid to admit temporary ignorance on any topic, whatever its level of importance, he will often surprise you with questions which may alternately indicate unusual perceptive insights or surprising lacunae in his knowledge. Though it is not always easy, his questions demand full and honest answers.

Innately courteous, helpful and considerate of others, he exudes an easy self-confidence which is instinctively felt by all those fortunate enough to be in his presence. This self-assurance is not born of conceit or the desire to impress, but is the natural expression of someone entirely secure in his own skin and cognisant of his place in the world.

His accomplishments are already impressive: a competent linguist and classicist, a practitioner of martial arts and a nimble-fingered master of prestidigitation – it is impossible to see how he does those amazing card tricks.

No description of him would be complete without an appraisal of his physical attractiveness, which mirrors his sunny personality. It is sad that in these dark times many who are capable of appreciating such exquisite beauty are afraid to admit it, even to themselves. It is just because of its transience that this unique glory should be proclaimed and acknowledged by all who are brave and honest enough to recognise it.

He has reached that sublime stage in a boy's development when female and masculine qualities merge into a glorious miracle of perfection. His soft dusky skin, partially-broken voice and meltingly beautiful limbs all contribute to the androgynous marvel that is his lissom body. Glowing fine features, longish dark hair, a small nose and fulsome lips frequently forming a dazzling smile before breaking into infectious bubbly laughter, filling all who have ears to hear with joy. Joy that in a world sullied by so much ugliness, there still exist such bundles of charmingly innocent sophistication.

Stephen went to stay with the Marlowes four times during the rest of 2018, helping Tancred with his ambitious film projects, besides seeing the family during their brief visits to England.

He also resumed contact with Colin Spencer, who, it now transpired, was Davidson's literary executor and, aged eighty-five and in poor health, was anxious about what to do with Davidson's unpublished writings. Stephen was instrumental in bringing together Colin and Edmund, who shared their admiration for Davidson, leading to an agreement that Edmund would not only edit and publish Davidson's unpublished manuscript, *Sicilian Vespers*, and his correspondence, but also republish his two old books, which had long been out-of-print despite having gone through several editions in freer days.

The other close friend whom Stephen continued frequently to visit abroad was Charles Douglas, who lived in Belgium and to whom he remained deeply attached for his "wicked sense of humour, robust intellect and heart of gold".

He also remained extremely fond of Isa, whom he had been back to visit a few times in Istanbul. Now a successful writer, Isa dedicated to Stephen, as his "mentor", his translation into Turkish of an English classic Stephen had introduced to him, so Stephen went there again to join in the celebrations connected to its publication.

He combined this with a visit to Adam, his original host in Bangkok. Adam had long since abandoned Thailand, when it became dangerous for boy-lovers, and was now settled in a beautiful part of the Lebanon unspoilt by tourism, where Stephen briefly joined him for an enjoyable exchange of memories.

The following spring, Stephen again joined the Marlowes on holiday, this time in Cyprus. The cancer had been spreading and he required stronger painkillers, but he was determined to travel as long as he could and even still considering living out his last days in one of the countries dearer to him than Britain, but working out how he might receive vital medical care elsewhere was a deterrent. He continued to pay frequent visits to his friends in France and Belgium, and then determined to spend the following Christmas and New Year in what he realised was likely to be his last voyage outside Europe.

He picked Thailand, where he had once been so happy. He could even remember some of the language after more than two decades absence. Most of his friends who had lived there had, like Adam, long departed for lands at least somewhat less hostile to who they were. A friend remained in Bangkok who had proven capable of transferring his interest to young men of just legal age, some others were willing to come there for a reunion, and it all passed happily enough except that poor Stephen was now subject to intermittent attacks of debilitating pain.

Back in England, he gave vital last assistance to the Marlowes when international borders were about to close down due to the Covid pandemic by rushing to Tancred's school to enable him to catch a flight from Heathrow he might well otherwise have missed. There had been a real danger of the boy being left isolated in England for a long time if his school shut down too, as of course it soon did. Instead, he was able to go home to his parents for over a year.

Soon afterwards, the hospital Stephen attended telephoned to tell him they could no longer give him any treatment, on the grounds that catching Covid would finish him off. From this time onwards, his health deteriorated more rapidly and he was in frequent agony, while hopes of seeing again any of his friends who lived abroad steadily evaporated. The only one of his soul mates he was still able to see was Roger C., and their visits to each other were one of his few great joys in his last months.

His last work on his memoirs was on 22nd August, by when he had a brain metastasis, which fast diminished his speech and ability to write. In the following weeks his emails became steadily shorter and it took him hours to write them, though they continued after his speech had gone. His courage in adversity remained extraordinary to the end.

A cleaning-lady who had been with him long enough to become a close friend had become his full-time carer, but eventually he was in such a bad state that he asked to be taken to St. Barnabas Hospice in Worthing, where, after five days spent mostly sleeping, he died on 27th October 2020, aged sixty-three.

Isa, who had been frantically trying to find out what had happened until Edmund told him the news, wrote saying:

Stephen was such a strong presence in my life, such a wise influence on my mind and such a compassionate companion of my heart in the last twenty years since my adolescence that I still can't believe he's no longer around to see, to chat, to seek counsel from and to talk from heart to heart … I wish I could have been there for him just to hold his hand as he went through all these complications of rapid deterioration towards his last breath in that hospice because he was with me as a guide throughout my most difficult times.

Others privileged to have been his close friends felt similarly.

Other books from Arcadian Dreams

Publisher of memoirs, biography, fiction and poetry challenging the dehumanising, puritan dogma of the twenty-first century.

All the books listed here can be bought from any branch of Amazon as paperbacks and, except for *My Love Is Like All Lovely Things*, as Kindle books.

arcadian.dreams.london@gmail.com

Alexander's Choice
by Edmund Marlowe

Sweet-natured, intelligent and good-looking, thirteen-year-old aristocrat Alexander Aylmer seems to have everything going for him when he goes to Eton, the prestigious English public school.

Within months, however, tragedy strikes, leaving him vulnerable, heartbroken and increasingly alone, forced to find his own emotional salvation in a world that is effectively uncaring despite its good intentions. The longings recently come with puberty aggravate his turmoil until he sees the solution to them is the key to everything. Two very different people seem to promise help.

Timid Julian Smith, three years older, nurses two secrets he is terrified the other boys might discover: his humble background as the son of a removals man who had saved all his life to send a son to Eton, and his being hopelessly in love with Alexander.

Damian Cavendish, a charming, young English master, is romantically only interested in women. He is conscious though of a special affinity with boys that has brought him to Eton determined to teach and befriend them. He burns too with a longing to find himself badly needed.

By luck and pluck, Alexander finds his way to unsurpassed happiness. But can he really get away with making his own choices as to how, without regard to what society has decided in advance is good for him?

Alternately uplifting and heart-wrenching, and at times erotic, *Alexander's Choice* candidly depicts a kind of passionate love the world is averse to recognising. It also reveals unflinchingly the brutal reality that can face a boy trying to have his emotional needs met in a society fallen into frightened confusion about the sexuality of early teens.

Edmund Marlowe, himself an old boy of the school, has in this, his first novel, accurately evoked the idiosyncratic but appealing world of Eton, which carried on in many of its centuries-old ways, but could not protect its own against the new spirit of the 1980s.

"Eton's homoerotic whodunnit! ... *Alexander's Choice* is being feverishly read by as many Etonians, past and present, as can get their hands on it. The 422-page potboiler is being hailed as the Etonian version of *Fifty Shades Of Grey* ...

OE author Guy Walters tells me: 'The book is set in the Eighties when I was there – David Cameron, Boris ... – were all contemporaries ... It's quite clear ... whoever wrote it was with us at school,' he says. 'It's great fun and is actually rather well written.' " – *The Daily Mail.*

"*Alexander's Choice* is an entertaining, engagingly written novel which confronts serious and controversial issues with an unprejudiced, fresh perspective, daring to question the rigid constructs of contemporary society." – S. P. Somtow, multiple-award-winning author of 57 books

"The sex scenes are thrillingly frank. And there's fun to be had ... in trying to identify who the people in the book might be in real life. Eton had a bumper crop of future statesmen and celebs in 1983 - David Cameron, Boris Johnson, Earl Spencer and Dominic West among them. Is *Alexander's Choice* a roman à clef? Is Julian, with his 'wavy dark brown hair and thick spectacles' a fantasy portrait of the future Detective McNulty? Alexander has 'dazzling white teeth' and 'golden-blond hair': is he based on Bojo? Earl Spencer?" – *The London Review of Books*

The World, the Flesh and Myself
by Michael Davidson

Michael Davidson (1897-1975) was an English foreign correspondent widely respected for his intelligence, keen observation and sympathy for the under-dog. He joined the Berlin communists against Hitler, crossed wartime Morocco in Arab disguise, and opposed the British authorities in Malaya and Cyprus. This autobiography, published in 1962 in an England where homosexuality was still illegal and widely reviled, caused a sensation with its opening sentence, "This is the life-history of a lover of boys," but impressed many with its candid accounts of his journalistic and sexual adventures.

"the twofold story of a courageous and lovable person's struggle to come to terms with his Grecian heresy and of a brilliant journalist's fight against colonial jingoism." – Arthur Koestler (author of *Darkness at Noon*), *The Observer*.

"Mr. Davidson ... is one of the frankest of autobiographers, and, as he is also a writer of impressive skill and sensibility, he has produced an uncommonly readable book." –*The Times Literary Supplement*.

"Candour and forthrightness are rarely found in autobiographies. Mr. Davidson is the happy exception." – John Davenport, *The Observer*.

One of the books that were "the only salvation and sense in my life" and "reflected my own emotional turmoil and my own circumstances." – Stephen Fry on himself as a teenager, *Moab Is My Washpot*.

After being taken on by seven different publishers in three countries, *The World, The Flesh and Myself* went out-of-print for a quarter of a century.

This new edition includes an introduction by the author's close friend, the artist and writer Colin Spencer, and fascinating biographical notes on the main characters mentioned (gathered mostly from Davidson's private correspondence) by novelist Edmund Marlowe.

Some Boys
by Michael Davidson

In 1969, Davidson followed the success of his first book with this even more revealing sequel, a fond memoir of his adolescent friends in sixteen cities spanning three continents over three decades. Written with the keen observation of a brilliant journalist invariably open to diverse customs and warmly empathetic with the young.

> "We should be grateful that in Mr. Davidson we have a highly intelligent writer with a sensitive awareness of his nature. As to his style, no other contemporary English writer of prose possesses such exact lyricism, wit and learning" — Colin Spencer, *The Evening Standard*.

For this edition, some explicit passages, cut from both previous British editions but included in the very rare American edition, have been restored, and explanatory background notes have been added by novelist Edmund Marlowe.

Sicilian Vespers and Other Writings
by Michael Davidson

Published for the first time in 2021 was Davidson's last book, left unedited at his death, *Sicilian Vespers*, a wonderfully evocative account of life on the tiny Sicilian island where Davidson lived in the sixties. To this has been added an unfinished continuation of his memoirs, the best of his correspondence over half a century with a range of colourful characters, reminiscences of him by four of those who knew him, and a brief account of his fascinating life by the editor, Edmund Marlowe.

My Love Is Like All Lovely Things:
Selected Poems of E. E. Bradford

Edwin Emmanuel Bradford (1860–1944) was one of the Uranians, that group of late-Victorian and early-20th-century poets and prose writers who, often taking inspiration from classical Greece, sang the praises of the love between boys and men and advocated its rehabilitation in society. Virtually his entire poetic body of work – twelve volumes that appeared between 1908 and 1930 – is dedicated openly to this theme. Rather than looking back to classical antiquity, it is rooted largely in his own time and experience.

Bradford's poetry is exhilaratingly fresh, original, joyful and touching. It is a self-assured, unapologetic

affirmation of what is good and beautiful, making it very relevant to readers today. This anthology draws on the entirety of his poetic output and includes the first in-depth look at his life and work, addressing questions such as how his boy-love poetry could have been received so favourably in early-20th-century Britain.

'Colossal. What a job of work and what fine illustrations.' – Timothy d'Arch Smith, author of *Love in Earnest. Some Notes on the Lives and Writings of English 'Uranian' Poets from 1889 to 1930.*

www.ingramcontent.com/pod-product-compliance
Lightning Source LLC
Chambersburg PA
CBHW021340150726
47989CB00005B/2053